IMAGES
of America

REEDSPORT

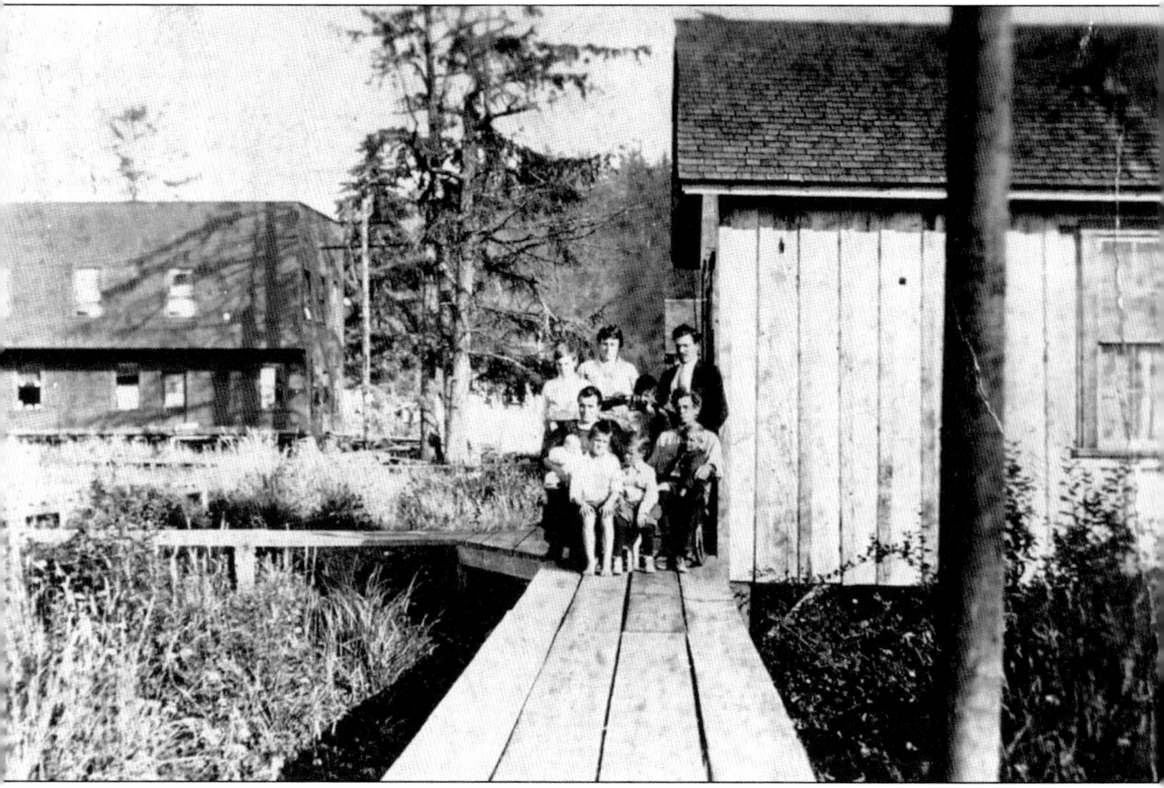

Members of the Balkema-Norris-Berlson family pose in 1919 to the right of the Riverview Hotel. Four plank boards, each a foot wide, make up the boardwalk in the foreground. These are the sorts of planks that made up the raised streets on which the original town of Reedsport sat. (Courtesy of the Douglas County Museum.)

On the Cover: Pictured is the confluence of Scholfield Creek and the Umpqua River at one of four operating lumber mills in Reedsport during the early 1920s, the Winchester Bay Mill, later the E.K. Woods Mill. Businesses in town were built on stilts six feet above the swamp and marsh that enveloped the area. (Courtesy of the Douglas County Museum.)

IMAGES
of America

REEDSPORT

Jim Akre, the Umpqua Discovery Center,
and the Douglas County Museum

ARCADIA
PUBLISHING

ISBN 978-0-7385-7604-6

Published by Arcadia Publishing
Charleston, South Carolina

Printed in the United States of America

Library of Congress Control Number: 2011925406

For all general information, please contact Arcadia Publishing:
Telephone 843-853-2070
Fax 843-853-0044
E-mail sales@arcadiapublishing.com
For customer service and orders:
Toll-Free 1-888-313-2665

Visit us on the Internet at www.arcadiapublishing.com

To the settlers of the Lower Umpqua River:

"Henry dried the paint with the heat of the burning note, and with one of the heavy red pencils used for marking the footage on the end of logs, finally put into words, into writing, what to Henry was nothing more than a good rule for his son to grow up under . . . NEVER GIVE A INCH!"

—Ken Kesey, *Sometimes a Great Notion*

Contents

Acknowledgments

This book would not be possible without the help of Diane Novak, director of the Umpqua Discovery Center in Reedsport, Oregon, and Gardner Chappell, director of the Douglas County Museum in Roseburg, Oregon. Their assistance in finding historical images and verifying historical accuracy was invaluable.

I also would like to thank the following individuals and families for their guidance and passion for their community: the Huebner family, the Harris family, the Thornton family, Joyce Brandon, Ann Hoile, Carol and Earl Plagmann, Bob North, Bill Mauldin, Merle Hausmann, Frank Barrett, Jeff Unger, Mindpower Gallery, Sunnie Heddon, the Dunn family, the Waggoner family, Nan Hanson, Reedsport Community Charter School, Bill Karcher, Ron Perry, Leslie Chapman, Barb Mills, the Henderson family, Doris Hedges, the Kaufmann family, Linda Noel and the Lower Umpqua Historical Society, and the Oregon Department of Forestry.

I would be remiss not to recognize all the pioneers in the Lower Umpqua River area for their grit and perseverance in weathering difficulty after difficulty in carving a civilization out of the wilderness.

Unless otherwise noted, all images appear courtesy of the Douglas County Museum.

Introduction

Originally, the Lower Umpqua River region was thought to be too remote to be civilized. Levi Scott, after whom the town of Scottsburg is named, wrote in his journal, "From the Hudson's Bay near the mouth of Elk River to the sea, the Umpqua River flows through a deep and rugged canyon in the Coast Range of mountains, where the river could not be navigated with boats, and it was, by man thought to be impossible to make a wagon road through this gorge. It was a serious and important question whether the Umpqua Valley could be put in anything like easy communication with the mouth of the river, which had never yet been examined by white men further down than the point where it entered the canyon in the Coast Range."

The Lower Umpqua River watershed was visited only by a variety of trappers, traders, and explorers until 1850. At that time, the *Samuel Roberts*, a ship carrying the Umpqua (Klamath) Exploration Expedition, financed by Winchester, Paine, and Company, entered the river. This was the first group of Americans to cross the treacherous Umpqua River bar, and they intended to plat townsites in the Lower Umpqua River area for future settlements that would help people to get to the newly discovered gold fields.

On August 4, 1850, seven Lower Umpqua Native American Indians in a canoe led Capt. Albert Lyman of the *Samuel Roberts* across the bar. The expedition laid out places for towns at Umpqua City in the dunes on the north side of the river and at West Umpqua on the heavily forested south side of the river. Other towns they platted were Gardiner at the big bend of the river, New Providence at the mouth of Scholfield Creek, and Middleton at Dean Creek. Umpqua City, the first of these budding communities, was located two miles north of the mouth of the river on the north bank. On August 5, 1850, Umpqua City was officially established, originally intended to be the port of entry. The *Oregon Spectator* wrote in 1850, "The proprietors are desirous of interesting men of enterprise and capital."

In July 1850, Capt. Levi Scott, a member of the group that laid out the Applegate Trail, platted his own town, and called it Scottsville. Later, it was called Myrtle City and then Upper Scottsburg. William Sloan had a land claim one mile west of Levi's that became Lower Scottsburg. In years to come, Scottsburg became a thriving supply town of 5,000 people that supplied miners going to and working in the gold fields south. Up to 500 pack animals would be in town on any given day to load supplies for the gold miners.

On October 1, 1850, the schooner *The Bostonian* was the first ship to break apart crossing the Umpqua bar. The survivors initially set up a tent city in the dunes until they could make their way to the site where the town of Gardiner stands today. George Snelling, nephew of *Bostonian* owner Mr. Gardiner of Boston, Massachusetts, suggested naming the original town after this owner. For years, settlers used the *Bostonian* timbers adrift in the river to help build structures in town.

Gardiner rapidly became one of the most important ports between San Francisco and Portland. In 1880, the Gardiner sawmill produced 12 million board feet of lumber and proved to be one of the most successful mills on the Oregon Coast. Even a fire that began in the pit of the mill on July 26, 1880, was not able to destroy the fervor of the town. The community was almost destroyed, with 37 buildings burned to the ground, including the Simpson Mill. Through the efforts of its citizens, Gardiner rebuilt and regained its prestige as a critical port on the Oregon Coast.

Fort Umpqua was established on July 28, 1856, two miles east of the mouth of the Umpqua River on the north bank. Originally, the fort was constructed to protect the southern part of the Siletz Indian Reservation and to prevent Indians from returning to their ancestral lands in southern Oregon. In reality, it served the purpose of protecting the Indians from local miners and community members who suffered from extermination madness. In 1862, Colonel Steinberger, commanding the District of Oregon, visited the outpost, only to discover no one at the fort. The few remaining troops were out hunting. Steinberger then decided to close the fort, since its purpose had long ago disappeared.

At the end of the 19th century, Gardiner was the dominant community in the Lower Umpqua River area. Umpqua City had long disappeared into the dunes. Fort Umpqua was abandoned, and citizens from Gardiner were using timbers from its blockhouse to construct new mills. Scottsburg had been washed away in a massive flood in 1861, and had never regained its place as a gateway to the gold fields. At this point, the Umpqua River was king of commerce and transportation. This was also the point at which Mr. and Mrs. J.F. Clark sold the marshy land across the river from Gardiner to A.W. Reed. The forested section above the swamp was referred to as Wade's Flat. The area below was an immense marsh.

This was also the point at which the railroad began to supersede the river as the future of commerce and transportation. In 1912, a British controlled firm called the Pacific Great Western Railway, headed by Sir Robert Perks, wanted to construct a railroad from the Willamette Valley via the Siuslaw River to the coast. The line turned south along the eastern shore of Siltcoos and Tahkenitch lakes and into northern Douglas County. This firm was purchased by the Southern Pacific Railroad, which in 1916 completed a line from Willamette Valley to Coos Bay, going through Reedsport and bypassing Gardiner. The arrival of the railroad proved the end for steamboat dominance in the economy of the area.

Gardiner had been the main commercial and industrial center of the region until the railroad came. Within years, the fledgling town of Reedsport emerged as the region's economic mainstay. Originally constructed on the marsh below Wade's Flat, the first town was constructed on stilts to stay above the wet and swampy ground, with the riverfront and Rainbow Slough as the center of activity in the town. Rainbow Slough was the backwater running through the swamp that connected the Umpqua River with Scholfield Creek. Before the swamp was filled with mud and sand, streets were constructed 4 to 7 feet off the ground and about 12 feet wide—just wide enough for a horse and wagon.

In 1927, Reedsport finally filled in the swamp with dredging fill from Schofield Creek and the Umpqua River. With this addition, many Scandinavian families came to the area and were quickly absorbed into the fishing, logging, and building in the community. This expansion of the town, combined with increased rail traffic and continued emphasis on logging and fishing, led to the golden age of the community.

One

The Past

Only two navigable rivers, the Columbia and the Umpqua, cut through the coastal mountain range on the Oregon Coast and connect the Pacific Ocean with the Willamette Valley. Since the Umpqua River was the furthest south, this was the most efficient route to the gold fields in Southern Oregon and in Northern California in the late 1840s. The Umpqua River is totally contained within Douglas County and displaces more water than any river in the state of Oregon, with the exception of the Columbia River. It is the most dominant geographical feature in Douglas County. Due to the river's prominence, settlement of this part of the Oregon Coast crept up the river from the ocean. The whims of the river dictated how much success original settlers were granted. Torrential floods, an ever-changing ocean bar, hidden reefs, and sudden fire all proved to be obstacles faced by the first settlers. Coexisting with the Umpqua was the only way civilization could make a stand.

Small communities also grow recounting tales of past citizens that are colorful, unique, and eccentric. Reedsport is no different in that a wide variety of characters have left their imprint on the personality of the area. Levi Scott founded the town of Scottsburg in 1850 and was part of the territorial government from 1852 to 1857. Cyrus Heddon, twice a survivor of Indian battles, opened a successful store in Scottsburg. John Bergman, a cannery worker, achieved notoriety by rescuing two boatloads of passengers from the stranded steamer *Tacoma* in 1883. W.F. Jewett was the owner of the Gardiner Sawmill and arguably the most powerful man in the Lower Umpqua area.

Although access to the gold fields was the first reason for exploring the Umpqua River, many found that with settling in the region they could not only provide supplies for gold seekers, but could also provide larger cities on the coast with valuable commodities such as timber and fish. It was this entrepreneurial spirit that convinced travelers to stay and to prosper.

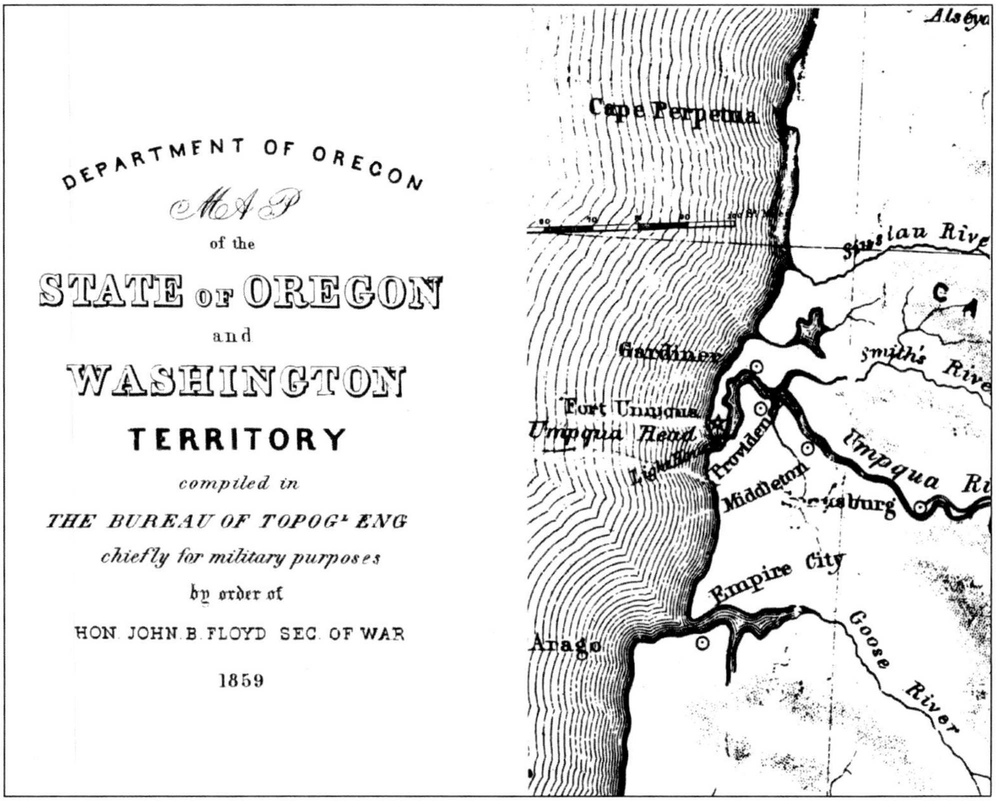

This 1859 map of the Lower Umpqua River indicates the potential townsites platted by the members of the Umpqua Exploration Expedition in 1851.

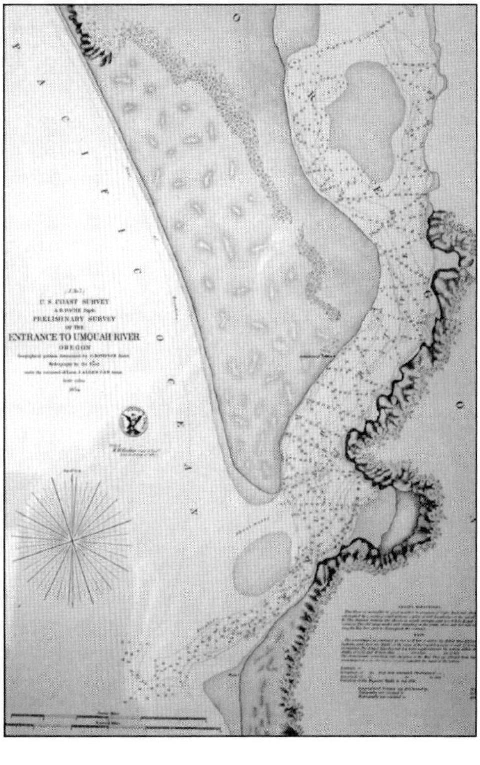

This is the 1854 map drawn by Lt. James Alden that was the result of the federal government's first survey of the Lower Umpqua River, called "The Preliminary Survey of the Entrance to the Umpqua River." This map shows that the most striking feature of the river bar was an enormous sand spit that dangled from the north side of the river mouth, forcing the Umpqua River to flow south in an attempt to reach the ocean.

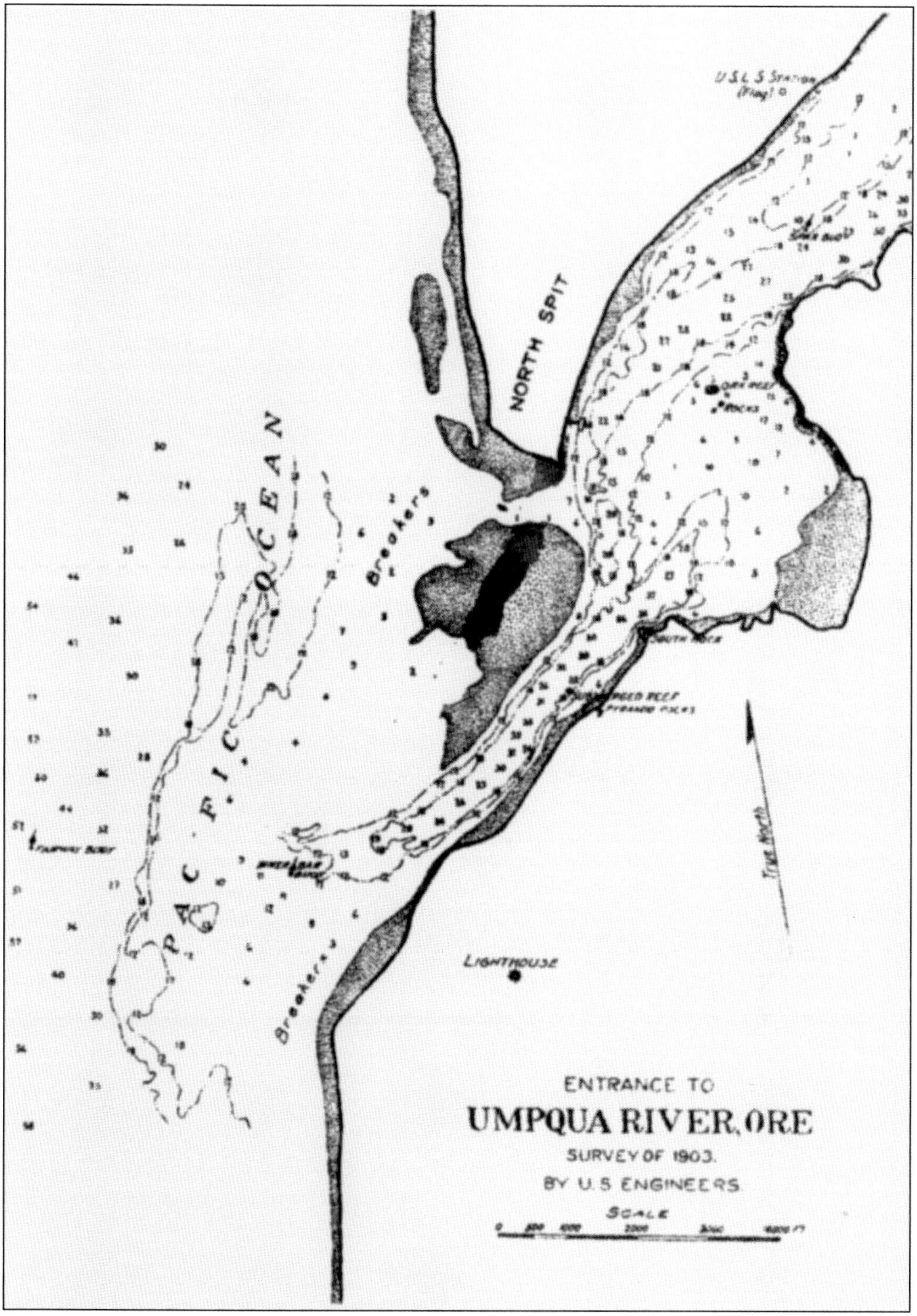

This 1903 map shows the entrance to the Umpqua River. The first wreck near the Umpqua River bar was on August 22, 1808. The *Sea Otter* was driven ashore just north of the Umpqua Bar, killing all but six members of the crew. Captain La Dalle La Valle and five men then walked across the continent until they found civilization in Red River, Louisiana.

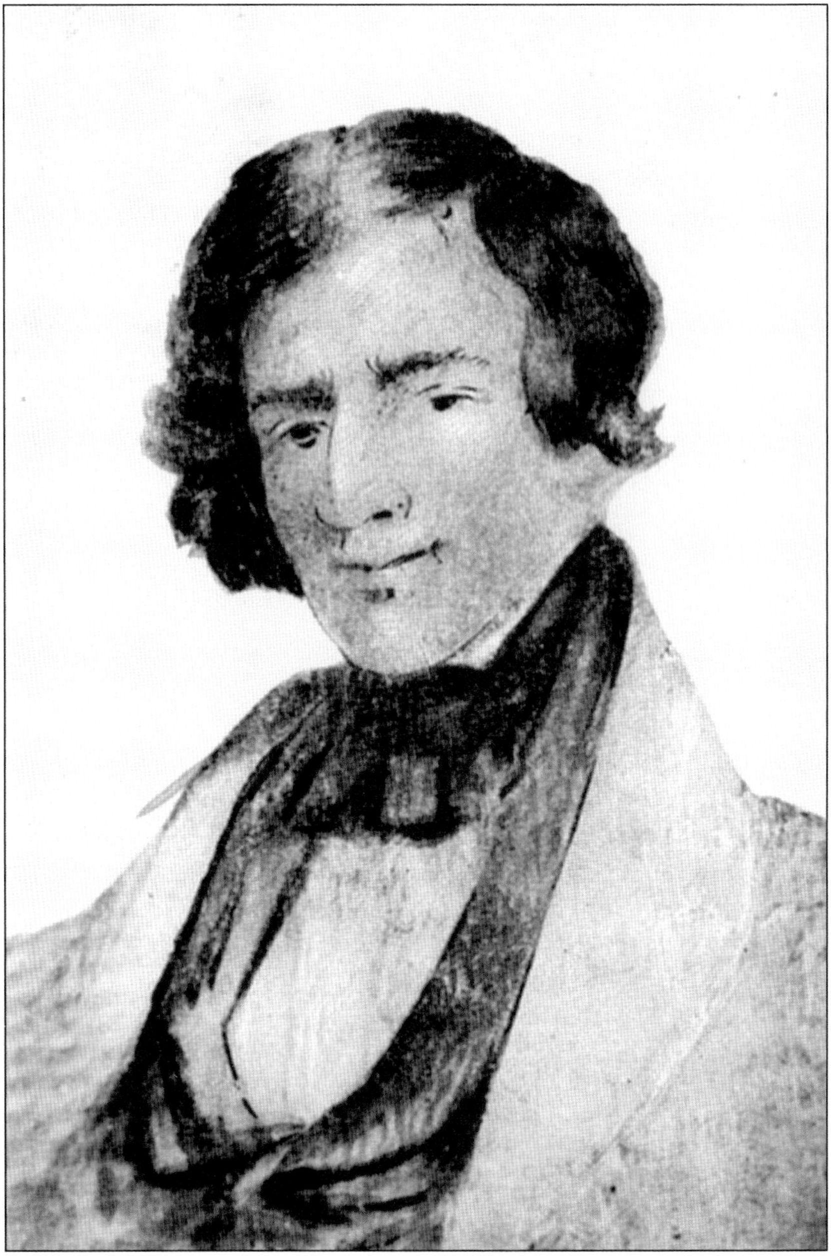

On July 14, 1828, explorer Jedediah Smith (above) had a violent encounter with the Kelawatset Indians at the mouth of the Umpqua River. There were a series of misunderstandings, involving the alleged theft of an axe, interference with some of the 250 horses Smith's group drove up from California to trade at Fort Vancouver, and attempted assaults on Kelawatset women. The Kelawatset killed 11 of Smith's 15 trappers, while Smith and two friends were off exploring the Umpqua River route to the Willamette Valley. Upon Smith's return, his group saw the atrocities taking place on the beach. They abandoned their canoe and swam to the far shore where they walked through the forest to Fort Vancouver, 185 miles to the north. Arthur Black, the only surviving member of the party from the beach attack, also walked to Vancouver from the river and rejoined Smith.

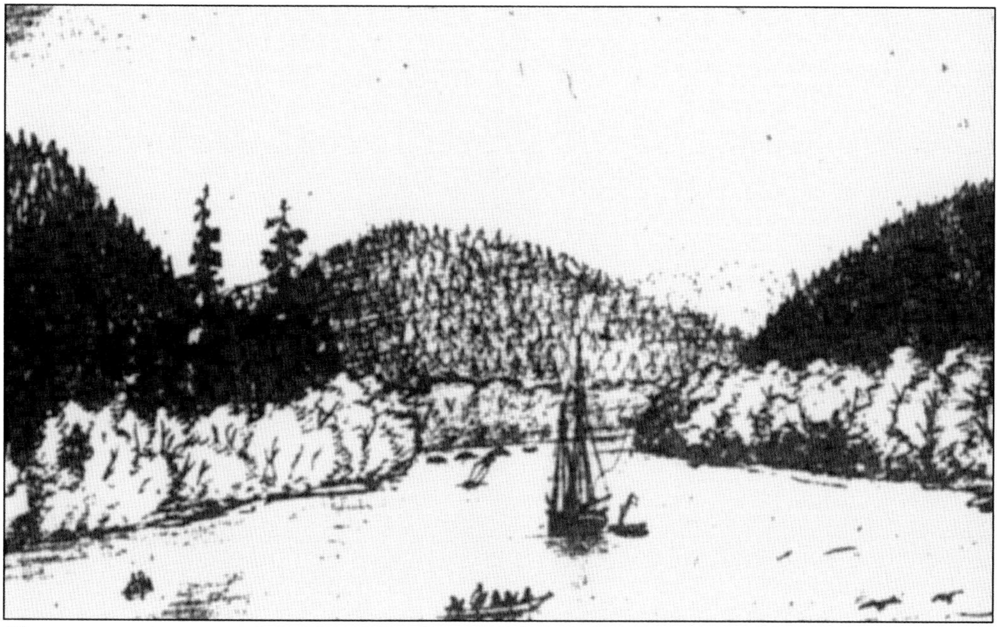

This is a woodcutting of the *Samuel Roberts* on the Umpqua River in 1850. On August 6, the *Samuel Roberts* grounded itself on a sand bar at night, several miles up the river. While waiting for the tide to float the vessel free, the crew helped themselves to casks of brandy on board and reportedly became quite inebriated. The crew named the island Brandy Bar, a name that still remains. The ship continued up the Umpqua River where Levi Scott founded the first American settlement on the south coast. Originally called Myrtle City, it was later renamed Scottsburg in honor of its founding father. In 1857, he became a member of the state constitutional convention. Scottsburg, being the nearest access to water shipments, became a major supply destination for adventurers going to the gold fields in Southern Oregon and Northern California.

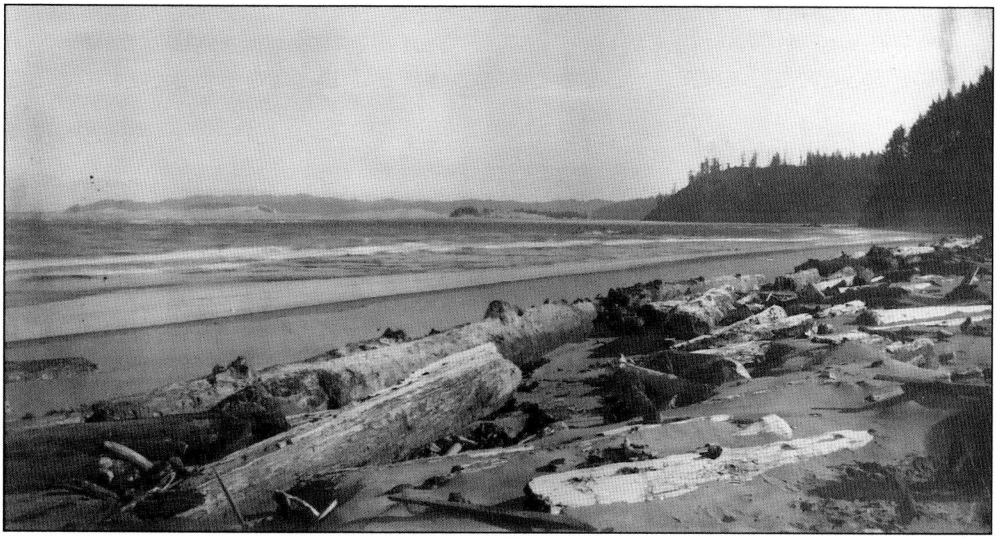

This is a 1932 picture of the site of the wreck of the schooner the *Bostonian*. On October 1, 1850, the *Bostonian* broke apart crossing the bar. The survivors initially set up a tent city on the dunes until they could make their way to the site where Gardiner stands today. For years, settlers used the *Bostonian* timbers to help construct structures in town.

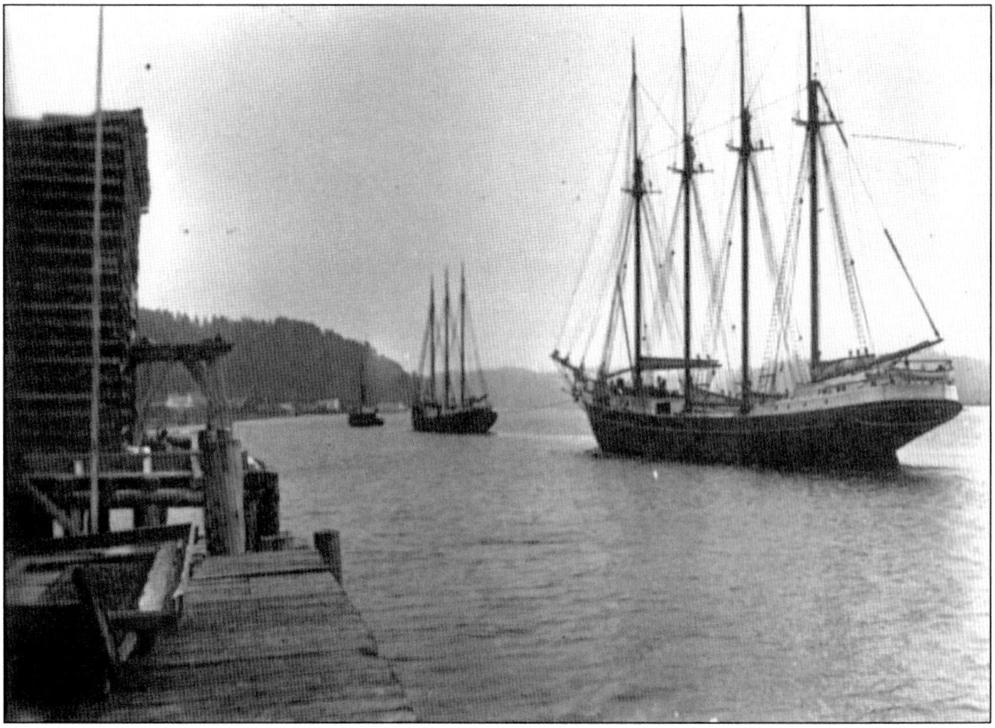

By 1879, five schooners regularly ran between Gardiner, California, and the Sandwich Islands. Gardiner was a major port on the Oregon Coast. This late 1800s photograph shows the busy shipping activity at the Gardiner waterfront during this time. This was Gardiner's golden age when it had a hospital, doctor, dentist, bank, post office, two stores, a haberdashery, a confectionery, a machine shop, a meat market, and a brewery.

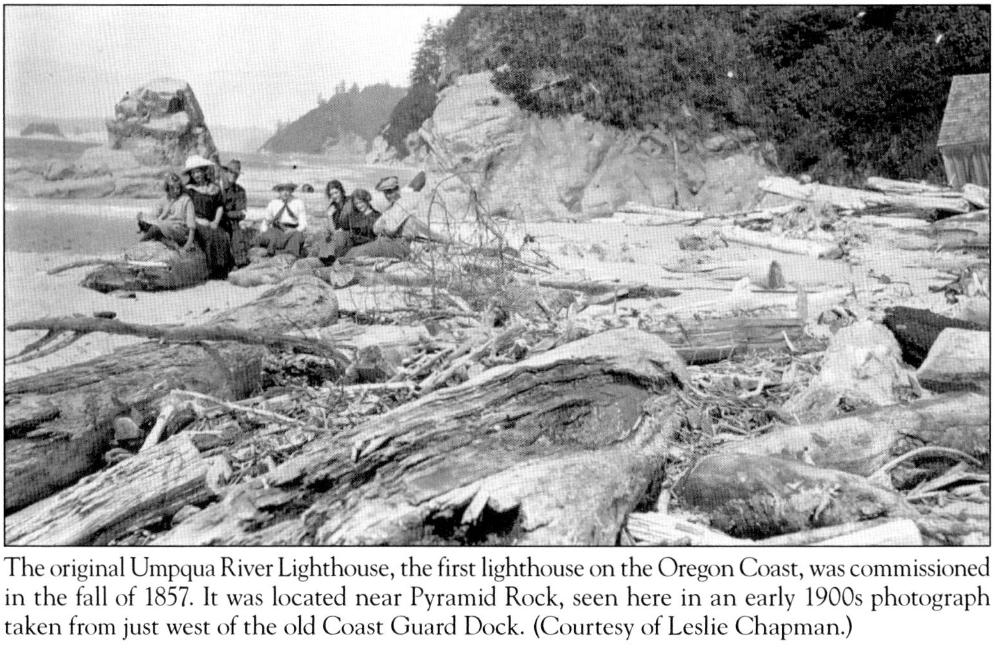

The original Umpqua River Lighthouse, the first lighthouse on the Oregon Coast, was commissioned in the fall of 1857. It was located near Pyramid Rock, seen here in an early 1900s photograph taken from just west of the old Coast Guard Dock. (Courtesy of Leslie Chapman.)

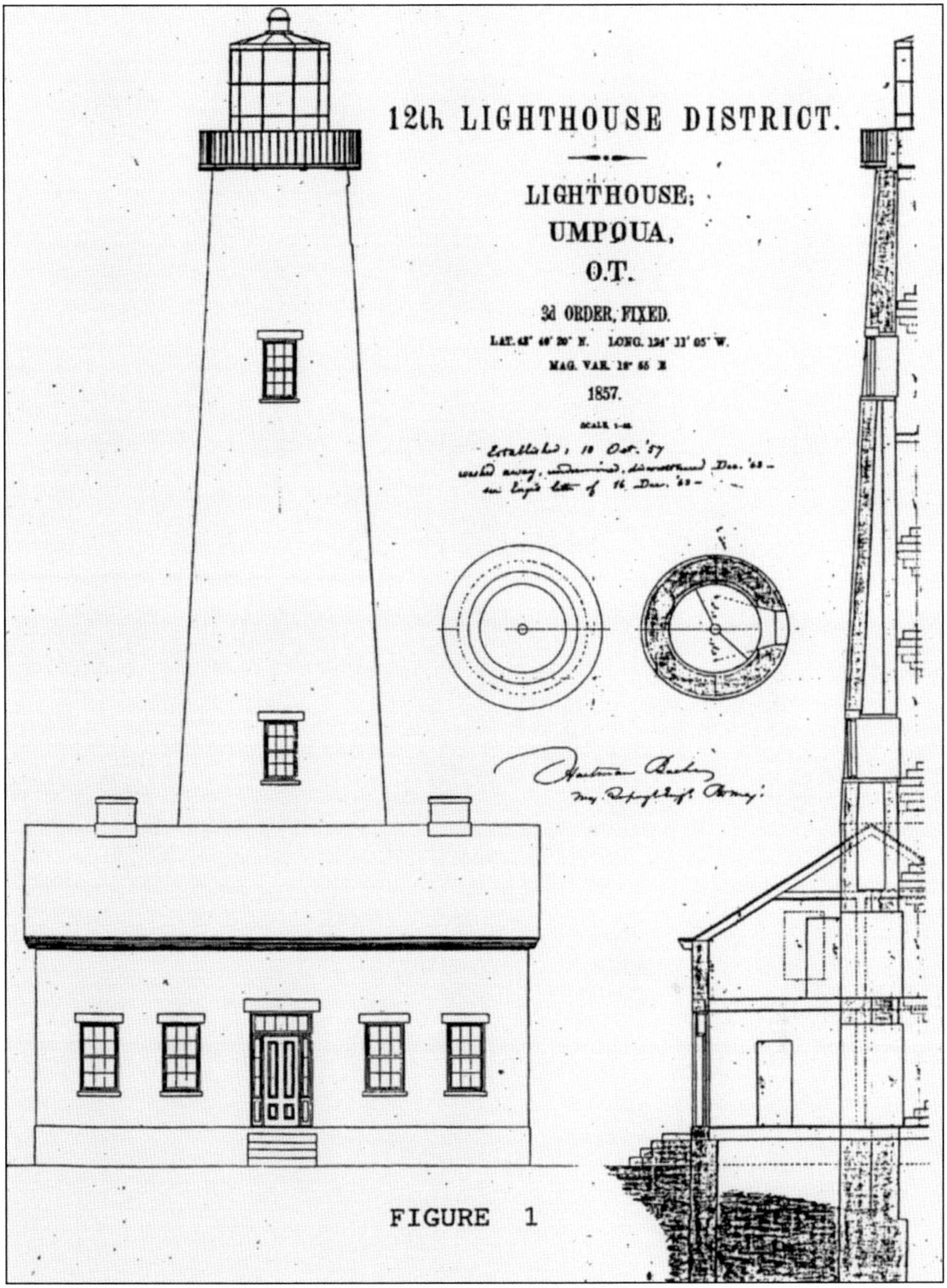

This diagram shows the design of the lighthouse, completed as a part of the preliminary survey of the entrance to Umpqua River in 1854. It had a tower 65 feet tall and housed a third order Fresnel lens. Beginning February 1861, there were 72 inches of rain in four months and the Umpqua River rose to flood stage, causing the building to list. Abandoned in 1864, the lens was moved; however, in the process of dismantling the iron lantern house, the building collapsed into the river. (Courtesy of Leslie Chapman.)

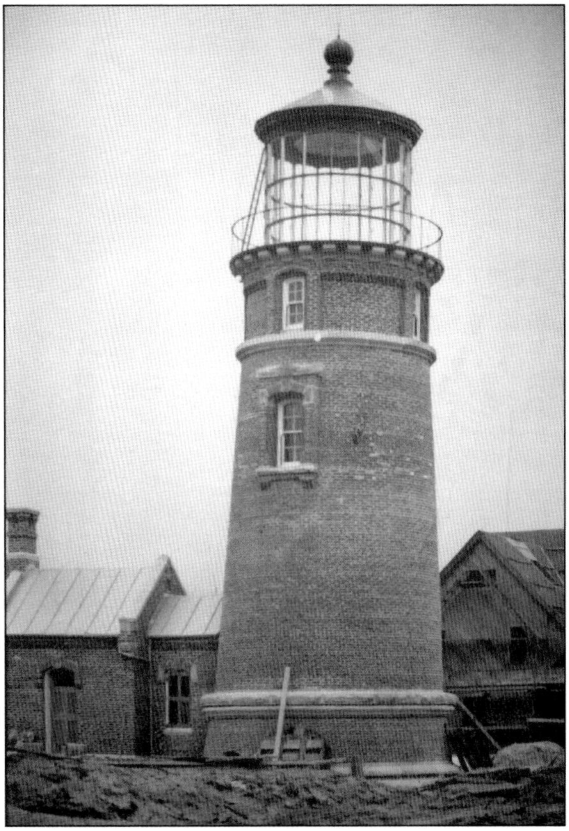

In 1888, the federal government agreed to pay $55,000 for another lighthouse at the Umpqua River. This facility, however, was constructed on top of the headlands just south of the river's mouth to avoid the disaster that befell the first Umpqua River Lighthouse. There were a myriad of problems constructing the second lighthouse. One contractor went bankrupt, one lost thousands of bricks because they were fired in the wrong kiln in San Francisco, and the tower was 15 inches short when the first-order Fresnel lens was lifted to the top. Carl Leick finally finished constructing the second Umpqua River Lighthouse, and it was commissioned on December 31, 1894. This is a c. 1890 photograph of the construction of the second Umpqua River Lighthouse. Its distinctive Fresnel lens flashed two white signals followed by one red signal. The lens is nine feet, seven inches tall and six feet, two inches wide. It weighs two tons, has 616 hand-cut prisms, and can be seen 20 miles out to sea.

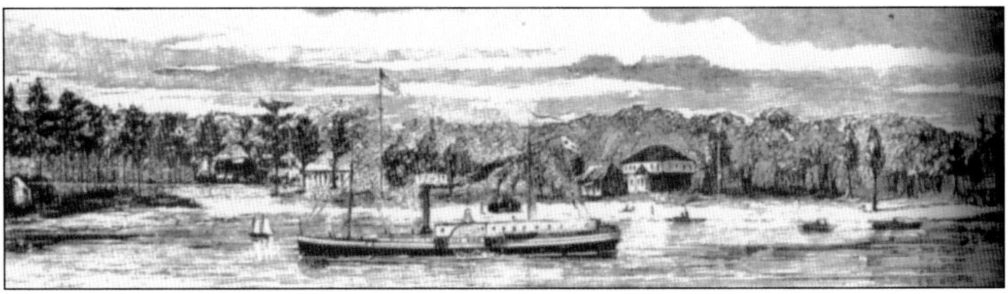

On August 5, 1850, Umpqua City became the first townsite platted on the Umpqua River, two miles north of the mouth. Originally, it had one of four Wells Fargo offices in Oregon, the Clark Hotel, and a general store run by Ed Breen just down the beach. This sketch appeared in the April 24, 1858, edition of *Frank Leslie's Illustrated Magazine*.

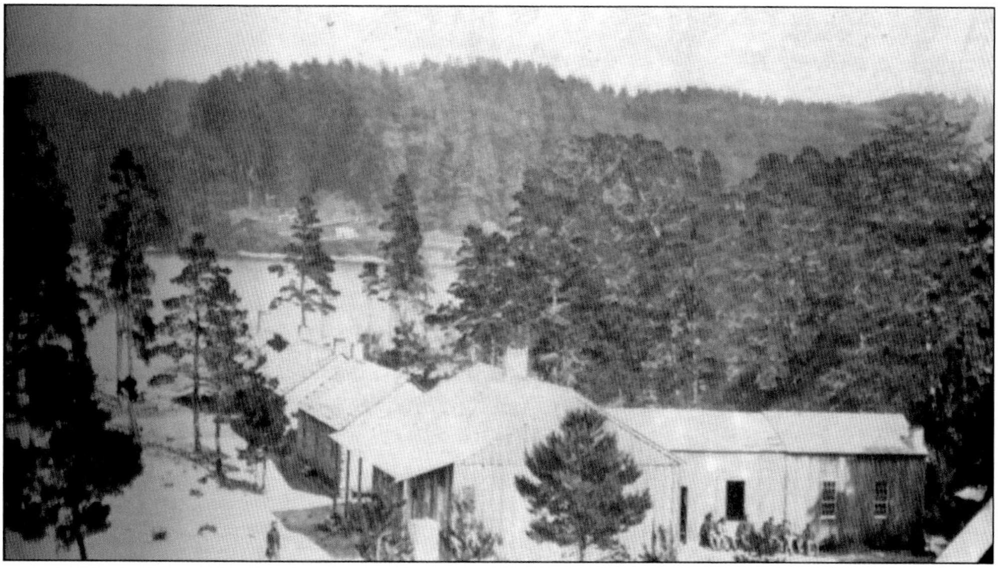

Fort Umpqua was established on July 28, 1856, two miles east of the mouth of the Umpqua River. This fort was to protect the southern boundary of the Siletz Reservation and to prevent Indians from returning to their ancestral homeland in Southern Oregon. In reality, it also served to protect the Indians from extermination-minded rabble in the mining settlements in Southern Oregon. Pictured above are the barracks that housed up to 100 men at the height of the fort's activity with the Umpqua River in the distance. Pictured below are the officers quarters, located a little closer to the beach. Fort Umpqua was closed on June 27, 1862, after Colonel Steinberger determined that their mission to guard the Siletz Reservation was no longer needed and he issued a statement that "Fort Umpqua serves no other purpose for military defense or protection."

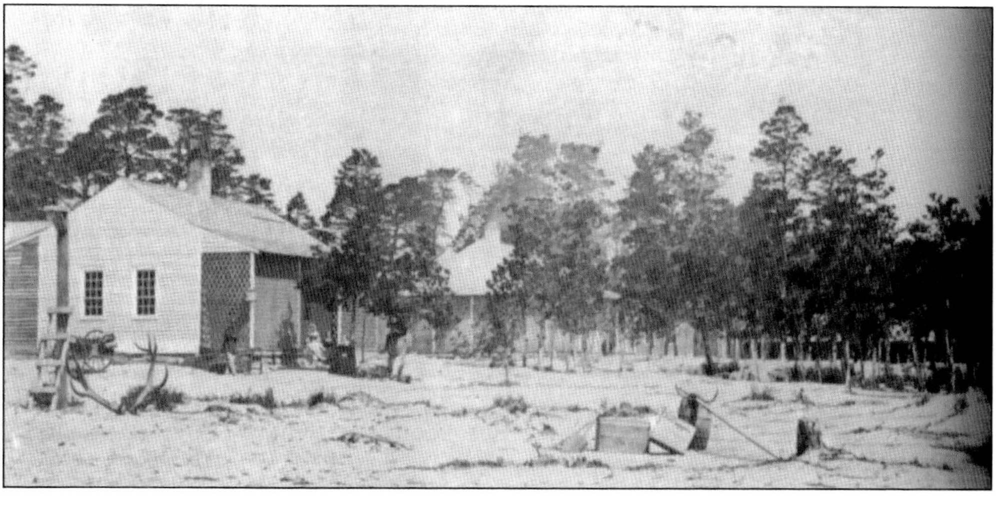

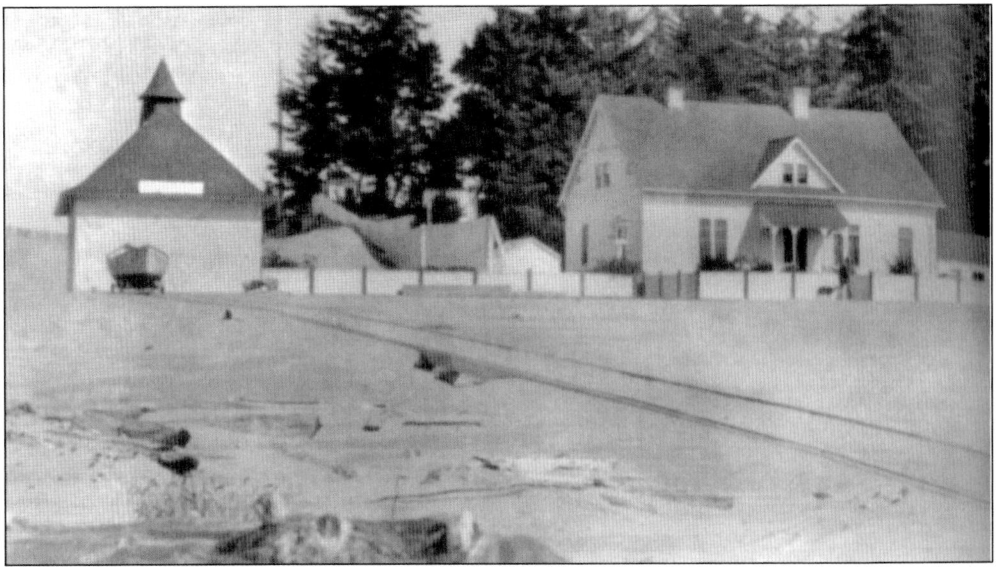

The Umpqua River Life Saving Station pictured here was established on the North Spit in 1891. The crews lived together in the crew's quarters and were allowed only one day a week with their families. Most work consisted of working on the boats and equipment, filling lamps, and running exercises and drills to keep in shape. If the lighthouse keepers saw a ship in distress, the keepers climbed down from the hill at the lighthouse and rowed upriver for a mile and a half to the Life Saving Station. The Life Saving Crew was then responsible for working on ships that were stranded or in peril.

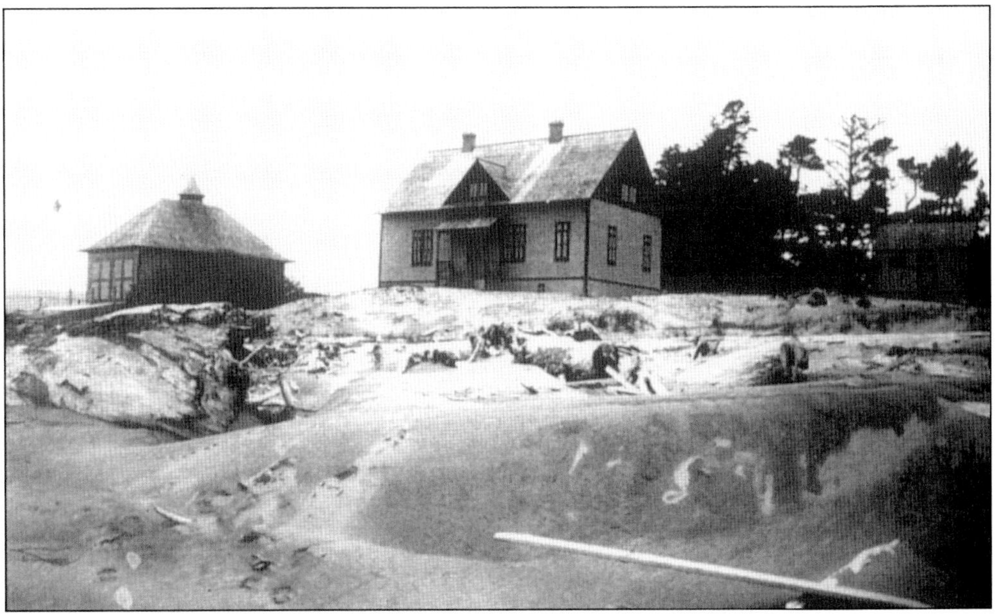

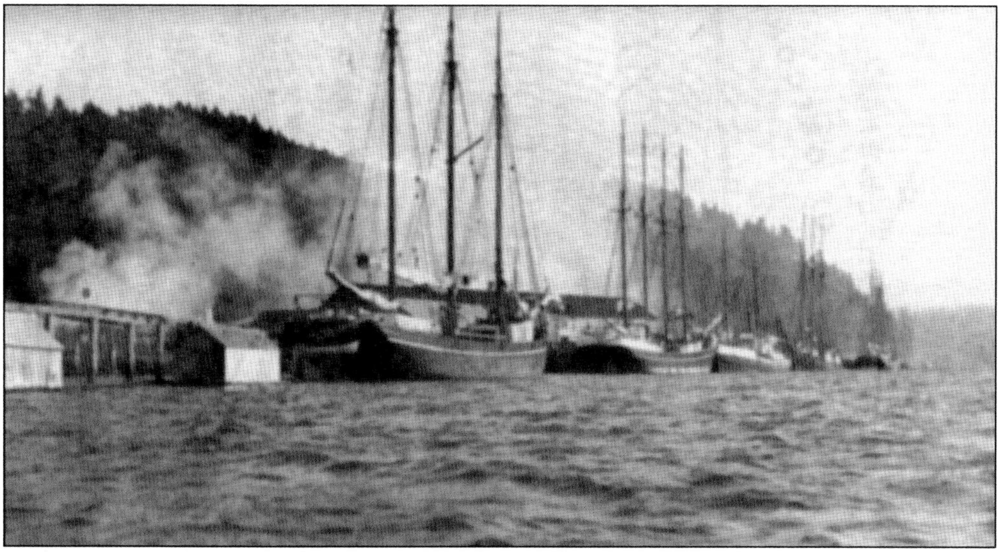

In the midst of Gardiner's prosperity, on July 26, 1880, a fire that began in the pit of the mill destroyed the town. There were 37 buildings, including the Simpson Mill, that were burned at the cost of $52,000. Owners of the mill offered free lumber and free white paint to any who would remain and rebuild. This is where Gardiner's nickname, the "White City," came from.

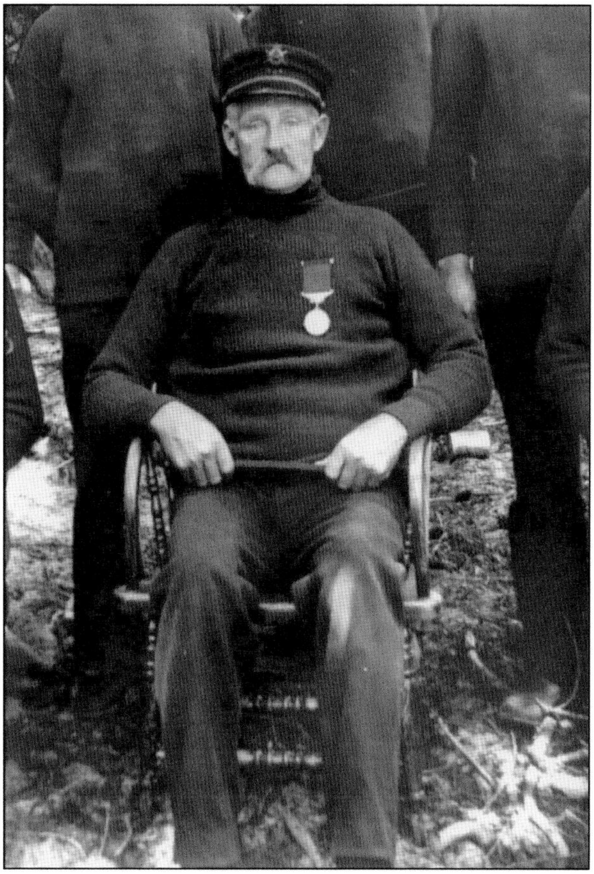

John Bergman, photographed here in the late 1890s, began a career as a cannery worker. When the *Tacoma* wrecked near Gardiner in 1883, Bergman heroically saved the life of several boatloads of passengers, despite his fishing boat being turned over six times in the surf. Bergman later became the keeper of the local lifesaving station.

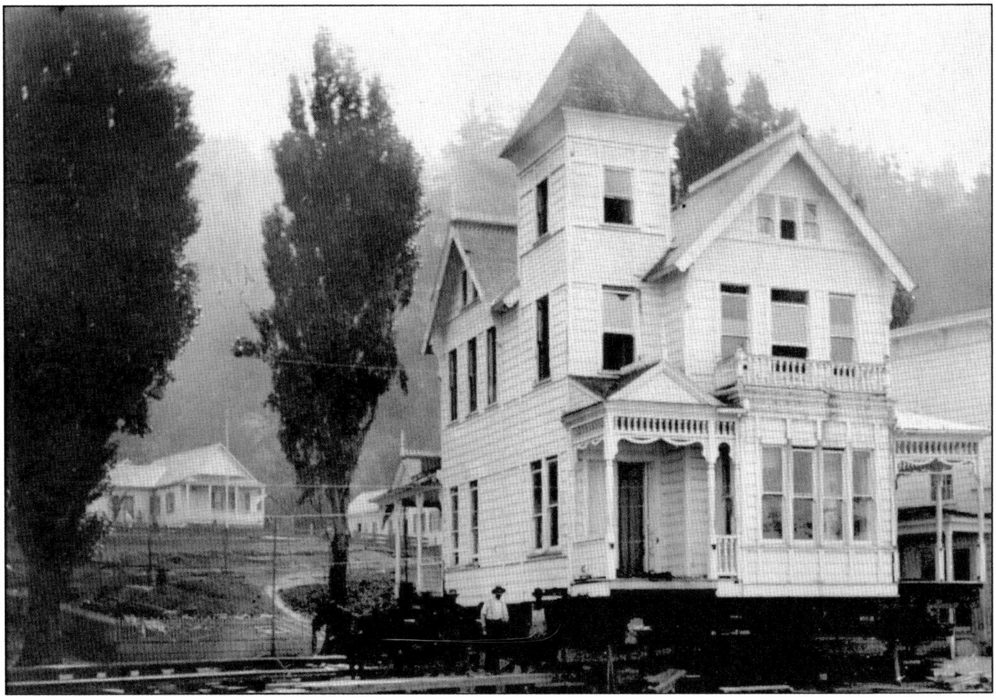

In 1886, the W.F. Jewett first home was moved from the corner of Jewett's land and given to John Bergman as a reward for his lifesaving efforts. The first attempt at moving the home was a failure, and it sat in the road for a year, as shown in this photograph.

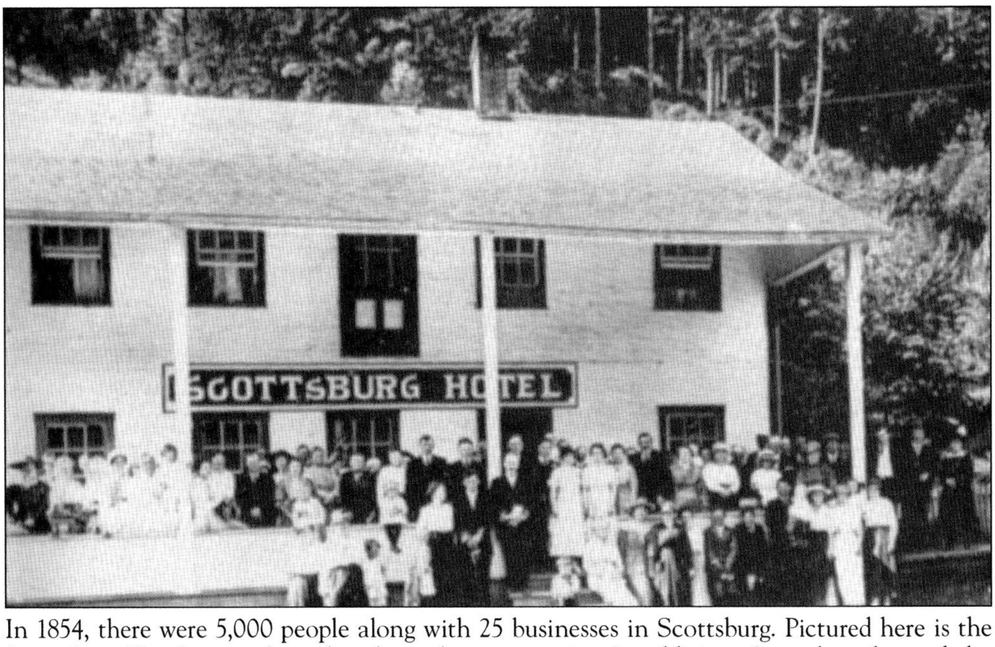

In 1854, there were 5,000 people along with 25 businesses in Scottsburg. Pictured here is the Scottsburg Hotel, one of two hotels in the community. In addition, Scottsburg housed the first newspaper in Southern Oregon, eight different merchandise stores, two attorney offices, a blacksmith shop, a carpenter shop, a harness and saddle store, a freight office, a mill, a saloon, and a bordello.

Two

THE RIVER AND THE MARSH

The Umpqua River is the lifeblood for the valley through which it flows. Ocean tides come 25 miles up the river to Scottsburg, and the entire 218 miles of the river are contained in Douglas County. Anyone who lived on the Umpqua recognized it was the artery for supplies, commerce, sustenance, and travel. Much of the inhabitants' lives revolved around the whims of the river. The salmon canning industry and timber industry based their livelihood on the ebb and flow of the river tides. Steamships used the river as the highway connecting local communities on the river. There was even an attempt to tame the Umpqua River mouth with the jetty construction in the early 1900s and the constant dredging to create a channel all the way to Reedsport. When Reedsport was just beginning to shape itself into a thriving community, the original riverfront businesses were the ones to move the town forward.

In the late 1800s, there was a triangular piece of property cut off from the mainland by a slough flowing east from Scholfield Creek to the Umpqua River in an arc shape, which looked like a rainbow; hence, it was named Rainbow Slough. Before the railroad came to Reedsport in 1916, businesses associated with the river grew up on Rainbow Slough and on the Umpqua waterfront. These businesses and the sidewalks that connected them were constructed on stilts four to seven feet above the marsh. These stilts were pilings driven into the marsh with planks laid on top for wagon and foot traffic.

With limited housing opportunities for the fledgling city when the railroad brought hundreds of workers to town, there came a cry to fill in the swamp, above which Reedsport originally sat. In 1925, a public hearing was held to discuss the feasibility of such a project. In 1927, the Port of Umpqua Commission levied a bond to construct a 16-inch, steam-powered dredge and used the mud and sand from the Umpqua and Scholfield to fill towns lowland.

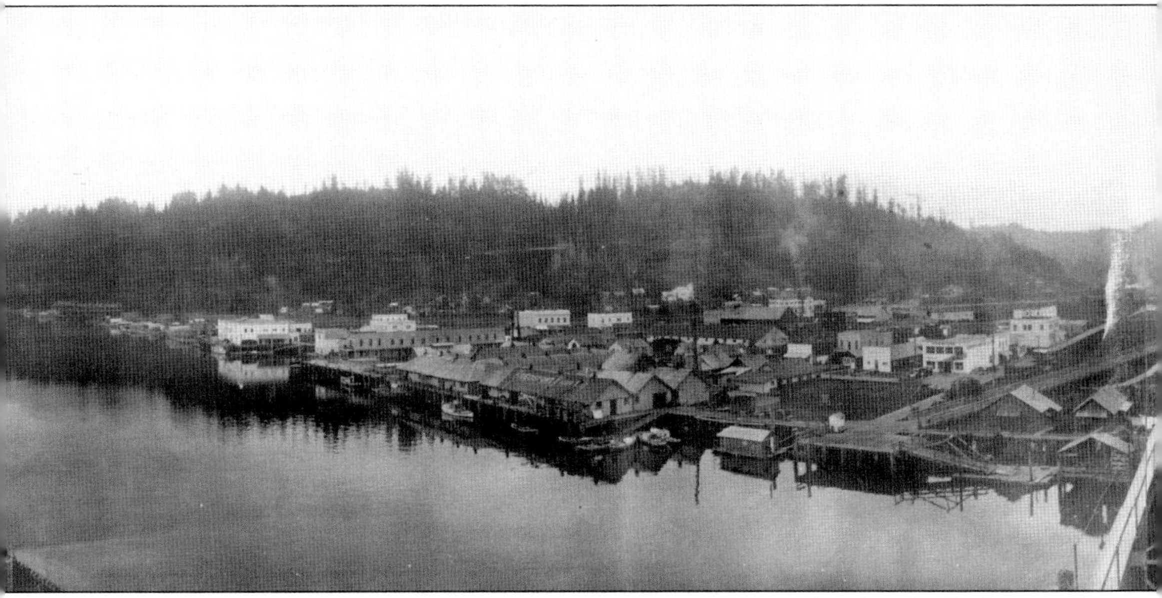

This 1923 panoramic photograph was taken from the top of the Railroad Bridge looking south over Reedsport's original waterfront and its initial businesses. On the far left is Hubbard's Mill, and next to it is the Reedsport-Janelle Merchandise Store. Lyon's Store was next in line. This is the point at which Rainbow Slough entered the Umpqua River with the Chase Cannery adjoining it. Looking up the tracks to the left were the J.R. Brown Furniture Store and then the first bank in town. To the right of the Railroad Bridge was the Gardiner Ferry slip, and later came the

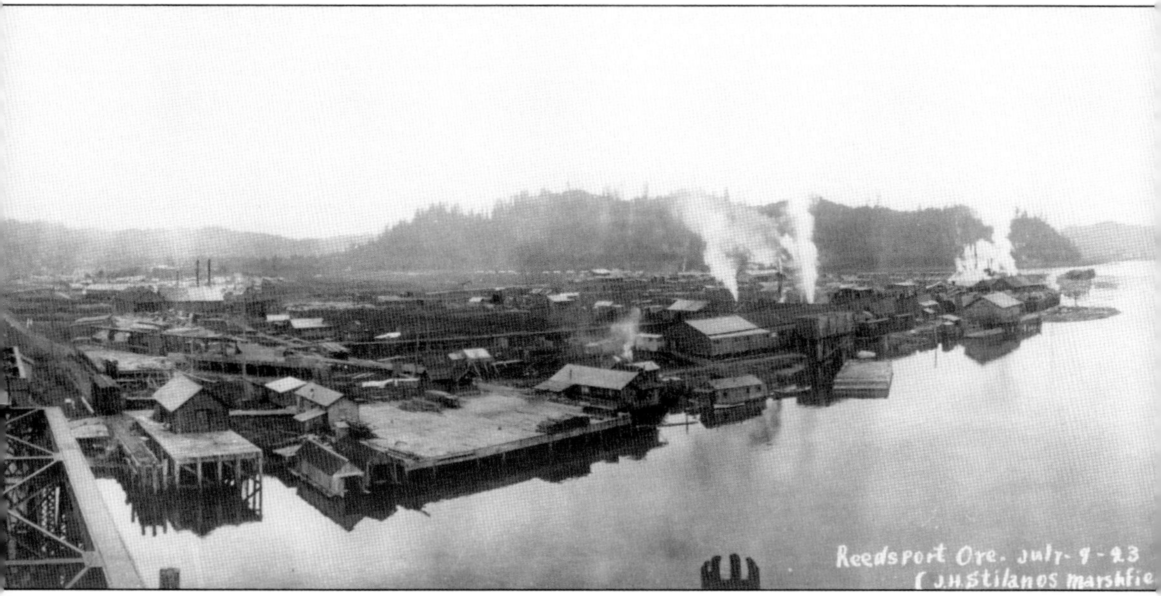

Bridge Mill. On the far right was the E.K. Woods Mill. In the distance, Crestview Heights is to the left, with the Reed Mansion just to the left of the tracks. Decker Point is directly ahead of the train tracks with Scholfield Creek entering the Umpqua on the far right. This was the point where, beyond the waterfront, much of Reedsport was constructed on stilts above the swampy ground. (Courtesy of Mindpower Gallery.)

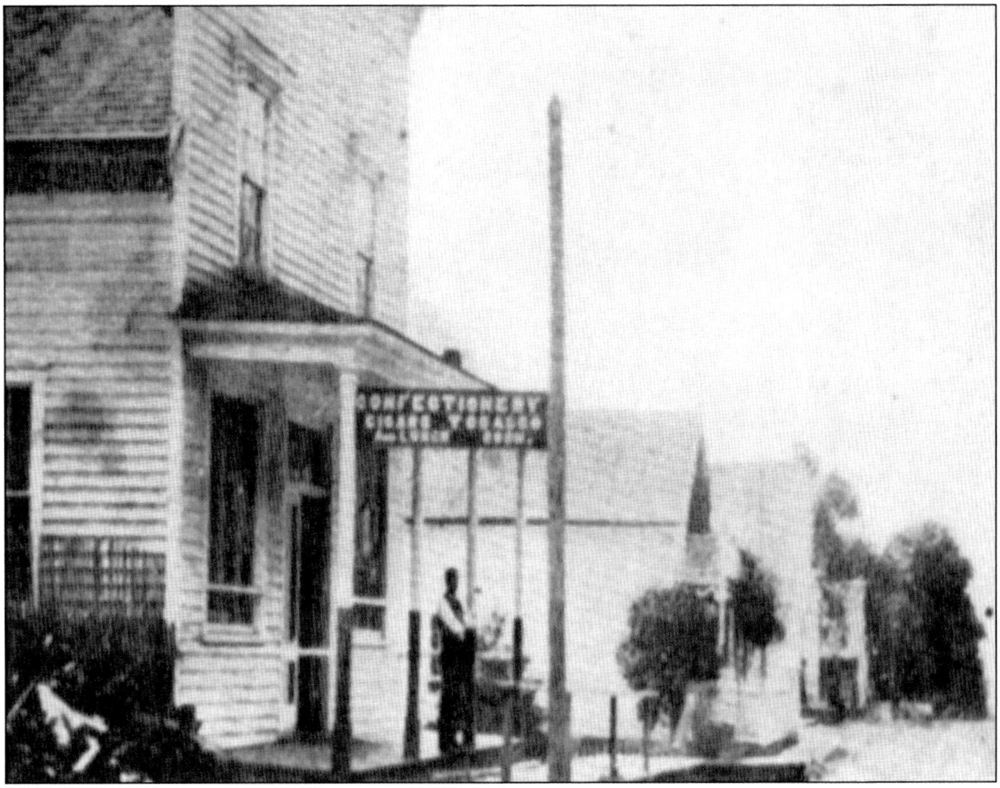

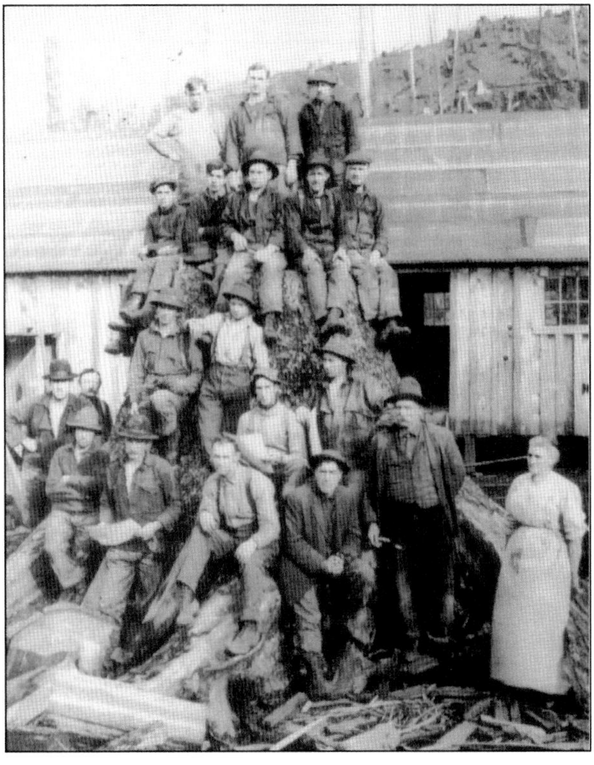

Pictured here in the late 1800s is the Scottsburg Confectionery along the main street in Scottsburg. Since Scottsburg was a supply point for the mining districts of southern Oregon, up to 500 pack animals might be in town for supplies for the gold fields. Up to $70 million was transported in bags on these animals.

In 1832, the Spanish ship the *Archive* sailed up the Umpqua River to the Scottsburg area and repaired their ship. The Spanish journals marvel at the timber available. Indian stories at this time revolve around men with beards and white faces. Early settlers in the 1850s commented on the huge stumps left by the Spanish timber cutting. This c. 1900 photograph shows Scottsburg residents sitting on one of these behemoth stumps.

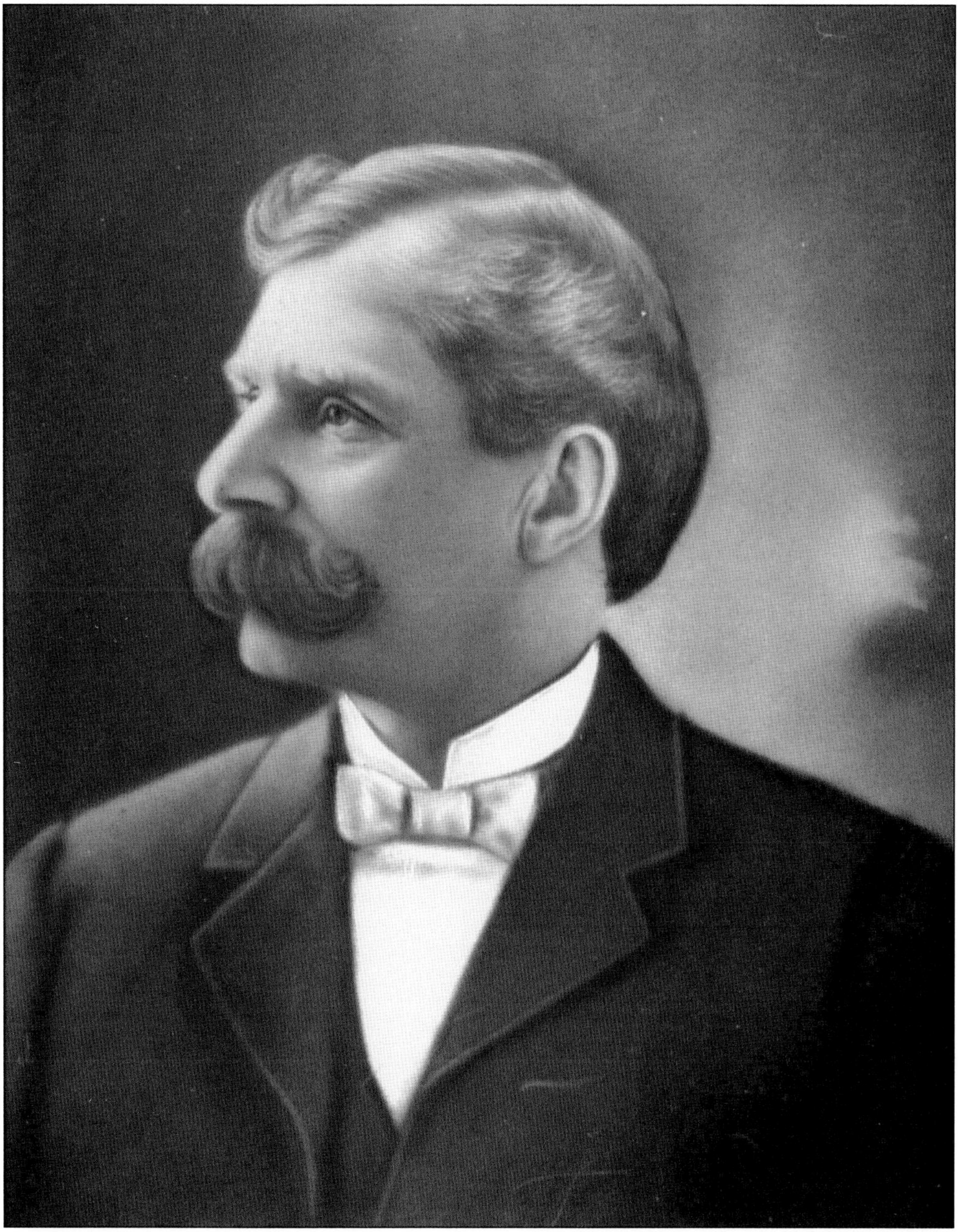

A.W. Reed came to Gardiner in 1870 as a sawyer in Simpson's Mill. He later ran the steamship *Argo* and had an interest in the steamship *Restless*. Over the years, he became an entrepreneur in the area, owning the Gardiner Creamery, a salmon canning plant, a mercantile, and a tannery. He was also elected a state senator before he drowned by looking for locations for a salmon hatchery in Winchester, Oregon.

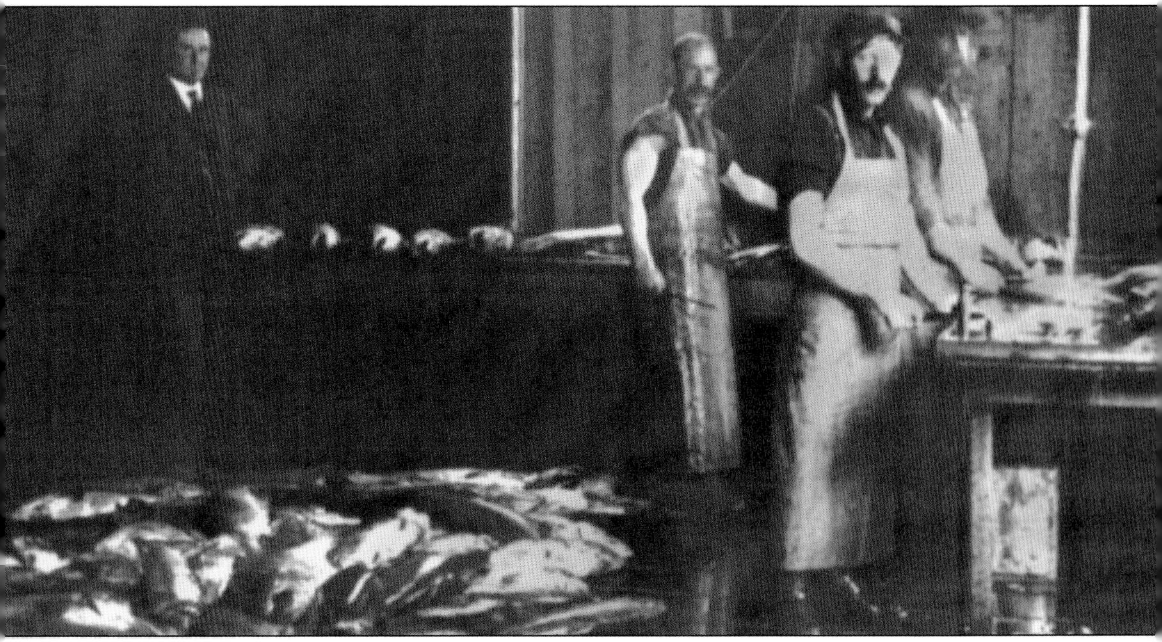

In this 1904 photograph, workers are processing the salmon catch under the watchful eye of owner Warren Reed, A.W. Reed's nephew, standing to the left at the cannery in Reedsport. The first rank of processing workers stood at long tables, scaling, cleaning, and chopping off the heads and tails of fish. This part of the processing eventually became the sole domain of Chinese and Japanese workers that came to Reedsport during the canning season. Warren Reed was the biggest owner and promoter of the Port of Umpqua in the early 1900s, and because of that, the other members of the board of directors decided to name the new town after him. Warren later inherited A.W. Reed's properties and pieced together key properties through which the railroad had to pass in its route to Reedsport and the coast.

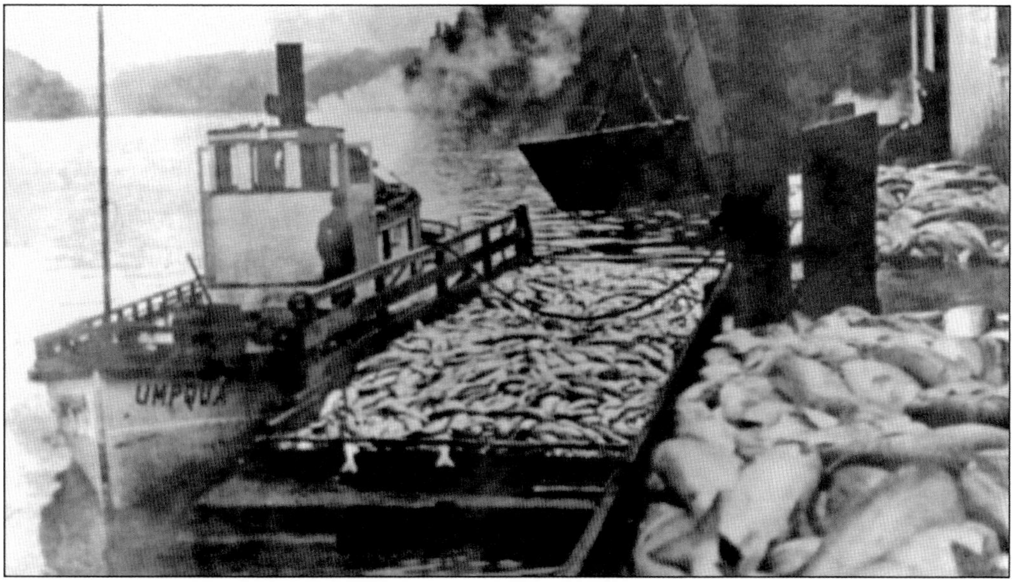

Every morning, the commercial fishermen unloaded the night's catch. This photograph is of a typical catch. The workers dressed the fish and packed them for shipping. Warren Reed's Umpqua Packing Company could put up 1,000 cases of salmon every 10 hours at peak season. Between 1923 and 1946, the Umpqua River fishery processed 17.4 million pounds of silverside salmon along with 4.4 million pounds of Chinook salmon.

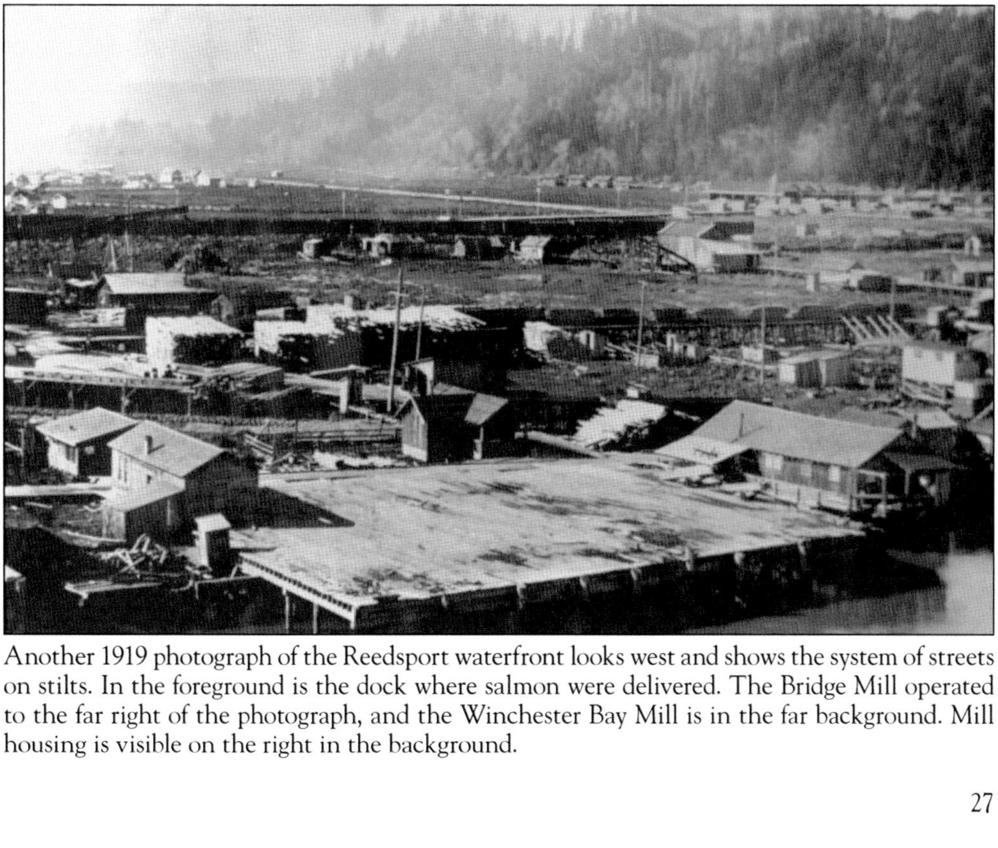

Another 1919 photograph of the Reedsport waterfront looks west and shows the system of streets on stilts. In the foreground is the dock where salmon were delivered. The Bridge Mill operated to the far right of the photograph, and the Winchester Bay Mill is in the far background. Mill housing is visible on the right in the background.

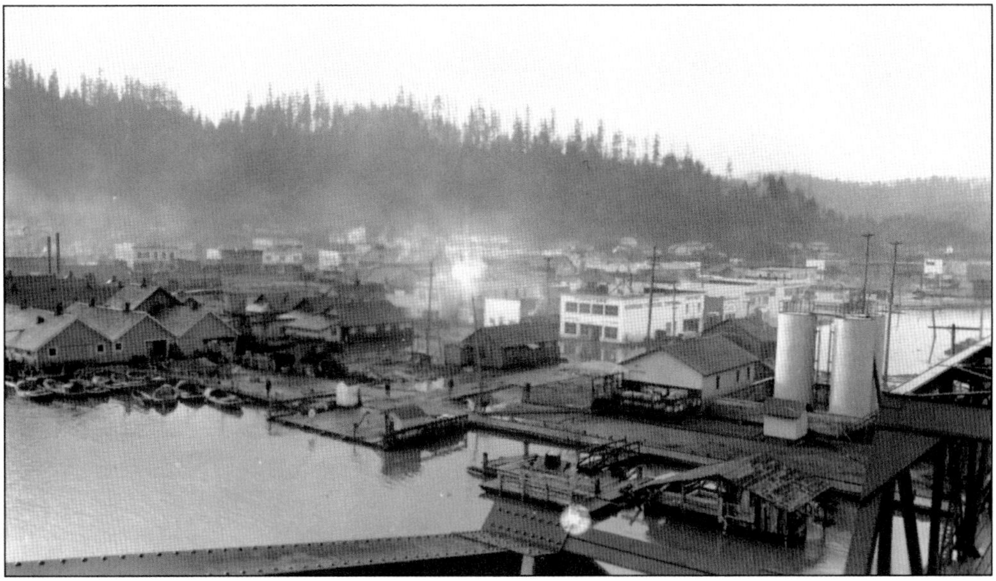

This is another photograph taken from the top of the Railroad Bridge. To the far left of the image, tied to the docks where boat repair shops operated, are the Columbia fishing boats that plied the Umpqua. The waterfront docks, where the catches of salmon were delivered daily, are clearly visible. Crestview Heights is in the background, and the Reed property is on the far right.

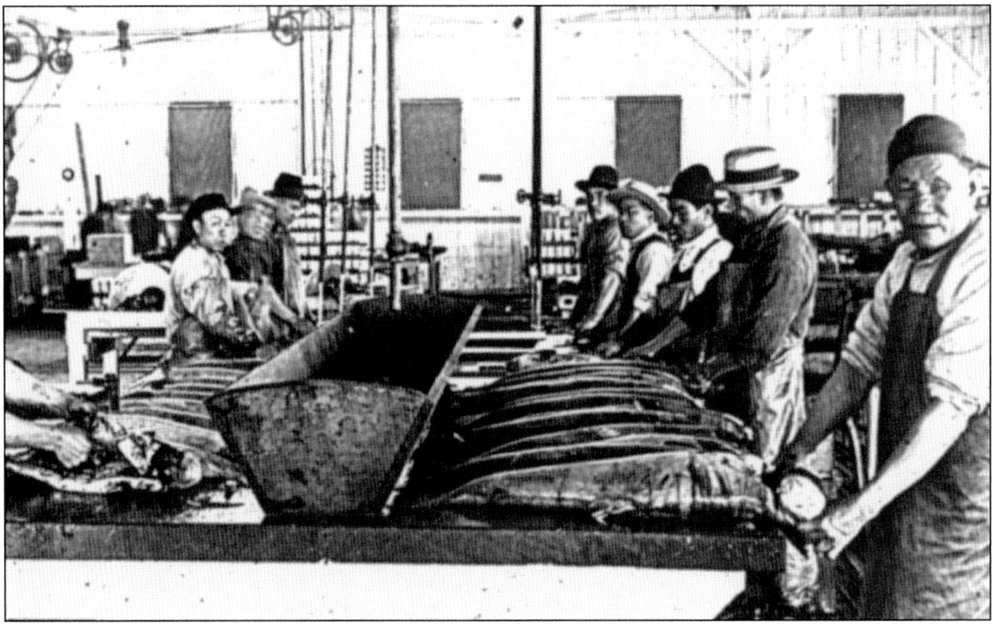

There was a strict division of labor between the Chinese, who were in charge of the cannery operations, and the Swedes, Finns, Germans, and Norwegians, who fished the river and the estuaries and were responsible for the nets. This c. 1900 photograph shows Chinese workers preparing salmon for the canning process.

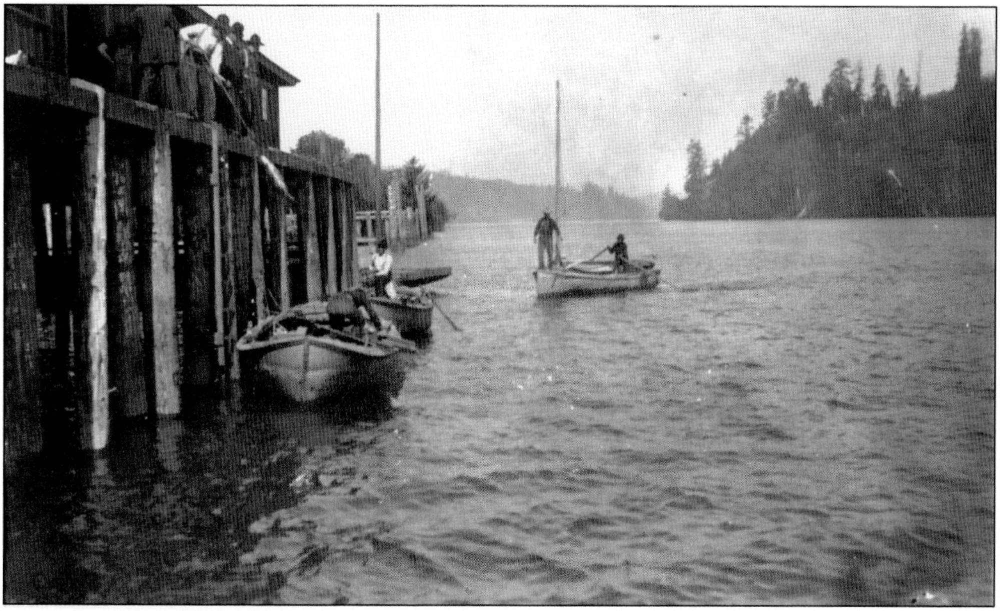

Most commercial fishermen used Columbia River fishing boats pulled by oars or small sails if there was a breeze. In this 1910 photograph, fishermen are seen unloading their catch at the Chase Cannery that used to sit on the location of present-day Umpqua Discovery Center. The fishery slowed when the state of Oregon began to harvest salmon eggs. In 1910, four million Chinook eggs were harvested.

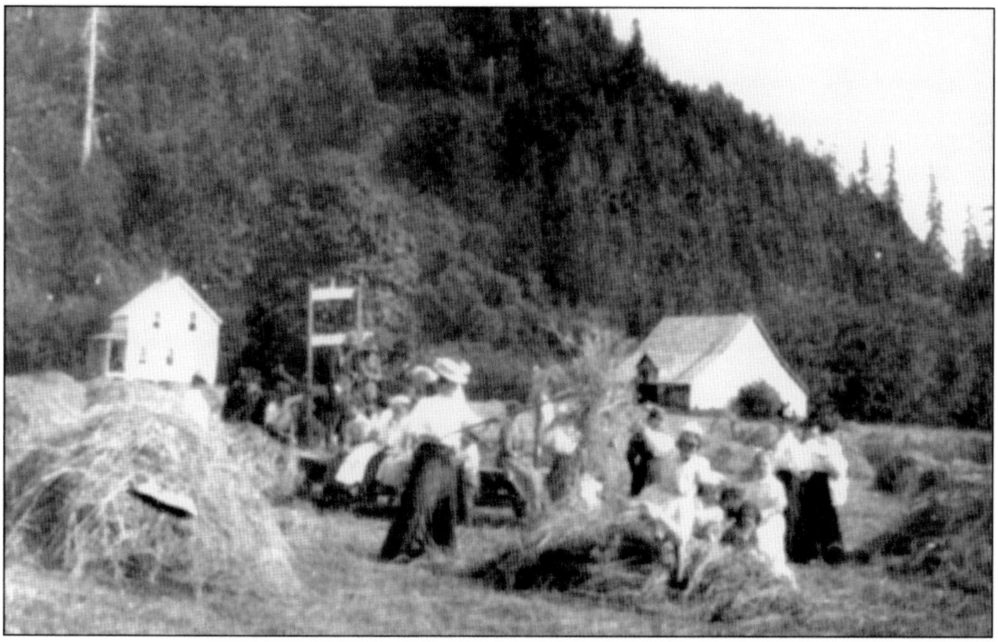

This 1912 photograph shows the dairy farm Oscar Hinsdale bought in 1906 that is located on the low-lying marsh just two miles east of Reedsport. The Dean Creek Elk Viewing Area is now situated on that site. Also owners of the Umpqua River Steam Navigation Company, Oscar and his wife, Evangeline, constructed a summer home on Spruce Reach Island that is just to the north of this dairy.

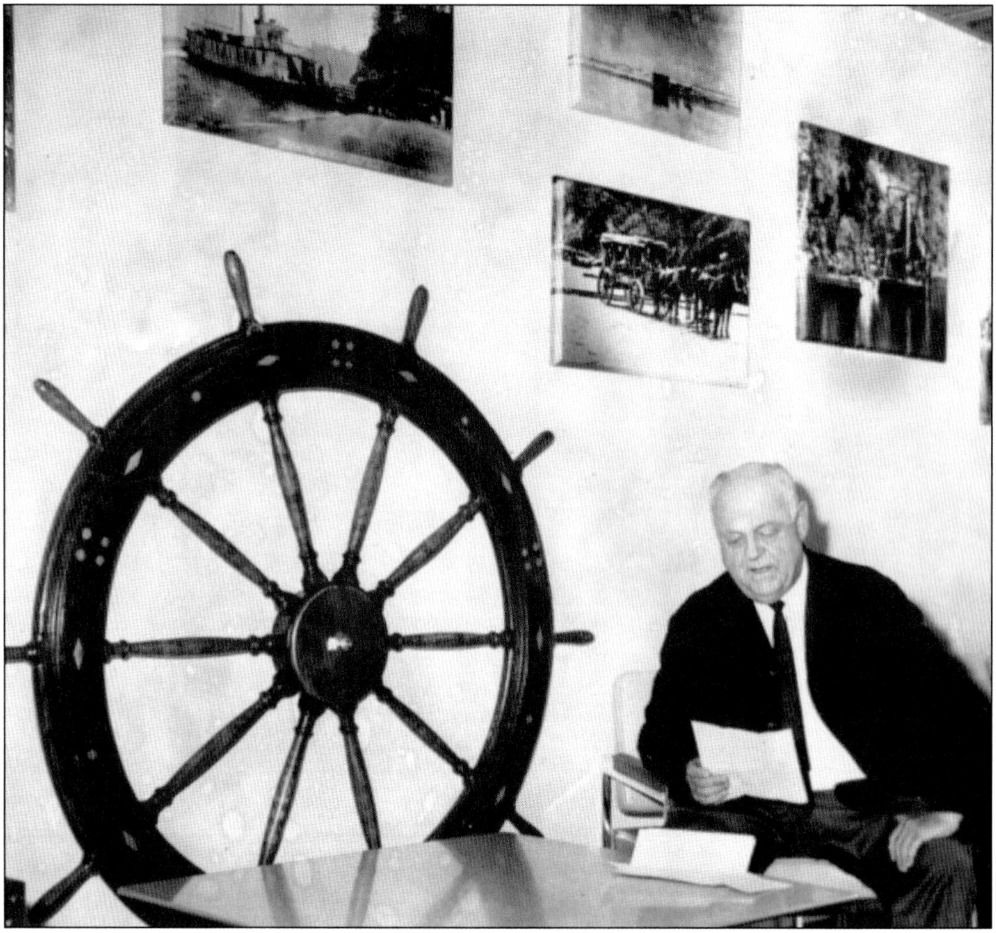

Oscar's son Howard, pictured here, created the National Bank of Gardiner. He owned the ferries traversing the Umpqua and operated Umpqua Navigation. He was responsible for the shift from hauling just freight to hauling logs and rock to help construct bridges on the Oregon Coast. He also constructed an internationally known Woodland Garden on Spruce Reach Island that contained a variety of rhododendrons, azaleas, and unique trees.

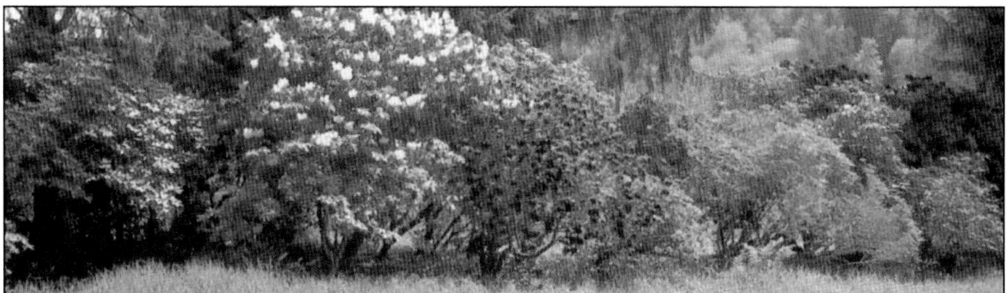

Hinsdale's Spruce Reach Island Woodland Garden reached international audiences. This garden is known for its rhododendrons, of which there are several hundred specimens. Some of these are now large, having grown over 40 feet tall with trunks a foot in diameter. However, the garden is much more than just rhododendrons. There are also almost 100 camellias, with blooms of various shapes, colors, and patterns.

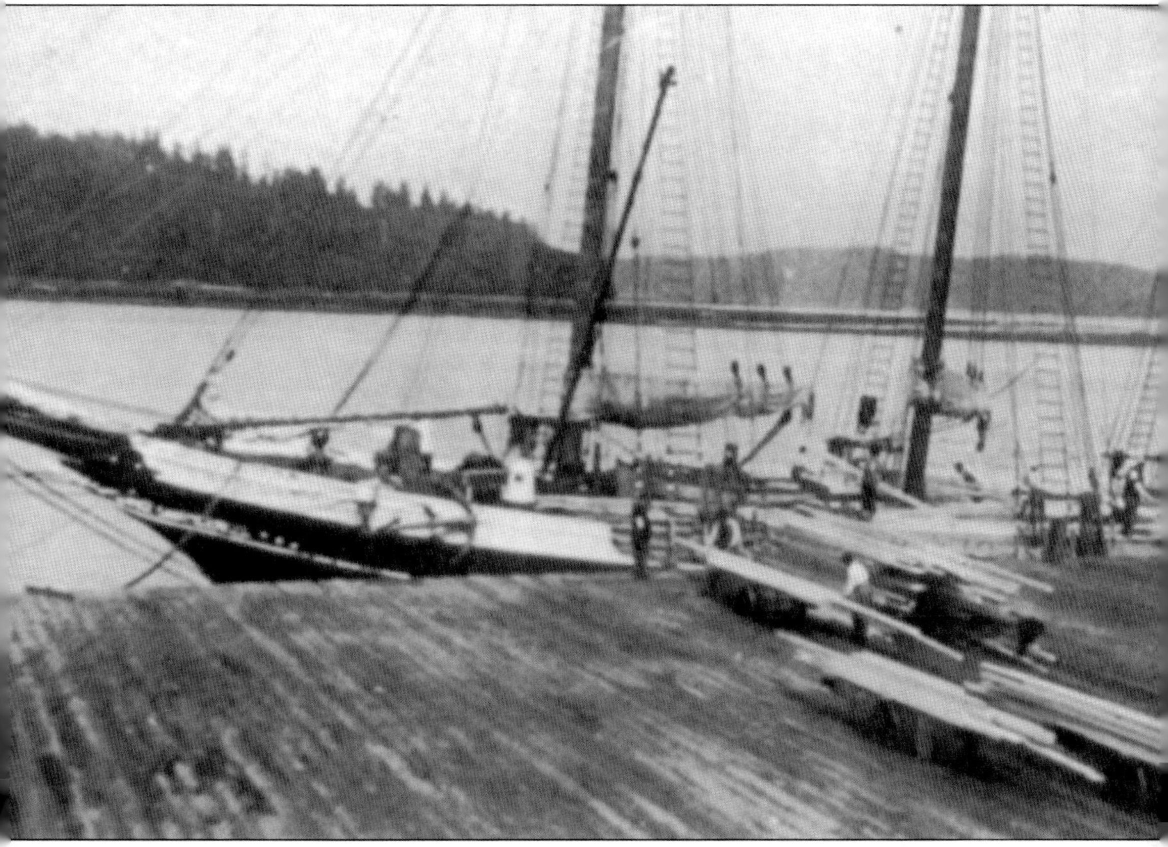

The vessel *The Caroline,* shown here in a c. 1900 photograph, was a trading ship that ran between Gardiner and San Francisco. It was a part of a fleet of ships operating out of Gardiner that carried 1,112,554 tons of exported goods over the Umpqua River Bar between 1892 and 1896. Timber that was being sent elsewhere took up 80 percent of this volume. The area's economy was, in large part, dependent on its ocean connection.

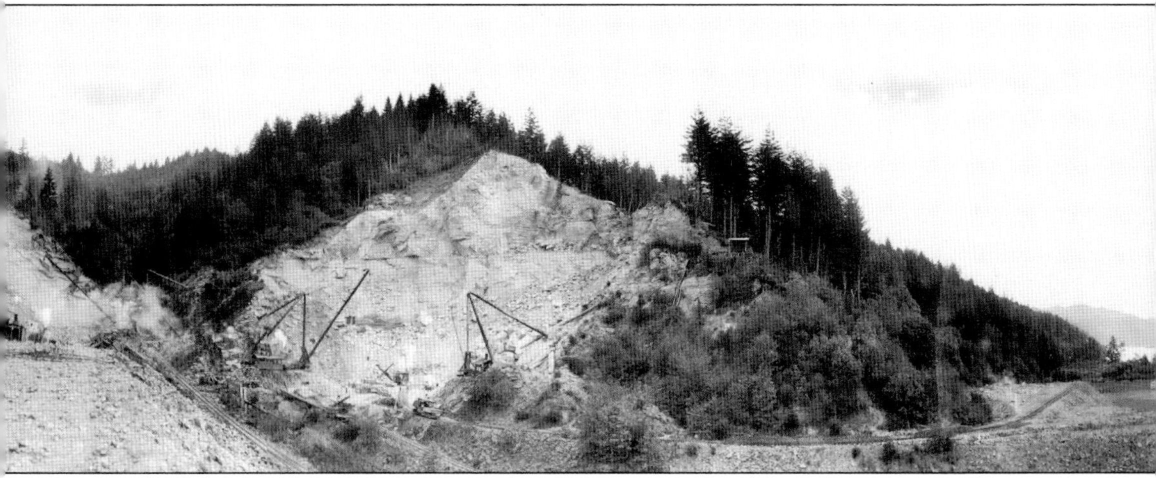

This is a c. 1940 photograph of the quarry system used to provide rock for the Reedsport area. In order to provide rock for the jetty-building projects, rock quarries were needed. This quarry was located east of Dean Creek at the six-mile marker on Highway 38. The original quarry was at the east end of Brandy Bar, but the ground proved too soft for heavy machinery to work. At the second site, rocks between 20 and 40 tons were used, and were sent by barge to the jetty sites. Steam-powered donkeys used swinging booms to move containers known as "skips" that were

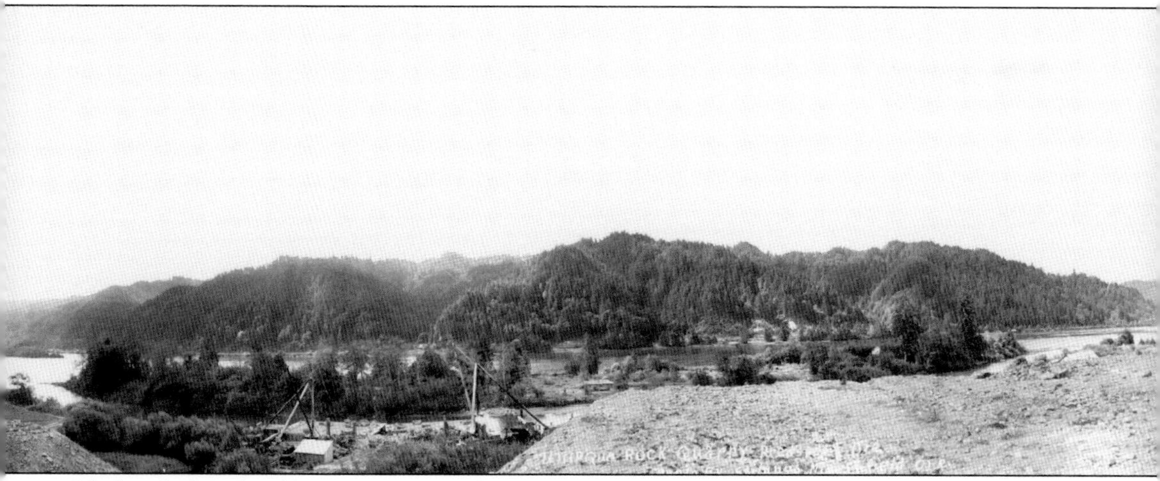

filled with these boulders. Oscar Hinsdale originally created the Umpqua River Steam Navigation Company in 1889, and their barges were heavily involved in the transportation of these rocks. The shift in hauling logs and rock from hauling freight was a major reason for the success of this business. The island seen in the middle of this photograph was largely destroyed in the flood of 1964. (Courtesy of Bob North.)

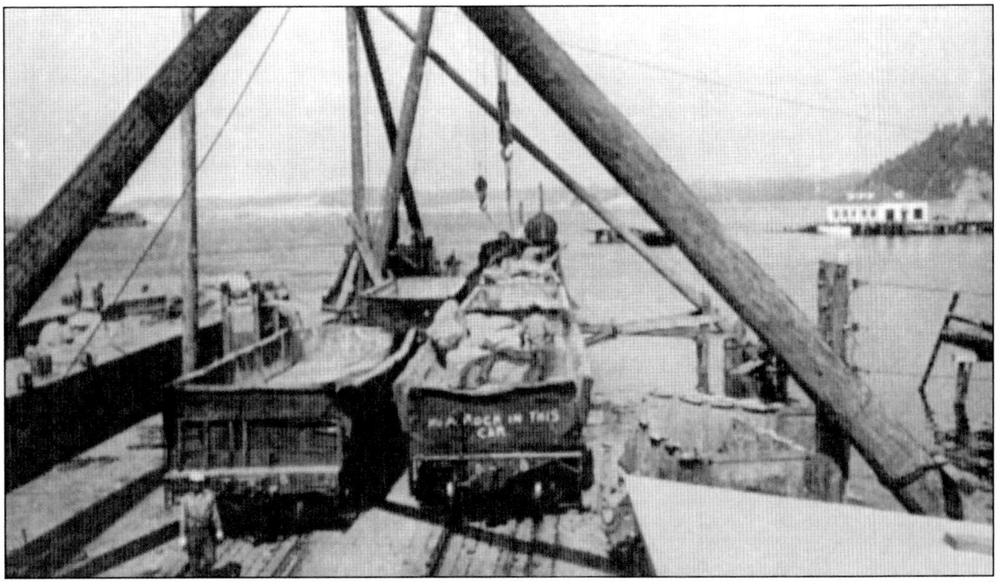

On June 22, 1916, the secretary of war issued the Port of Umpqua a permit to construct a wharf, tramway, and a 3,390-foot rock jetty on the north spit of the Umpqua River mouth. This project was completed in 1926. The jetty was to prevent sand from washing out and blocking the mouth of the river. Each rock weighed up to 40 tons, so a railroad spur was constructed to haul rocks to the ocean. This c. 1920 photograph shows the jetty tram hauling these rocks for the project. An A-frame was made with two big fir logs, a pulley and cable system was installed, and rocks could be lifted from the train to the jetty with the use of a steam donkey. The *Port Umpqua Courier* wrote in 1926, "With the improvement of the harbor channel, the completion of the North Jetty, and the dredging of the channel, Reedsport is able to make tremendous strides within the coming few years."

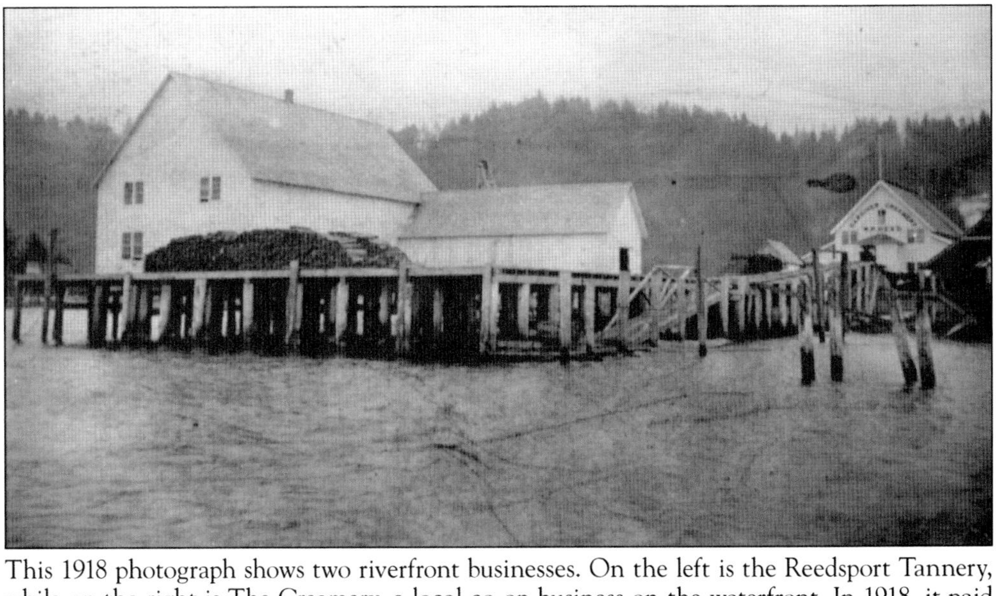

This 1918 photograph shows two riverfront businesses. On the left is the Reedsport Tannery, while on the right is The Creamery, a local co-op business on the waterfront. In 1918, it paid $80,000 to 75 members of their co-op for the crops and livestock they brought in to sell. They had cheese, hogs, and 5,600 turkeys that they sent to Portland at 40¢ pound.

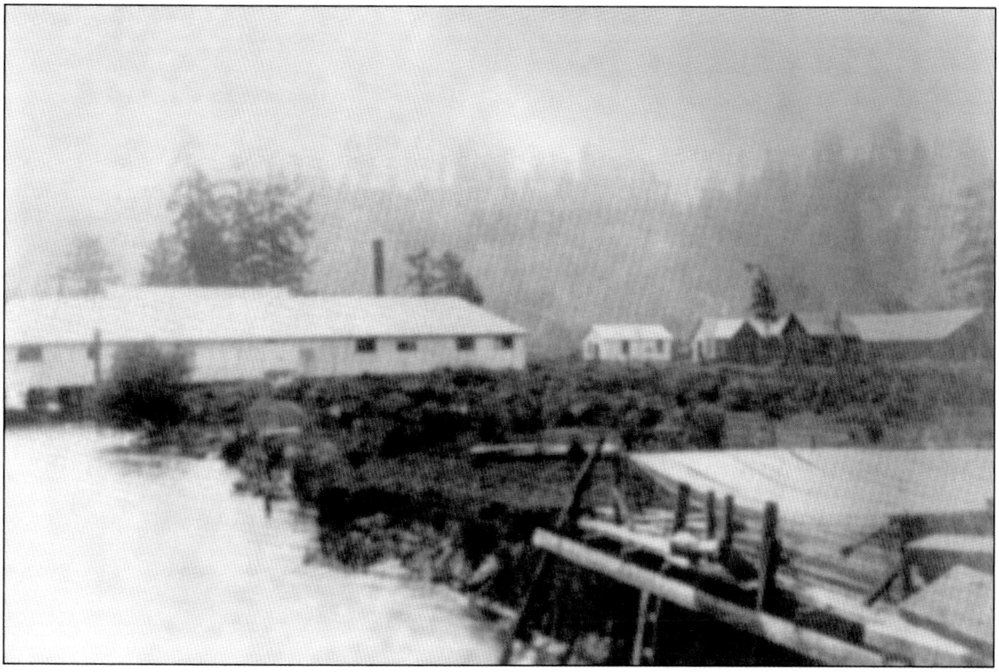

This photograph shows the Elmore Packing Company, one of two canneries on the river. Nets are stretched to dry next to their processing facility. Note the building in the middle of the image, which was the China House that housed Chinese salmon canners during the season. The Elmore Company had a small steamer that ran from Portland to Reedsport, bringing supplies and returning with canned salmon.

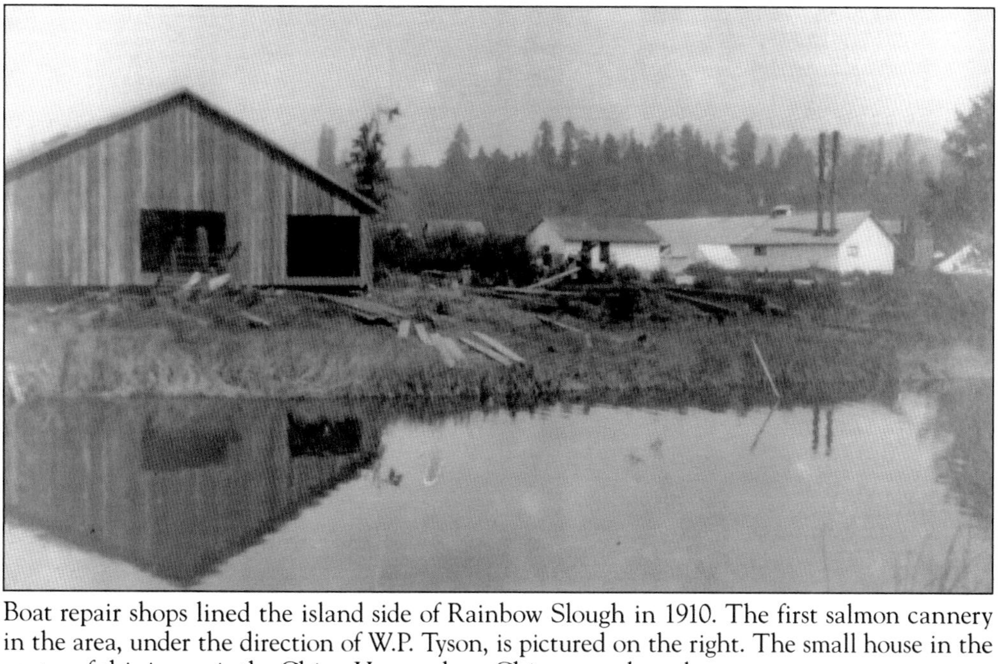

Boat repair shops lined the island side of Rainbow Slough in 1910. The first salmon cannery in the area, under the direction of W.P. Tyson, is pictured on the right. The small house in the center of this image is the China House where Chinese workers slept.

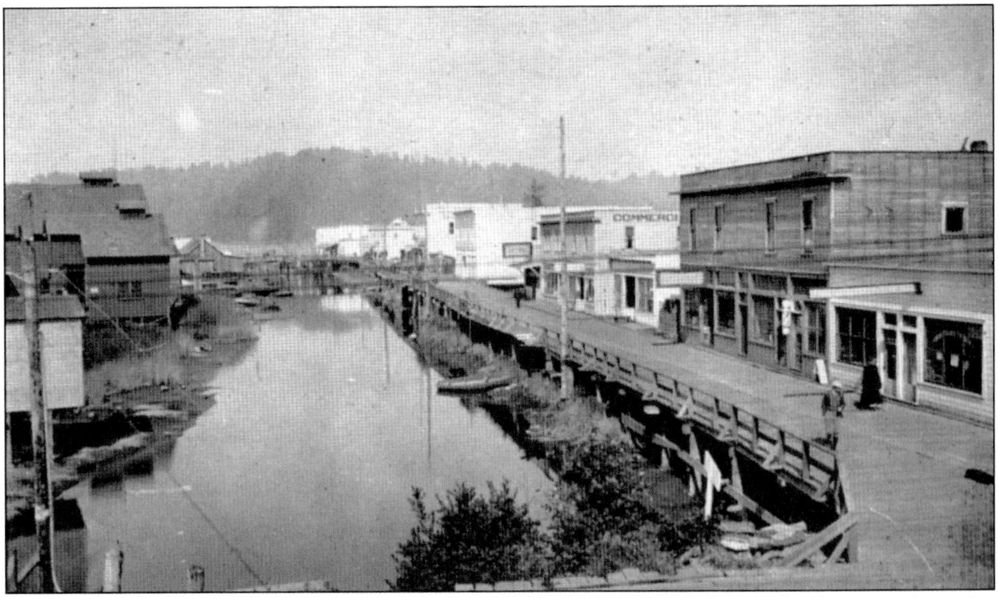

This 1920 photograph was taken from the boardwalk on Rainbow Slough, looking north to the Umpqua River. Juniper Street currently follows the course of Rainbow Slough. The Commercial Hotel (with Snow White's brothel located on the second floor) and other businesses face the boat repair shops and the China House across the slough. The post office is at the far end of the boardwalk on the right.

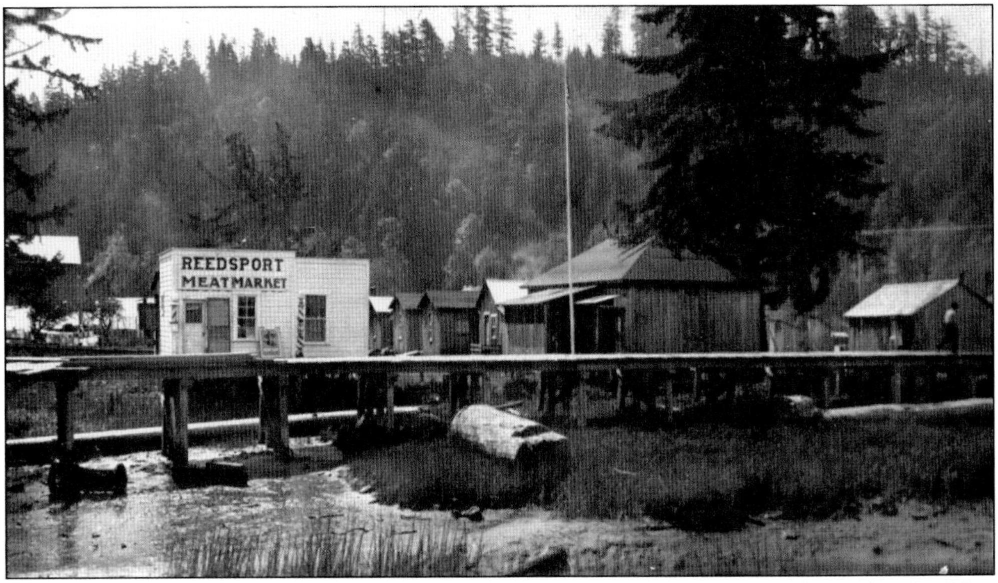

The Reedsport Meat Market pictured to the left was also located on Rainbow Slough. Glen Caley had his barbershop in the corner of the meat market. The building with flagpole was the school, while the post office was in the big building to the left. The post office was actually on the waterfront and not on Rainbow Slough.

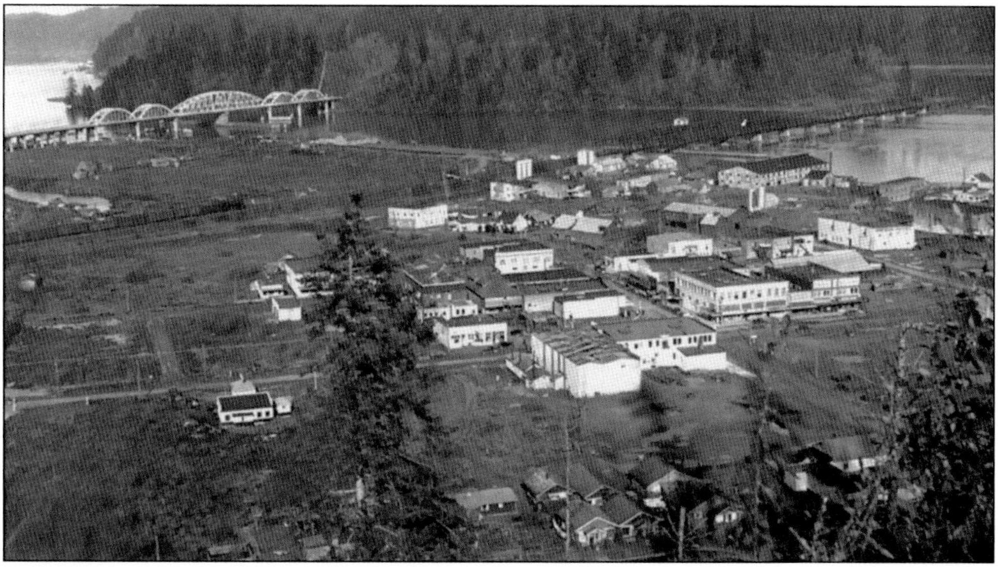

With Bolon Island in the background, the Conde McCullough Bridge to the right, and the Railroad Bridge to the left, the Reedsport waterfront facing the Umpqua River is visible in this late 1930s photograph. Most of downtown Reedsport rests on the fill that eventually covered the original marsh.

In this c. 1915 photograph of Reedsport's dominant businesses on the waterfront, Bill Burdick's store is on the far left. Next to it is the Reed and Janelle General Merchandise Store, and on the far right is the Lyons Store, a two-story general merchandise store. The family lived upstairs.

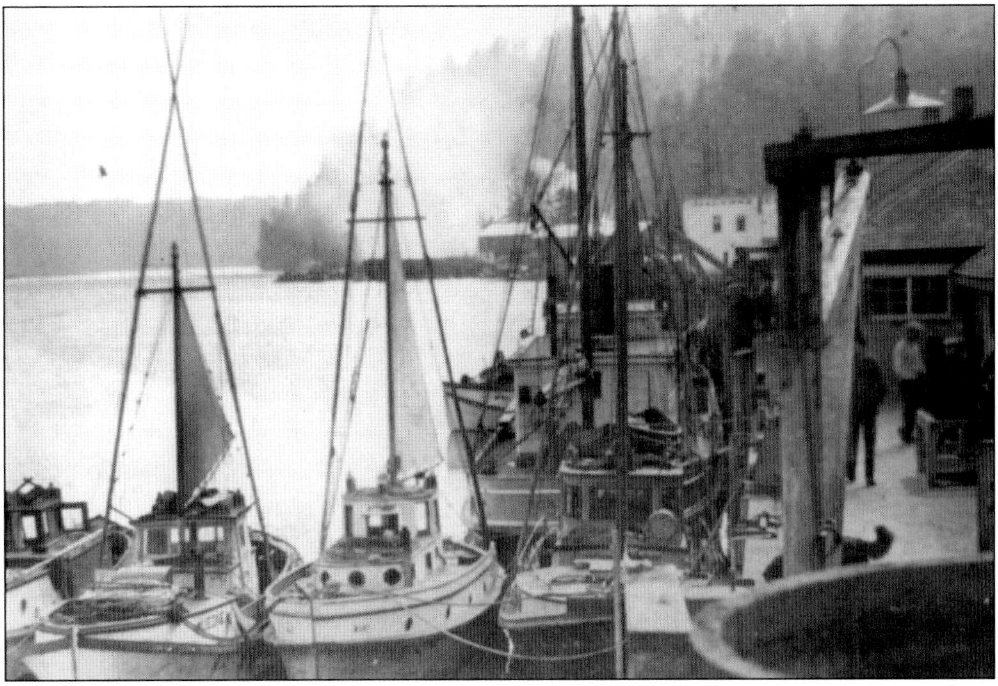

Looking east up the Umpqua River, fishing boats are tied side by side to the Reedsport riverfront boardwalk, having unloaded their daily catch. In the background are Hubbard's Mill and the Reed and Janelle General Merchandise Store. Riverfront activity was bustling with timber and fishing businesses thriving on local resources.

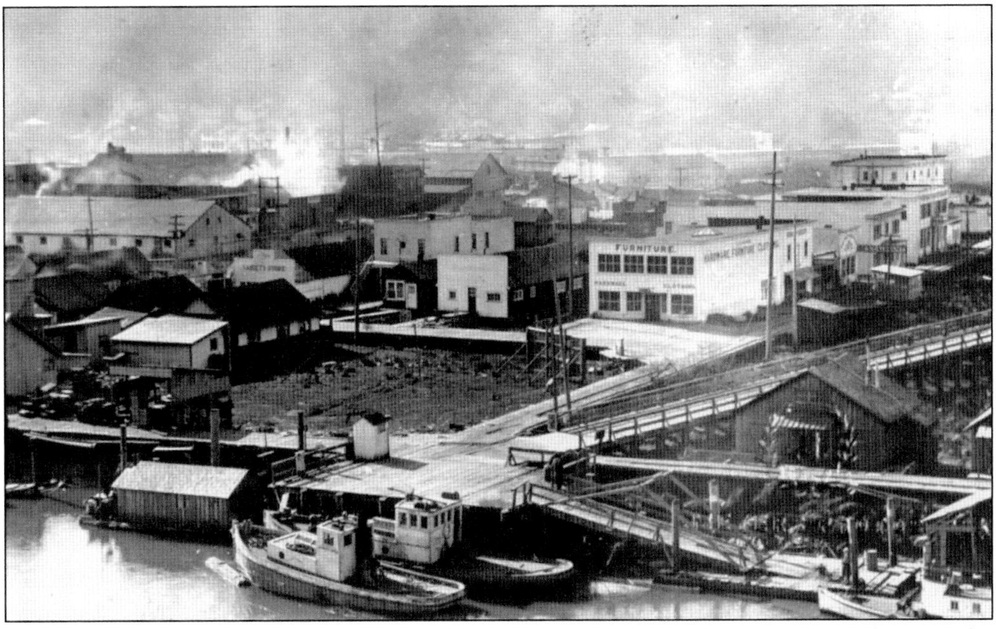

This is the Reedsport waterfront in the early 1920s. Since the town was constructed on marshy ground and was prone to flooding, it was elevated on stilts. Kennedy and Brown are in the front and center; Sorne's Variety Store is to the left, with the China House next to it. J.R. Brown Furniture Store is to the right, and the two-story Umpqua Bank is on the right.

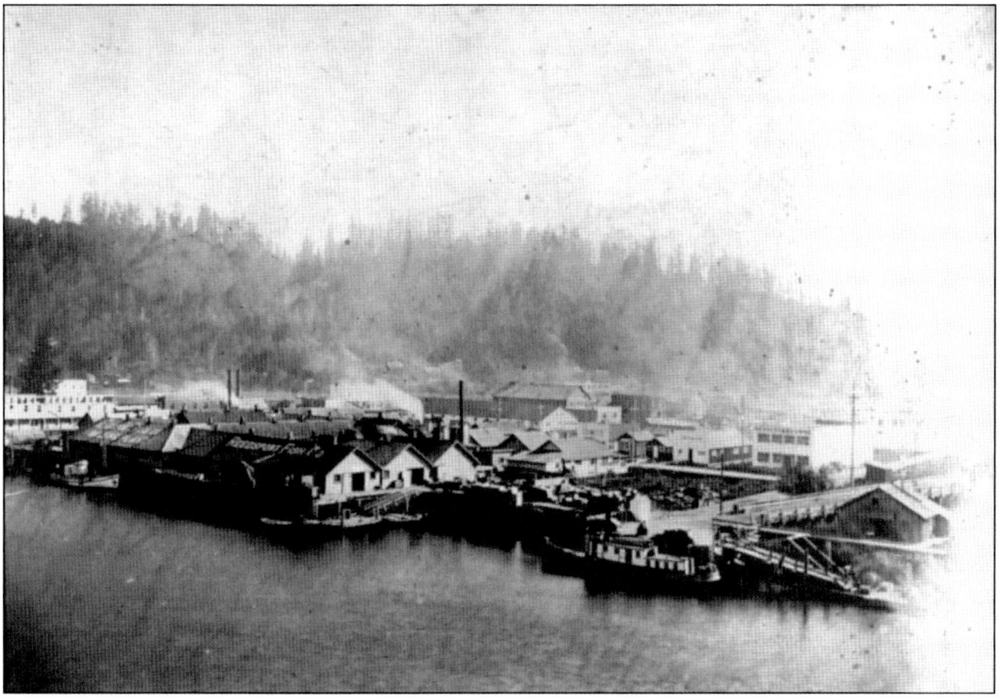

Crestview Heights is in the background of this 1920s photograph, rising behind the town. Before water was taken from Clear Lake, the town's water supply was piped from springs on Crestview Heights to the boardwalks where there was an occasional faucet. Eventually, E.K. Woods, the largest mill at the time, filled large tanks and the town got their water from them.

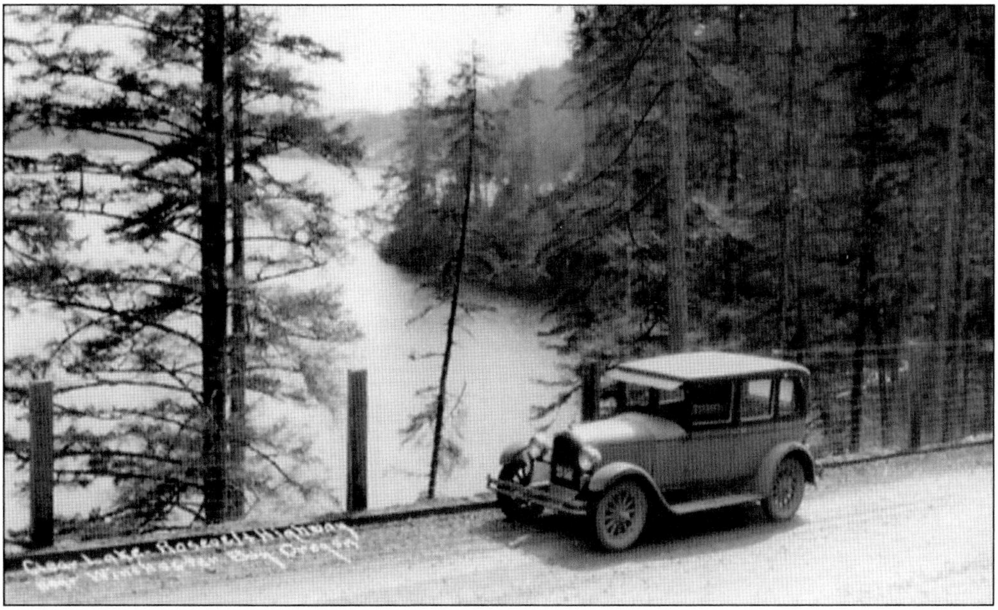

This is a 1923 photograph of Clear Lake, from which Reedsport gets its water. Warren Reed secured water rights to Clear Lake just one day before Coos Bay tried, with the city establishing pipes made from redwood logs to run water to the city. These pipes were wrapped in heavy wire and then buried in the swampy ground between Reedsport and the lake. (Courtesy of Tom Huebner.)

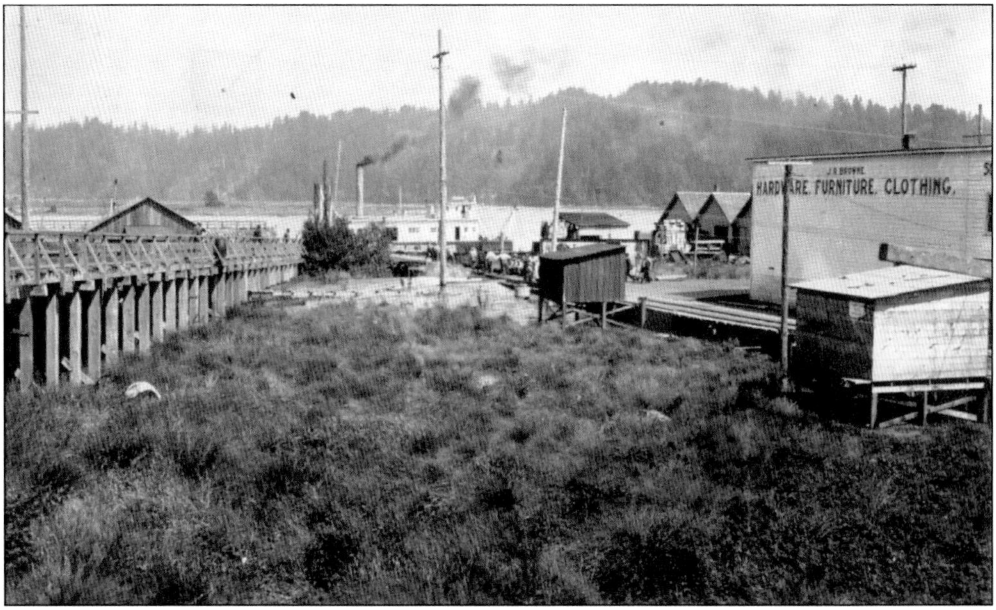

The camera looks north at the Umpqua River from the boardwalk, above the swamp in this 1919 photograph. J.R. Browne Furniture Store is located on the right, with one of the steamboats that still ran up and down the river is moored in the distance.

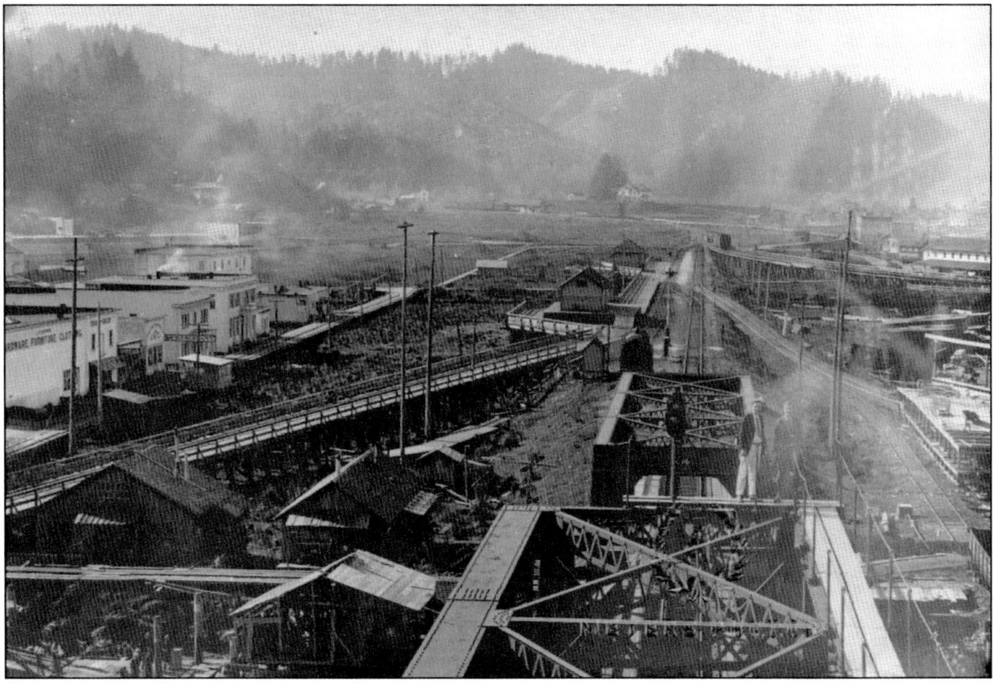

This image is taken from the top of the Southern Pacific Company Railroad Bridge facing south, looking at the swamp and the streets on stilts above the marsh. On the left sits the Umpqua Furniture Company. In the far rear of the photograph is the Reed House, located on its estate near Scholfield Creek.

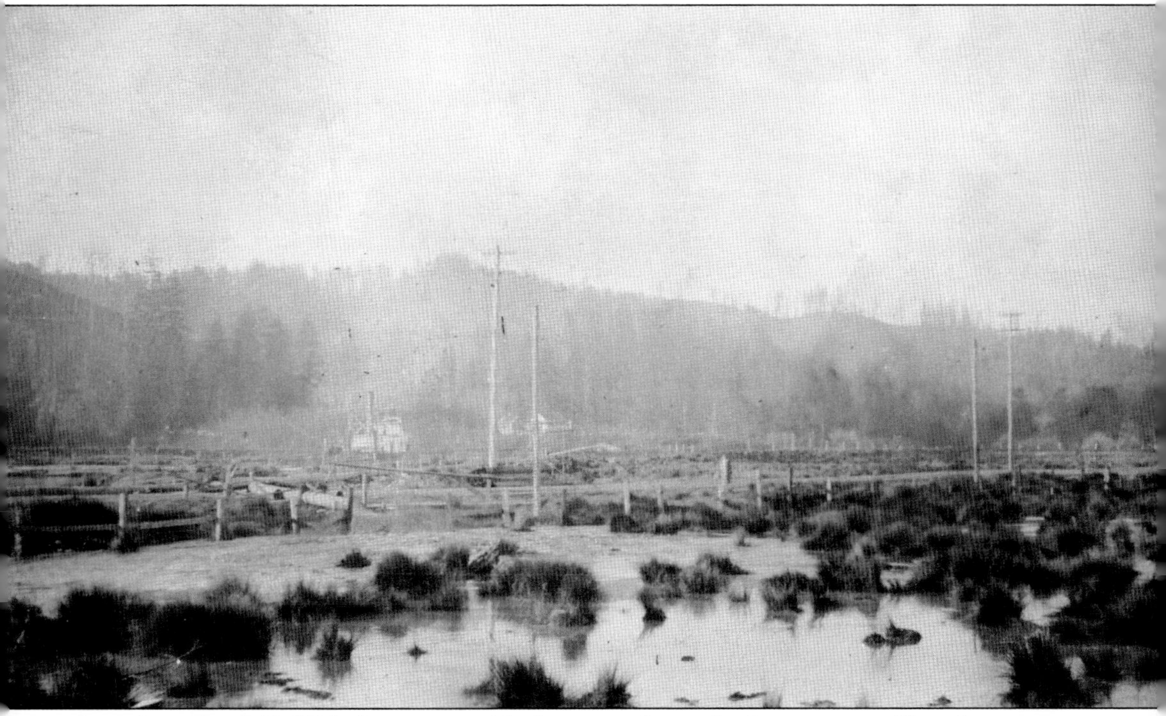

As early as April 17, 1925, there were public hearings about whether or not to fill in the swamp on which Reedsport sat. The dredging process eventually began in 1927, when this photograph was taken. The dredge that is collecting material from Scholfield Creek to fill the swamp in the Reedsport area can be seen in the distance to the left. Wade's Flat is in the far background, while the soupy texture of the Reedsport swamp is in the foreground.

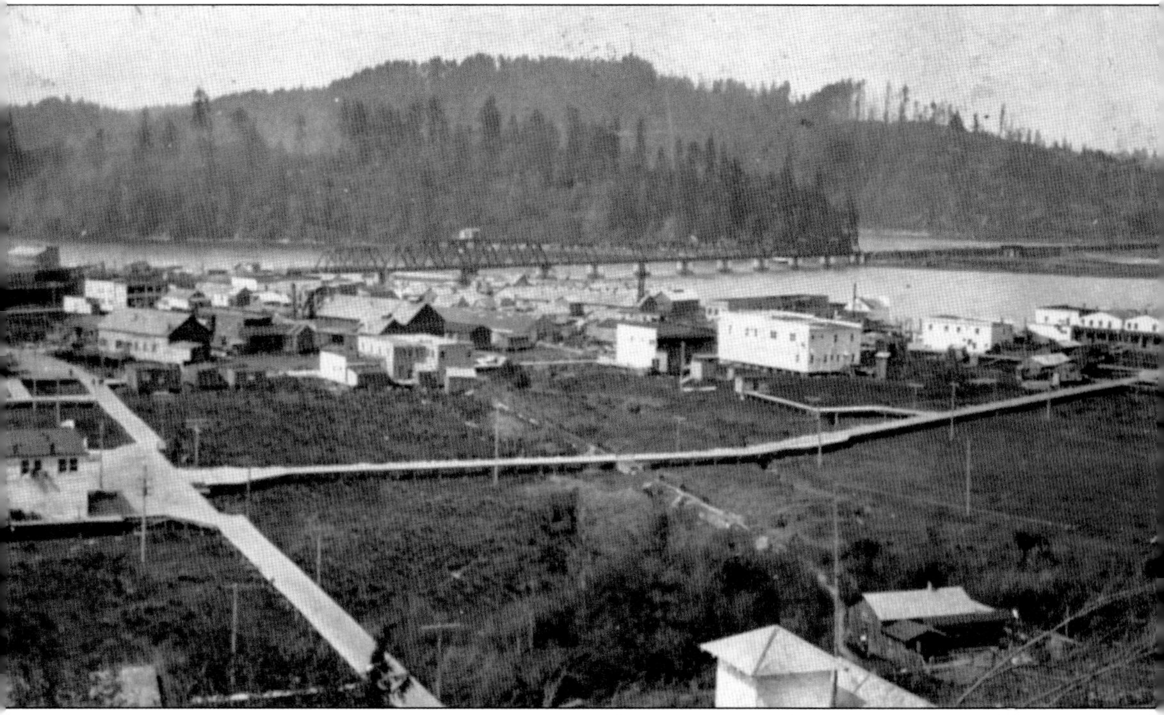

This is a 1922 view of Reedsport from Crestview Heights. One of the problems created by filling the swamp was that the community's infrastructure would be completely without regulation. Pipes ran everywhere with no overall design. Street improvement was also a problem, and the town had to vote on whether to lay two planks lengthwise or to tie planks together to create the boardwalks. Laying two planks lengthwise won. There was no real sanitary service or sewer system, only numerous old-fashioned outhouses along the sidewalks. If there were cesspools behind houses, citizens would use dynamite to make the pits bigger. One of the anecdotes local travelers would use about the town is, "This is Reedsport. I can see the garbage for the seagulls." The belfry for the Reedsport Community Church is in the foreground.

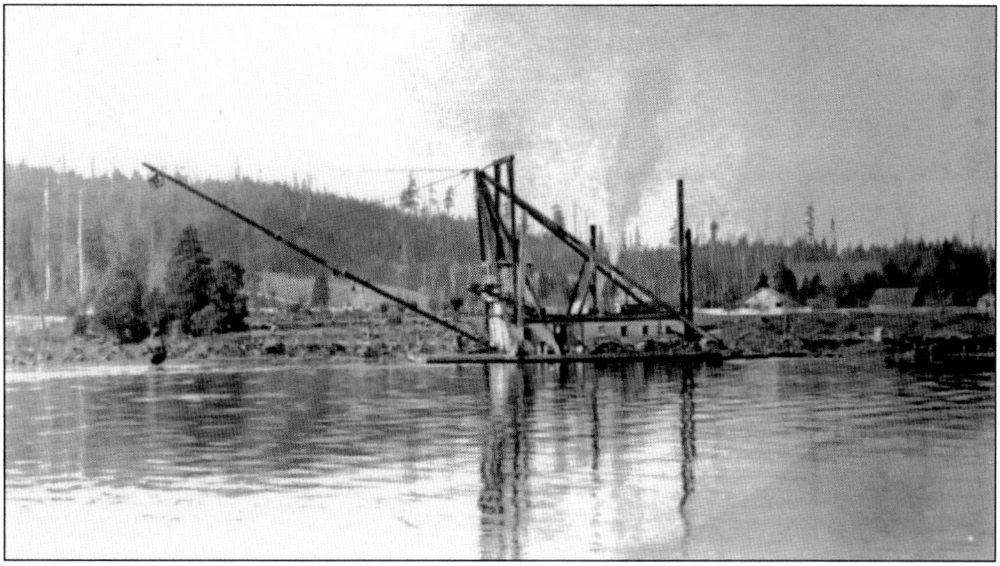

In 1927, the Port of Umpqua Commission levied a bond to dredge the shoals in the river channel between Reedsport and Winchester Bay. They then used the mud and sand from the Umpqua and Schofield to fill town's lowland. This was in an attempt to fill in the swamp on which rested the town's infrastructure at this time. This is a 1928 photograph showing the dredging process around Scholfield Creek. The dredging was to be financed with Bancroft bonds. A.W. Reed had laid out the whole lower part of town in lots for sale, because it was hoped they would sell quickly when word of the dredging got out. When the lots did not sell, Reed was unable to pay the taxes on the Bancroft bonds. The result was that Reedsport was the only town in Oregon to ever default on a Bancroft Bond.

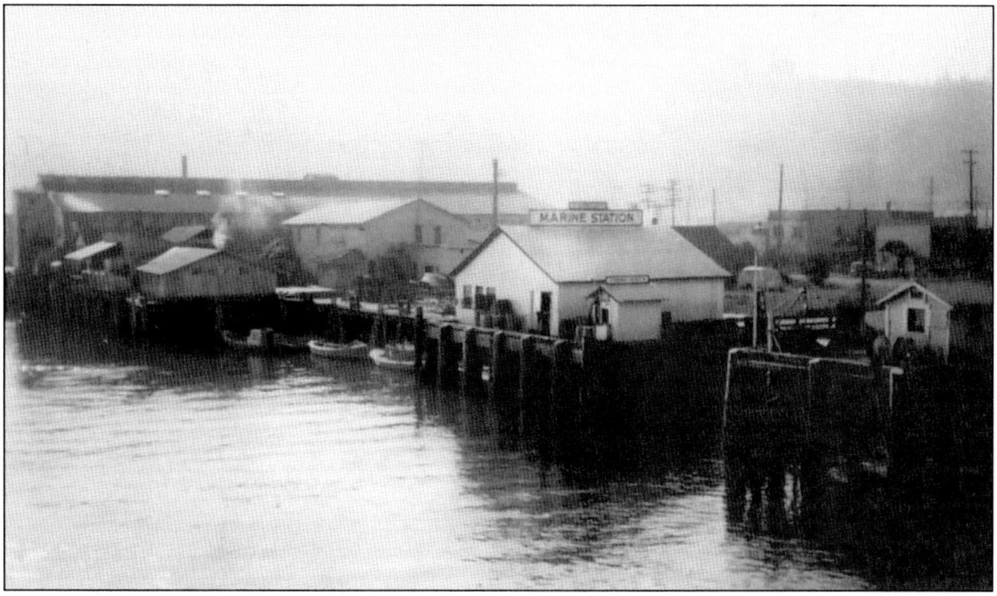

Pictured here around 1931 is the Standard Marine Station, run by Sherman Smiley. The pilings can still be seen on the boat ramp near the railroad tracks and Fred Wahl Industry in Reedsport. For years, the store was a critical repair shop that sold gas, oil, and candy bars on the waterfront. (Courtesy of Carole Plagmann.)

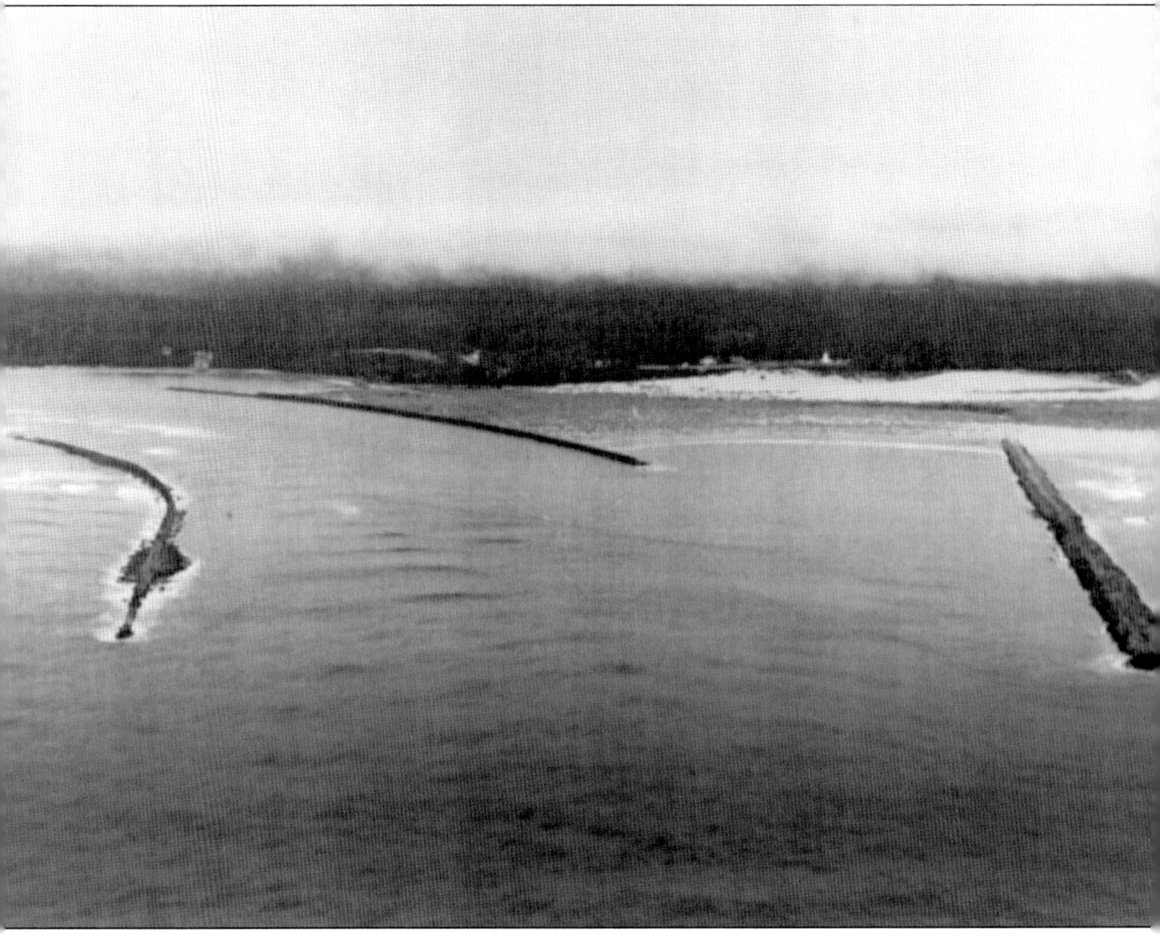

The 3,390-foot north jetty at the Umpqua River bar to the left in this photograph was built in 1916 to prevent sand from accumulating on the river entrance. When this did not work, a second jetty was constructed in 1935. This 4,200-foot jetty, visible to the far right in this photograph, was equally inefficient in keeping sand off of the river bar, so a training jetty (center) was added in 1979, forming a triangle between the south jetty and the training jetty when it was completed. Commercial oyster beds currently occupy the space in this area.

Three

The Entrepreneurs

The building of the Southern Pacific Railroad from 1913 to 1916 certainly sparked a huge increase in business in Reedsport. There was an influx of population, and both housing and service industries became commodities that were in huge demand. Business expanded from riverfront and Rainbow Slough stores, canneries, and repair shops to a new and forward-thinking Reedsport.

The first store in Reedsport was the 1912 Kennedy and Brown Store on the banks of Scholfield Creek. In the back of the store was the first Reedsport Post Office. The Reedsport Confectionery soon joined this establishment on the slough. The housing shortage created a need for hotels. The Franklin Hotel had rooms upstairs, while a dining room was downstairs with a confectionery and a pool hall. Hotel Reedsport was located downtown and had a restaurant with the Riverview Hotel nearby. The Winchester Bay Mill Company constructed a hotel for men on Mill Street that had a dining hall attached.

In addition to the existing industries of timber and fishing, support businesses grew on the boardwalk. Varrrelman's Dry Goods Store was one of the first dry goods establishments available in the area. There was also a sash and door factory, a cheese factory, a box factory, a creamery, a brick-making business, a shingles mill, and a dance hall. Frank Taylor opened a hardware store, and the Sornes brothers opened a variety store. Hinsdale had the Umpqua River Navigation Company, and Isaac Staples had a 44-by-80-foot building with a dance hall on the second floor and shops occupying the space below.

Unique buildings like the Edwards Theater, the Hogan Garage, the Umpqua National Bank, which also housed the post office and jail, and the Municipal Light Plant were spread throughout town. The Burdick and Lovelace Drug Store was the only place to buy prescription drugs in the area. Previously, these drugs had been available at Markley's Drug in Gardiner.

Other notable businesses and businesspeople were Jack Unger's Mortuary, Butch Thompson's Ford Dealership, Ley's Variety Store, Edgar Stevens' Grocery, and Maurice Kelly's Hardware Store.

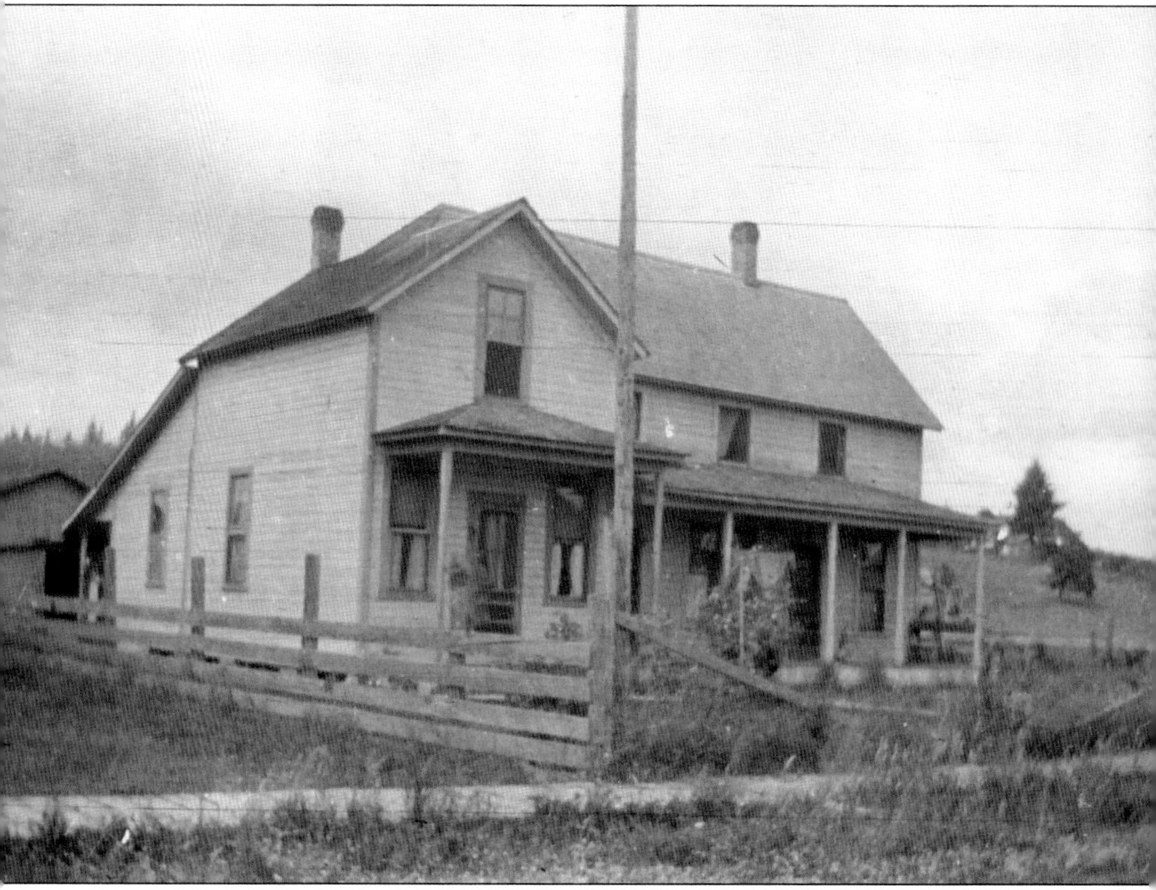

Wade's Flat was the area on the south side of Scholfield Creek that lay above Reedsport and the swampy land. The first home in this region, built in an area called Scholfield Heights, was the Wade Home. This c. 1905 photograph shows the wooden structure as it sat alone on the flats above what would ultimately be a part of Reedsport. This became the area where Gardiner and Reedsport residents would picnic and play baseball. (Courtesy of Sunnie Heddon.)

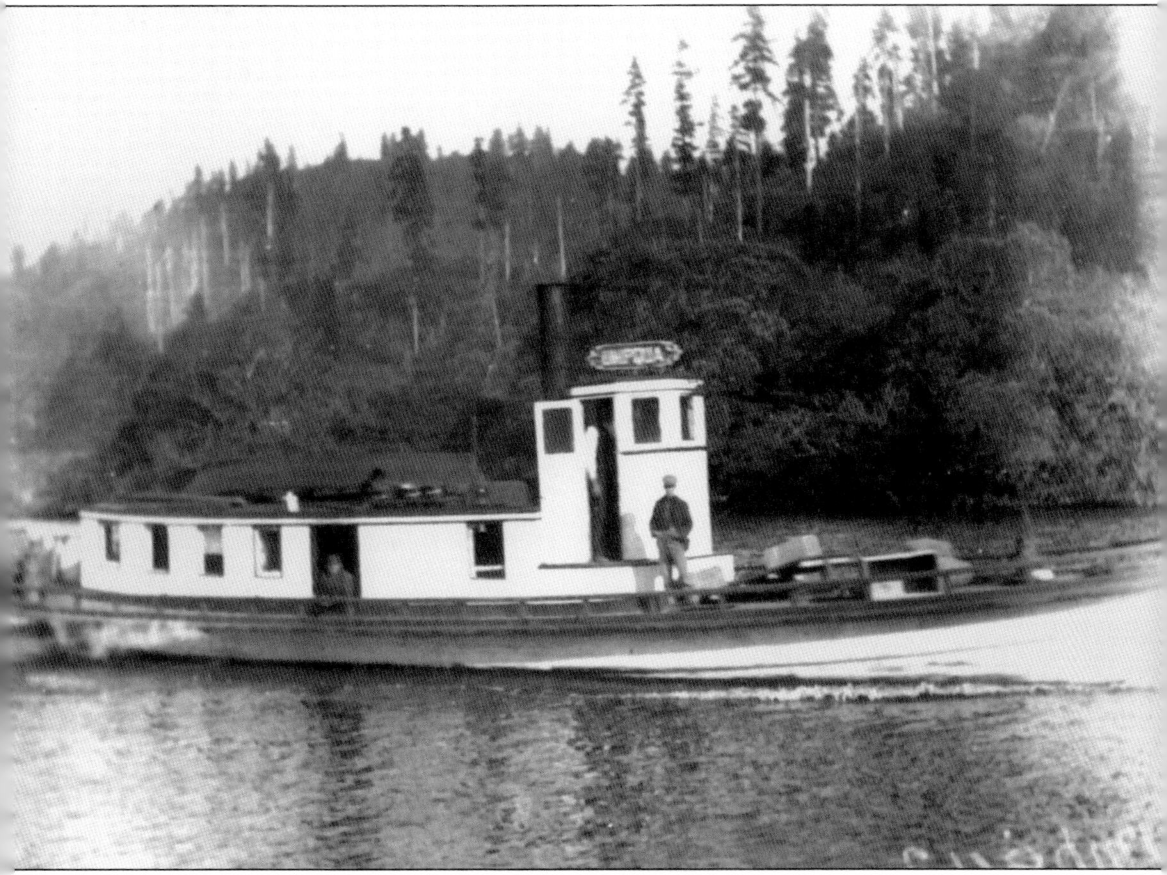

Steamboats were critical for transporting people and goods up and down the river. This 1914 photograph of the steamboat the *Umpqua* shows it as it approaches the lower river near Winchester Bay. The *Umpqua* was best known for transporting goods from the ocean beaches to Gardiner, Reedsport, and Scottsburg. (Courtesy of Sunnie Heddon.)

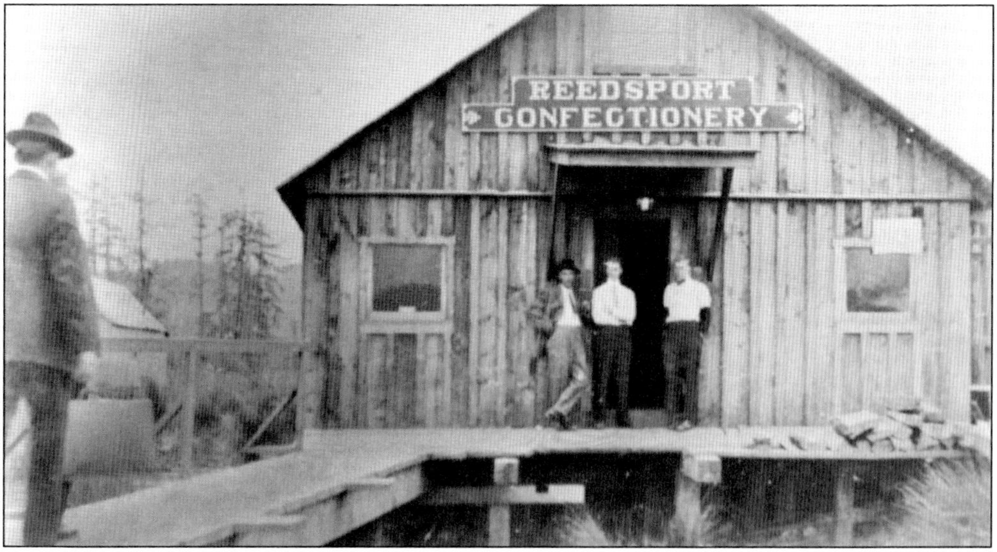

The Reedsport Confectionery was located on the Umpqua riverfront, carrying a wide assortment of candies and sweets for the public. Seen here, owner Oscar Anderson and Everett Anderson chat with a customer. The store was moved to the back of the Kennedy and Browne Store around 1917 and was used as a butcher shop. The Kennedy Brown Store opened on the south side of Scholfield Creek, just below where the Umpqua River Bridge is now, and was the first store in Reedsport. Owners Ted Kennedy and John Brown had a Columbia River fishing boat and made free deliveries up and down the river as a public relations ploy to attract more customers. Joseph Lyons had the post office in the corner of the store. Most of the early commerce in Reedsport was centered in these facilities.

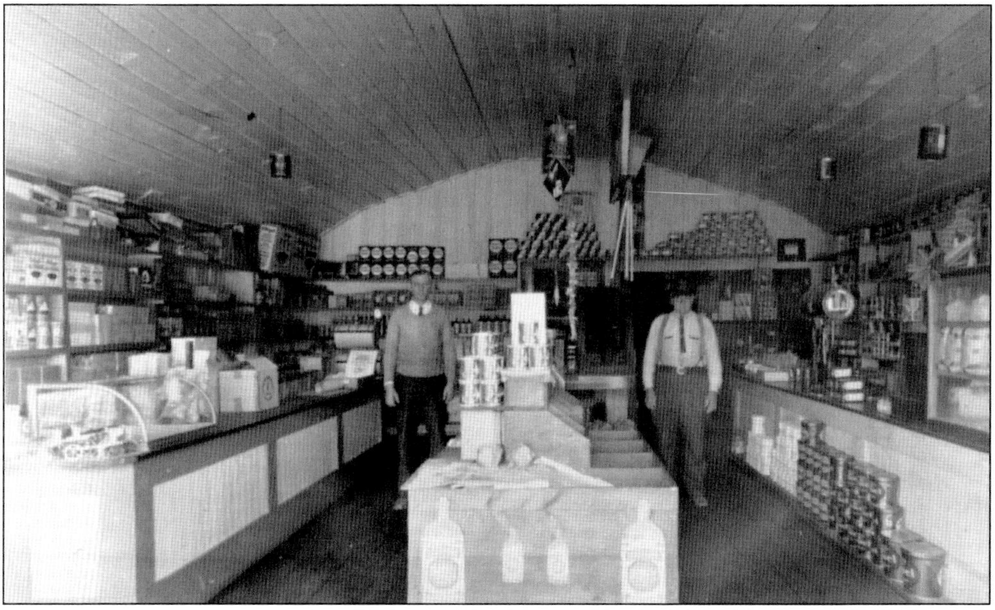

The Sornes brothers are pictured here in their Sornes Variety Store. It was one of the earliest variety stores in the area with a wide assortment of canned goods, hardware items, pots, pans, and gifts. It had an excellent location on the river boardwalk next to the China House as it faced the Umpqua River.

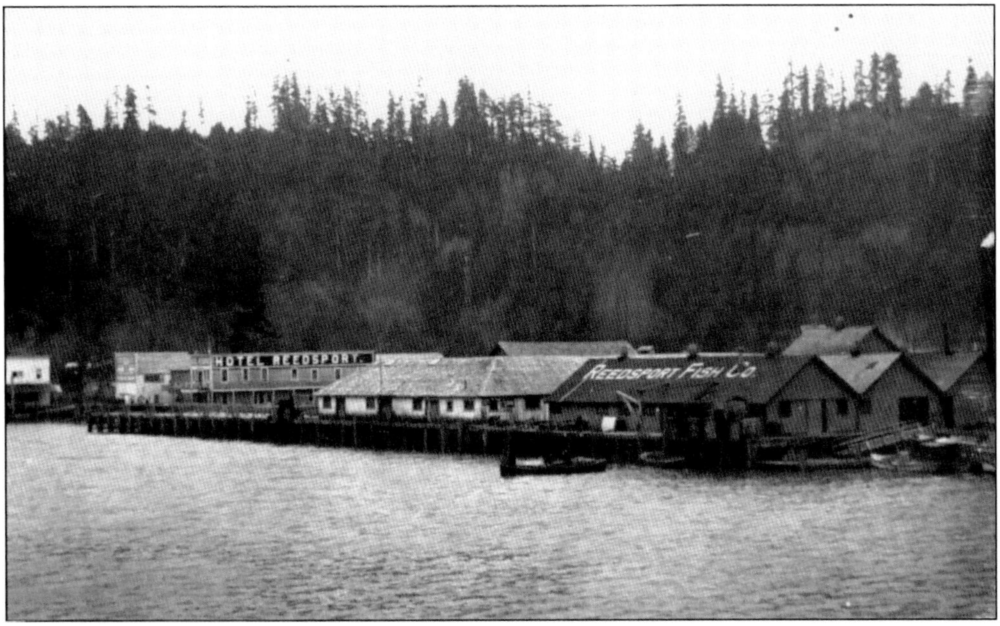

Some of the new additions to the boardwalk of the fledgling community are shown in this 1914 photograph. Hotel Reedsport is facing Rainbow Slough, while the Reedsport Fish Company, one of the fish processing businesses in town, faces the Umpqua River. The inlet to Rainbow Slough can be seen just in front of Hotel Reedsport.

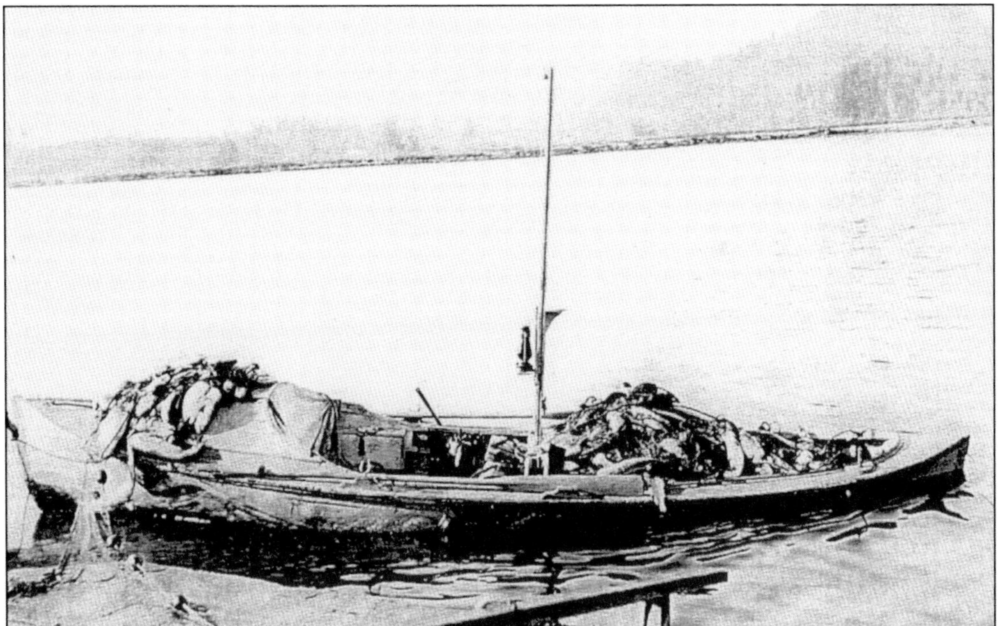

In the early 1900s, fishing was a major business on the Umpqua River at Reedsport. This is a c. 1920 photograph of a Columbia River fishing vessel in the early morning after a night of seining for salmon on the river. In one night's time, the fisherman had completely filled his boat to the point of almost sinking.

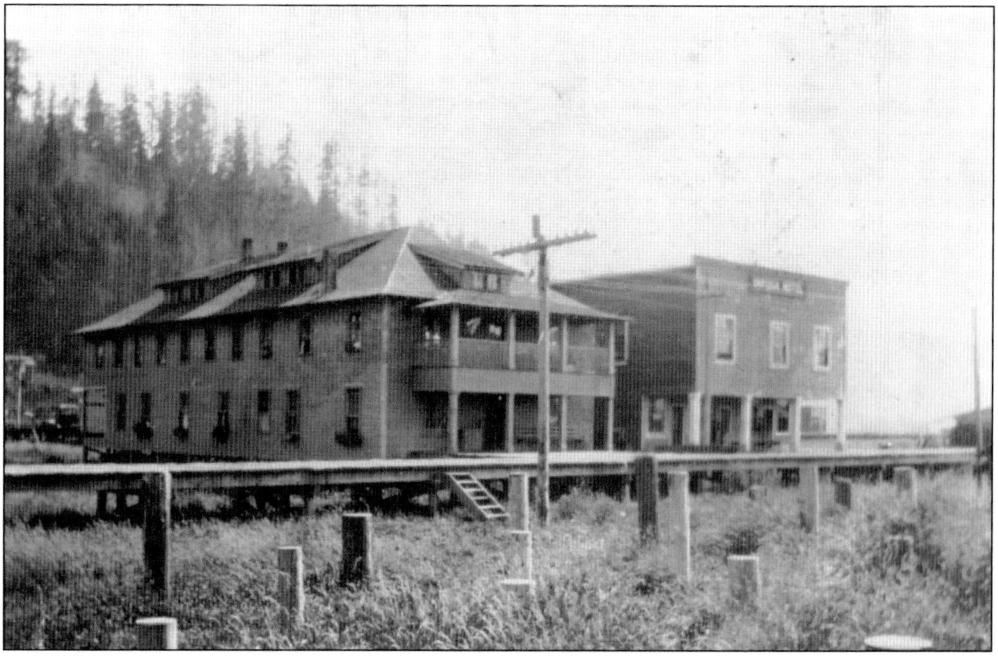

This 1920 photograph shows the riverside view of the Umpqua Hotel. A two-story affair, it was kept busy with all the men in town constructing the railroad. Note the boardwalk, which allowed customers to enter without having to walk in the swamp below. There were also numerous stumps in the swamp where trees had been cleared.

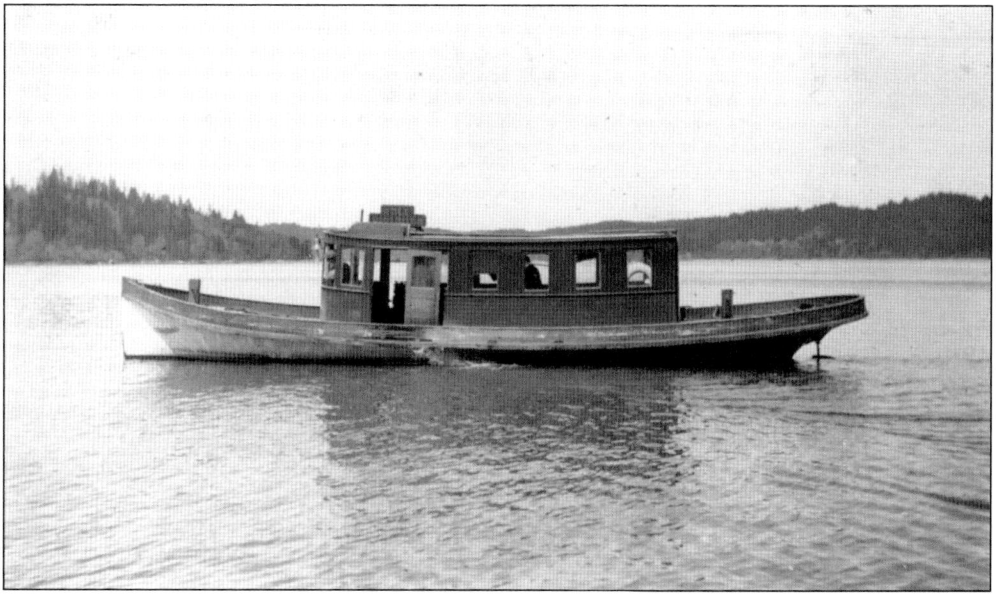

The *Adel Coos River* was the Smith River milk boat in the late 1920s. It left the Ray Dailey ranch at 6:00 a.m., and arrived in Reedsport around 1:30 p.m. The return trip left Reedsport at 2:00 p.m. and arrived at Dailey's at 7:00 p.m. Milk was brought into the creamery and empty cans were taken back to each ranch on the route. Frankie Boye was the boat pilot. (Courtesy of Sunnie Heddon.)

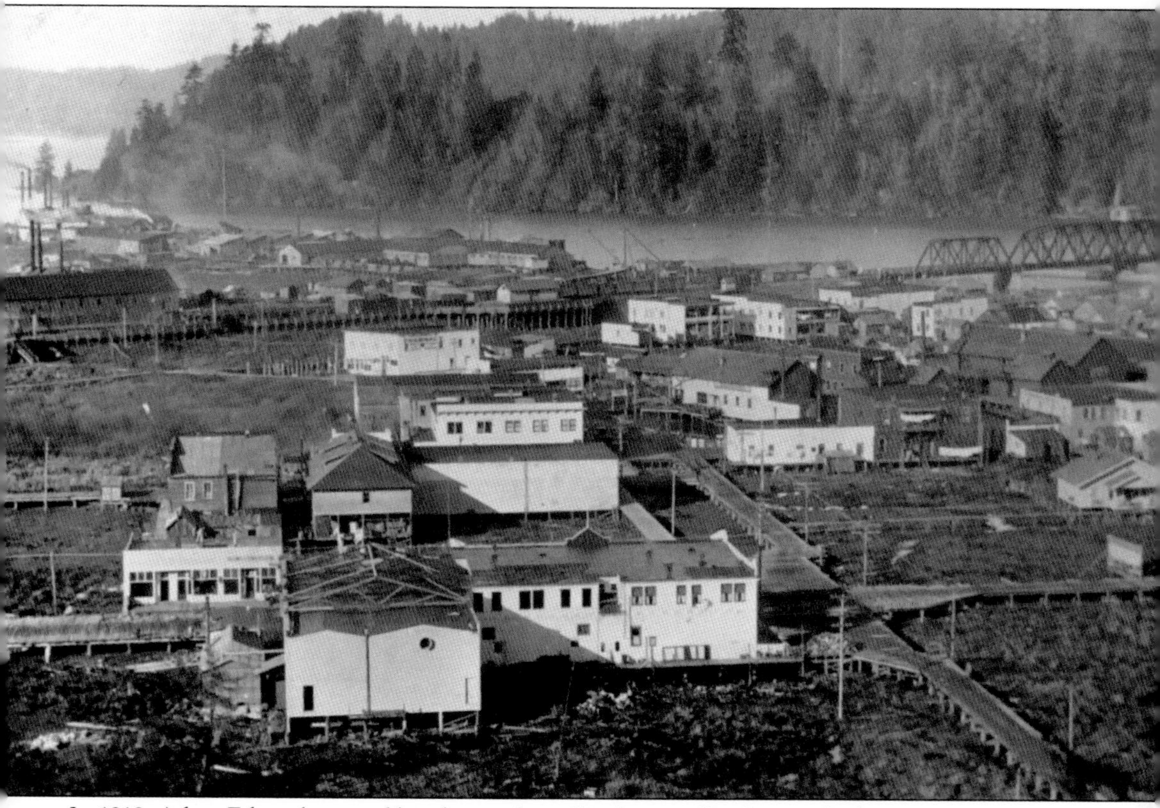

In 1918, Adam Edwards moved his theater from Gardiner to Reedsport. At first, it was in a tent, but a building was constructed in 1925. It is located below left in this 1929 photograph. When constructed, the building was slanted so that at high tide those in the front row could splash their feet in the water while watching the film. It was built on top of a colony of frogs in the swamp, so croaking could be heard during the movies. Edwards later opened theaters in both Elkton and Drain. A drive-in theater on Bolin Island opened some time later. The building to the right of the theater had the telephone office downstairs and Doctors Amick and Howett upstairs. The building across the street near the top of the photograph is the Rainbow Tavern and Restaurant. The building beyond that was the Reedsport Hotel that later became a secondhand store. Fourth Street runs north and south on the right side of the photograph.

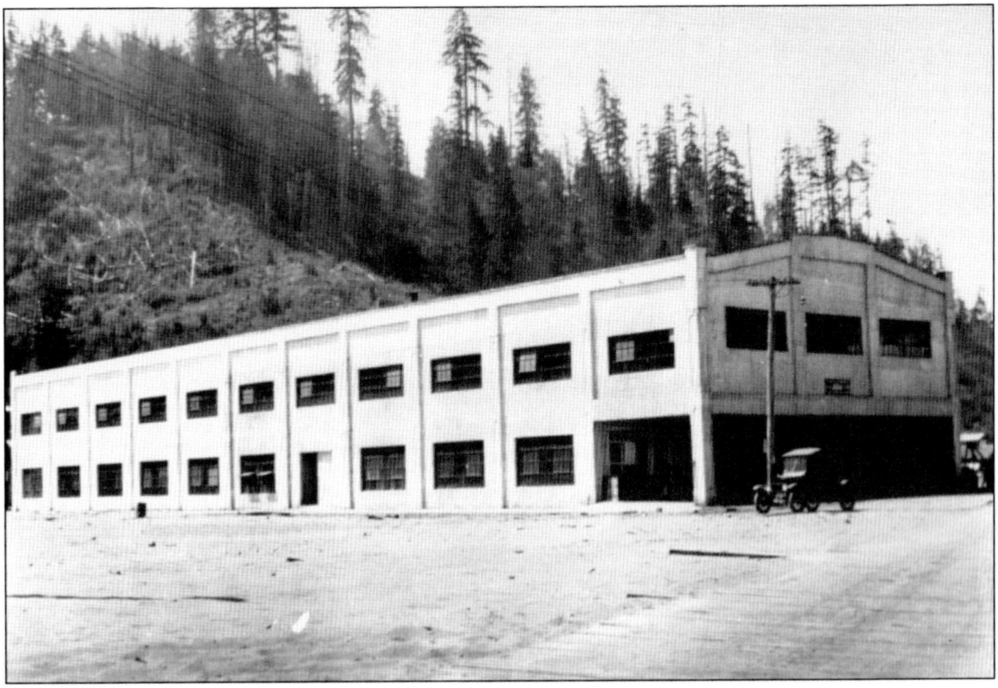

Another landmark in town was the Hogan Garage, later the Reedsport Garage, which is pictured above in 1927. It was the Model T Ford Agency in the area and was a state-of-the-art facility with two stories, mechanics that worked upstairs and downstairs, and a ramp on which they drove the cars to the second floor. The ramp also allowed young children on bikes to race into the street. Below is a 1931 photograph showing the garage on the right and its relationship to the rest of the town. In the forefront is the belfry of the church and to the left is the Edwards Theater. The Railroad Bridge is in the distance to the right.

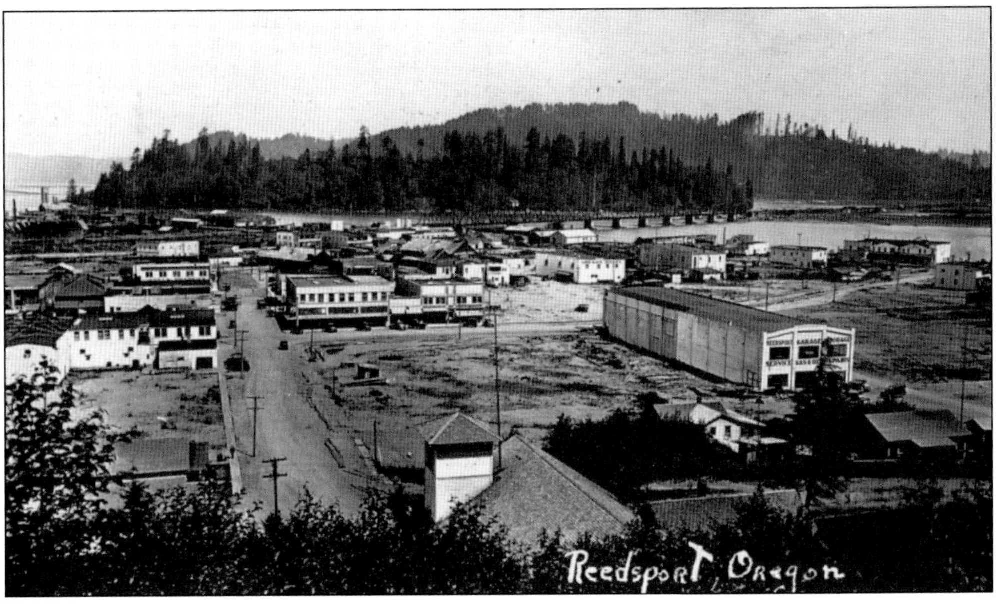

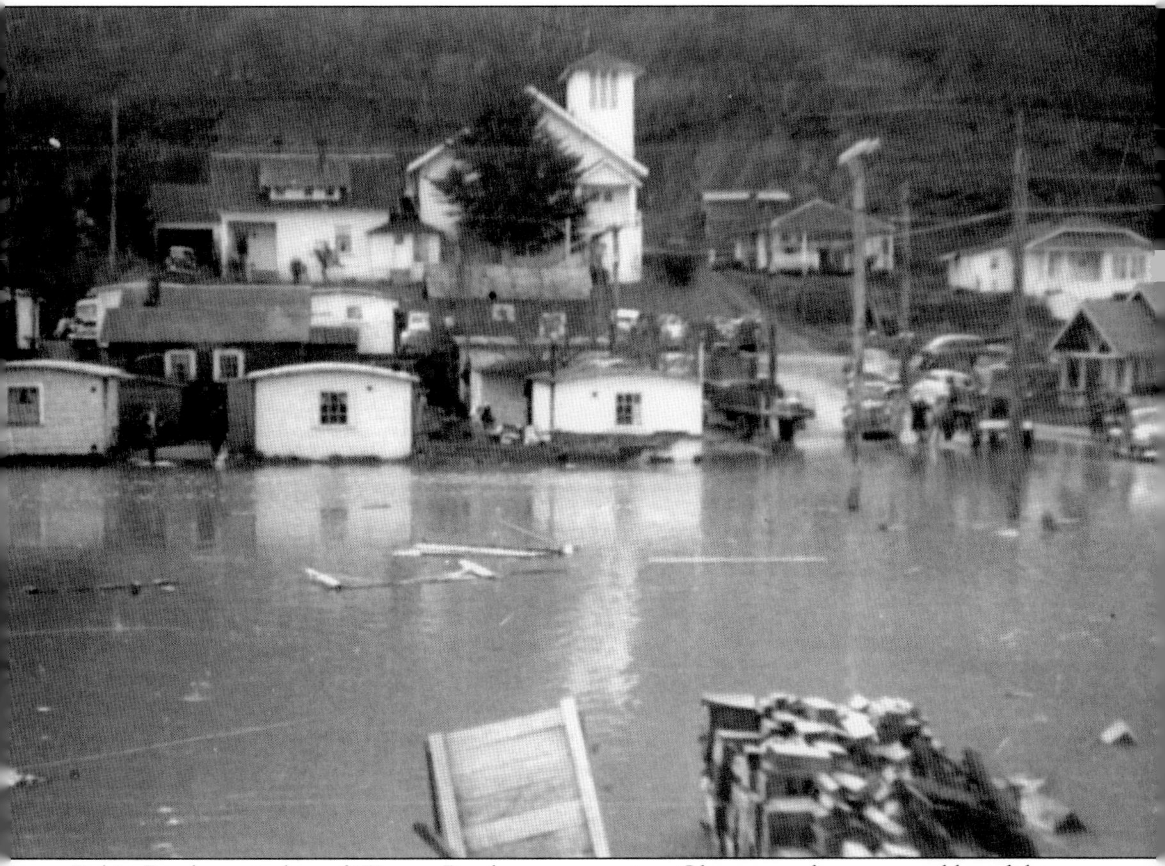

Robin Reed, son-in-law of Warren Reed, was a two-time Olympian who won a gold medal in wrestling at the 1924 Paris Olympics. He was considered by some historians as the best US wrestler prior to World War II at any weight. He was known for his pinning ability and rugged, take-no-prisoners style. After coming to Reedsport in the late 1920s, Robin became one of the first grass-seed farmers in Oregon, the mayor of Reedsport, had a part interest in the town newspaper, owned real estate called Reed's Cabins, and was a professional wrestler. This is a photograph of the 1927 Reedsport flood where Reed's Cabins, a property owned for a long time by Robin Reed, was threatened by the flood. Reed later moved to Salem, where his wife divorced him. Distraught, he went to the basement, put a noose around his neck, climbed on a box, and shot himself in the heart with a .22. His housekeeper heard the commotion and came downstairs and saved him. He lived until he was well into his eighties and was later inducted into the Collegiate National Wrestling Hall of Fame. (Courtesy of Tom Huebner.)

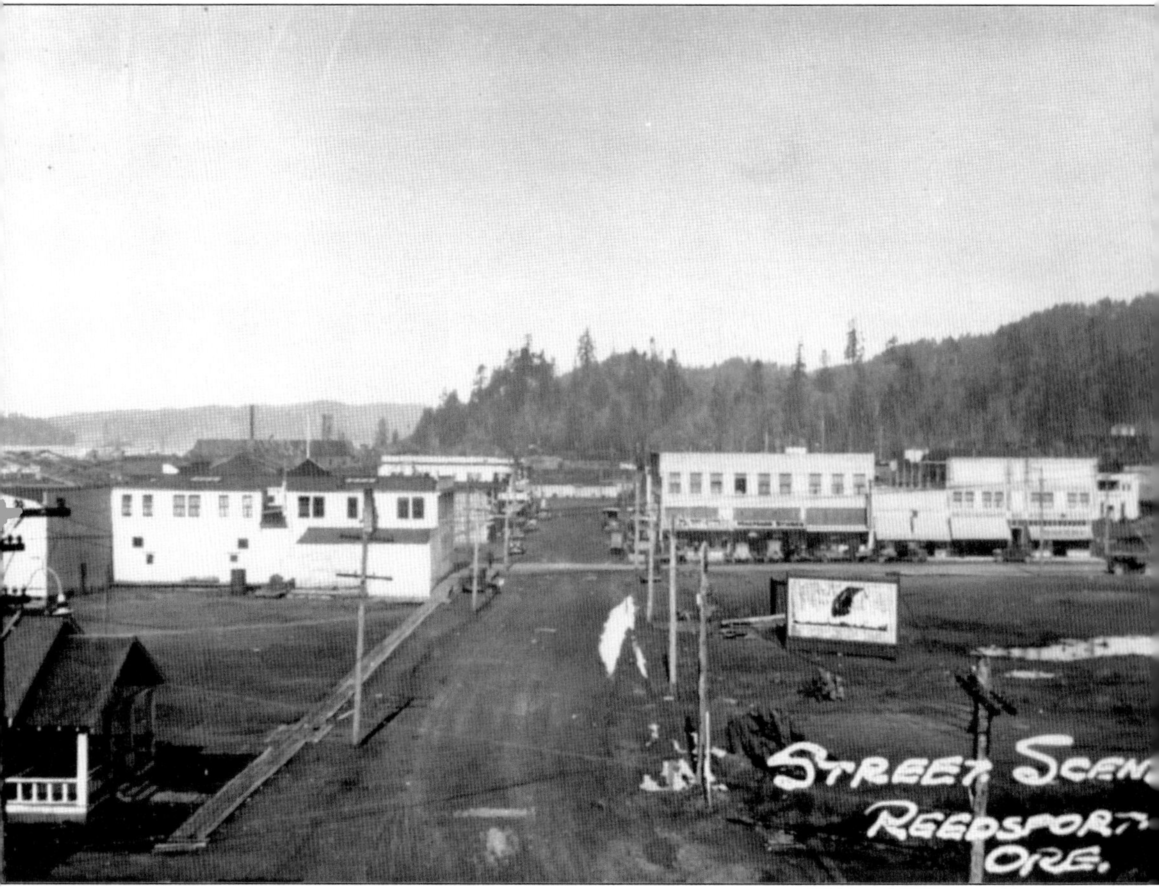

This c. 1930 photograph looks north from the Community Church at Lyons Street, the main street of business. Mr. and Mrs. Bill Burdick owned the Rexall Drugstore on the corner on the right side of the street. Their building also included a grocery store and the post office. Next to it was Bill Lovelace's clothing store. The Welcome Hotel was next with rooms upstairs and a five-and-dime store downstairs along with a bakery. To the far right is the little white house that was the operator's place on the Railroad Bridge. The building catty-corner to the drugstore is the bank building with doctor's offices and attorney Wallace Benson's office upstairs. Downstairs were the city hall offices. The long building to the side was Edward's Theater. Behind the Burdick Building was the Thompson Square Deal Café, and next to that was Frank Taylor's Hardware. Mr. and Mrs. Bendele's Meat Market was beyond that.

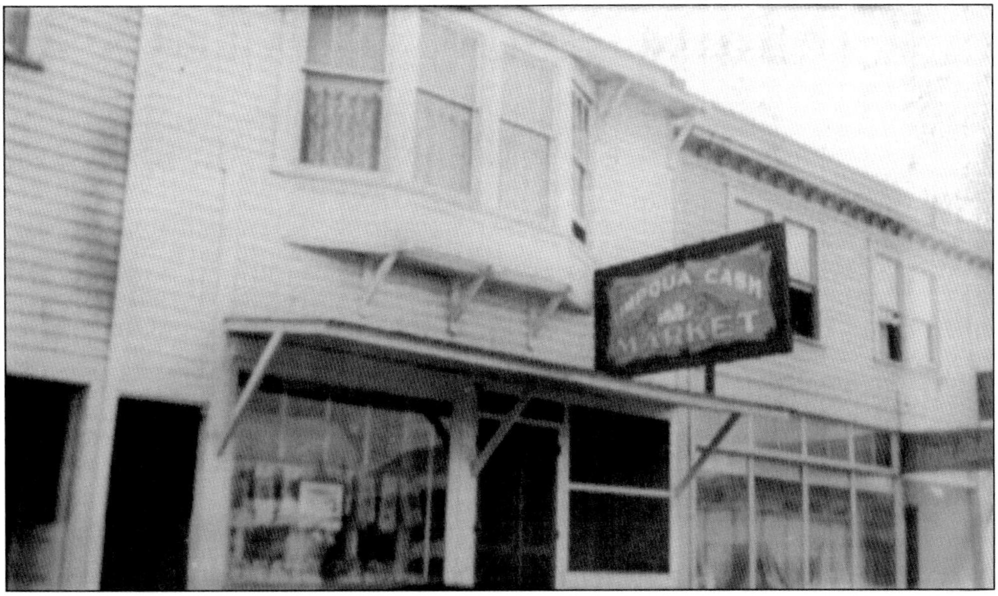

This 1920s photograph shows the Umpqua Cash Market that was one of the town's first grocery stores. Their advertisement proclaimed they were the best in meats. Wiley Mauldin and Ray Lucas ran the establishment. Just to the left is the Wakefield Store, located next to where Manthe's Furniture is today. (Courtesy of the Dunn family.)

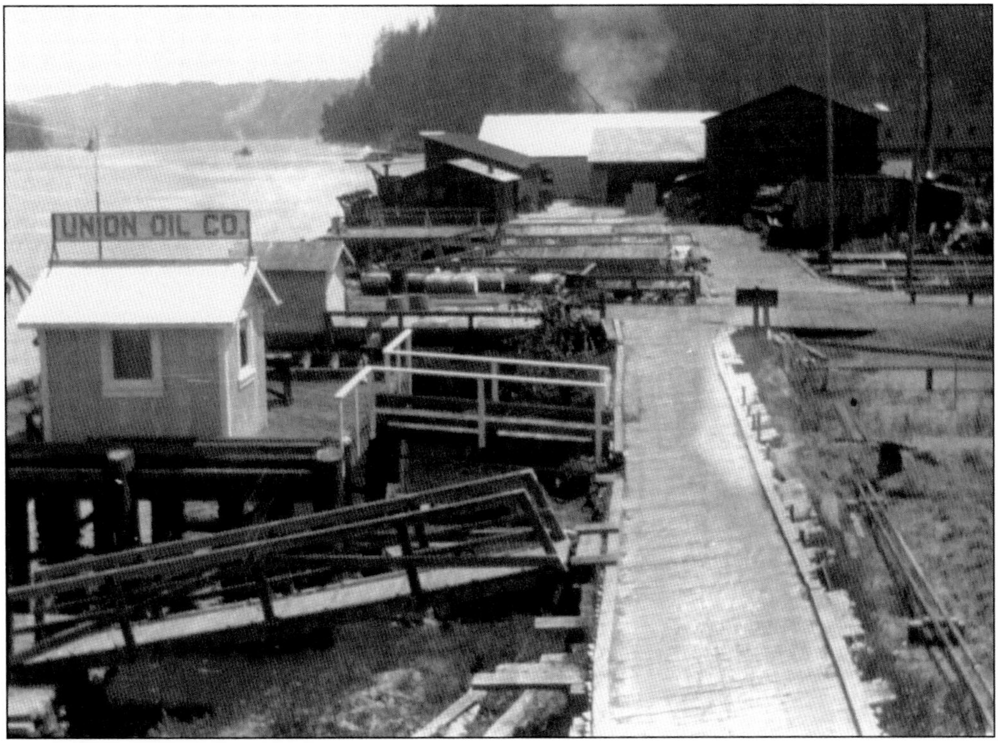

The Union Oil Company shop was a fixture on the boardwalk in this c. 1930 photograph of the Reedsport waterfront. Looking east down the boardwalk are fishing nets drying next to the Chase Cannery. Beyond the cannery was the ferry slip for people coming to and from Gardiner.

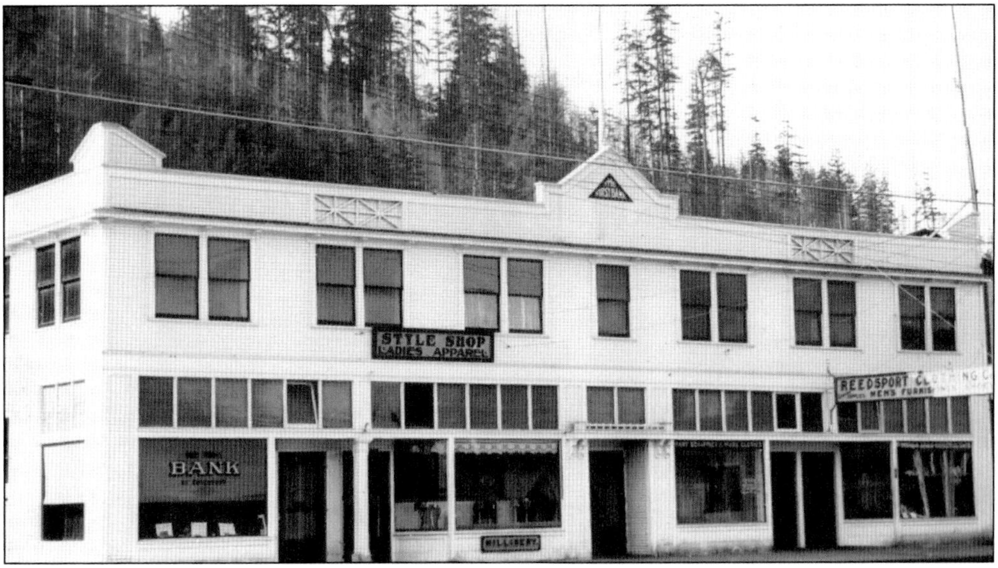

The first bank in Reedsport was constructed on the corner just down from the theater. When the bank went bankrupt, it became the city hall with a new jail built in back. Above were Andy Anderson's, Mothers Style Shop, and Reedsport Clothing. Dunn's Clothing Store and Ley's Variety Store were directly across the street, while Frank Taylor's Hardware Store was farther down the street.

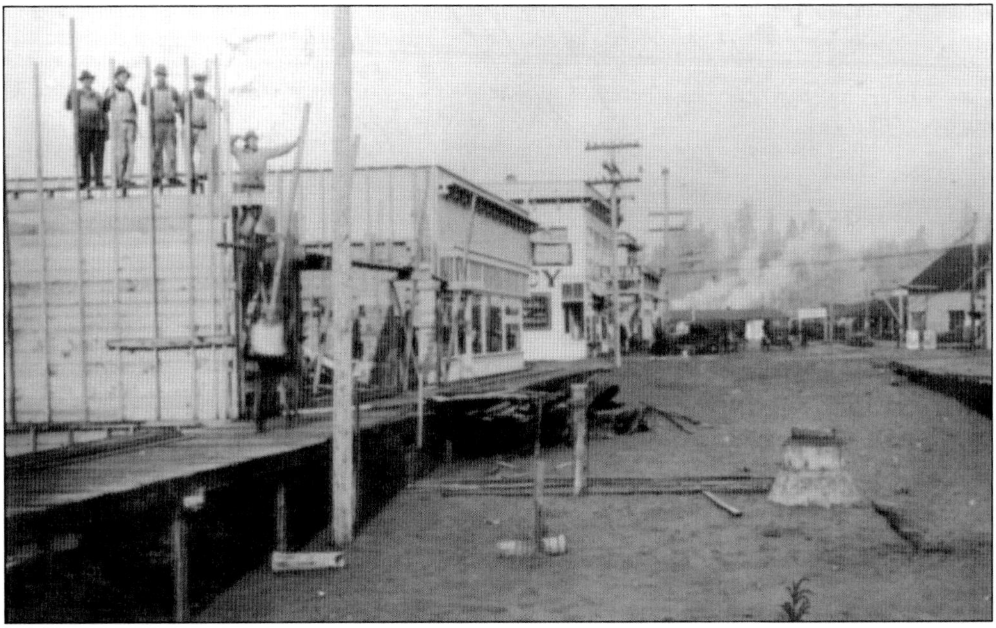

This 1920s photograph, looking west toward the Railroad Bridge and the mill, shows a construction crew building the Rainbow Tavern on Fourth Street. The Rainbow's advertisement read "Cigars, Tobacco, and Lunch." Note the sidewalks keeping people off of the marsh. Across the street is the first machine shop in Reedsport, run by Uno Leppanen, a Finnish immigrant. His wife was one of the popular midwives in town. (Courtesy of Tom Huebner.)

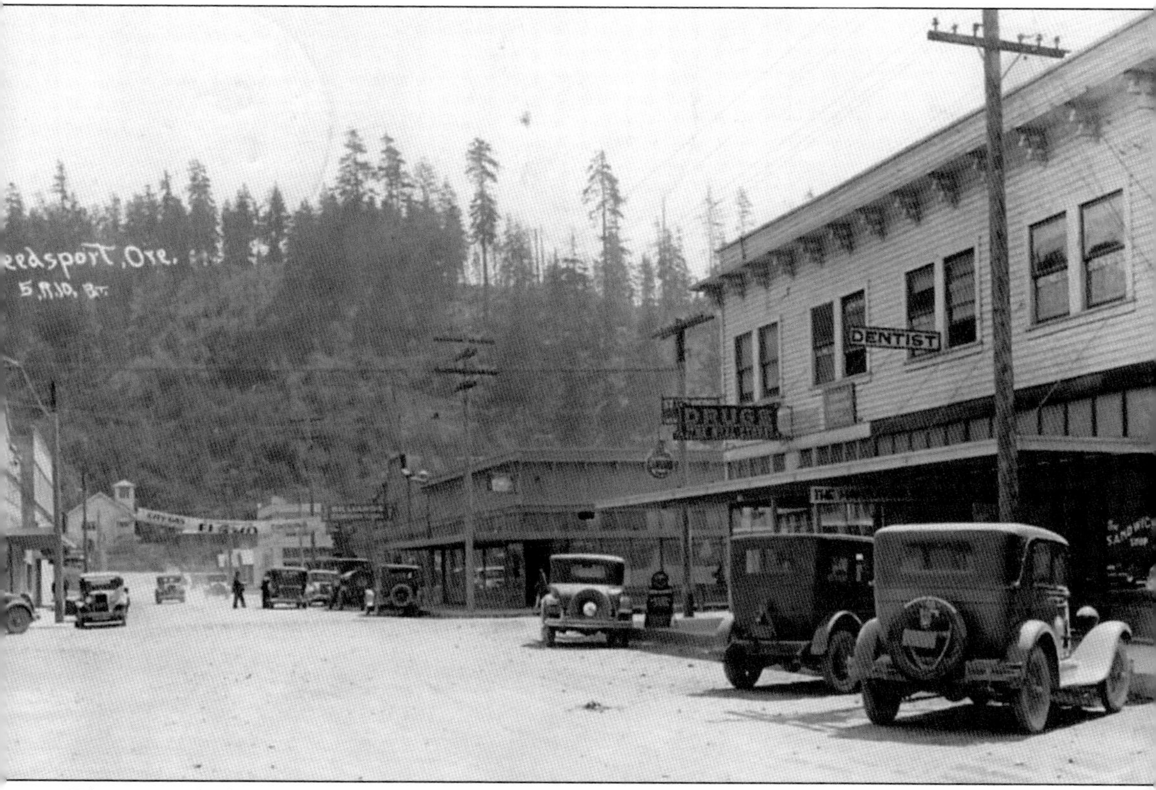

This view is looking south on Fourth Street in the 1920s. Fourth Street was the main thoroughfare at this time. The Rainbow Inn is on the right at the far side of the street, and Burton's Pharmacy is on the corner to the right. It was one of the places where citizens could buy liquor in town. The Square Deal, owned by the Thompson family, is on the left-hand side of the street across from the Rainbow. In the distance is the Reedsport Community Presbyterian Church, constructed in 1919 on the Crestview Heights hillside on the south side of the town. In addition to religious services, it was a gathering place for seasonal programs and acted as the first town library. Reverend Lamb was the first pastor. In later years, after Highway 38 and Highway 101 were completed, Fourth Street was not the center of town as highway traffic dictated emphasis in other areas of the community.

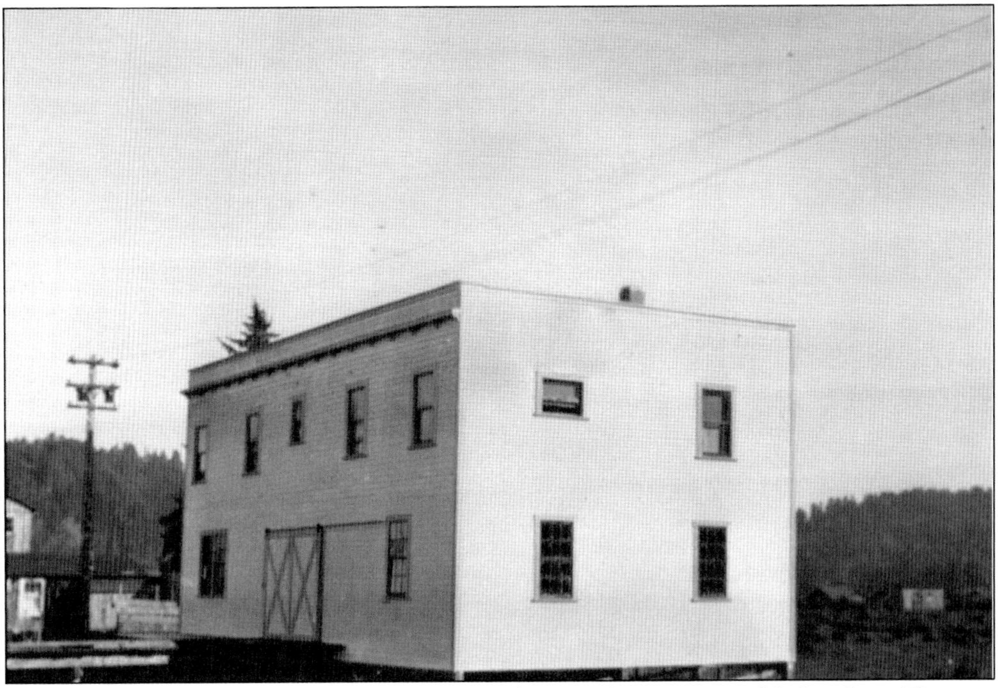

In 1920, the town voted 76 to 32 for a bond of $50,000 for a municipal light plant. This is a photograph of that original building. At that time, power was only available after 4:30 p.m. Crestview Heights is on the left, with Decker Point in the background on the right.

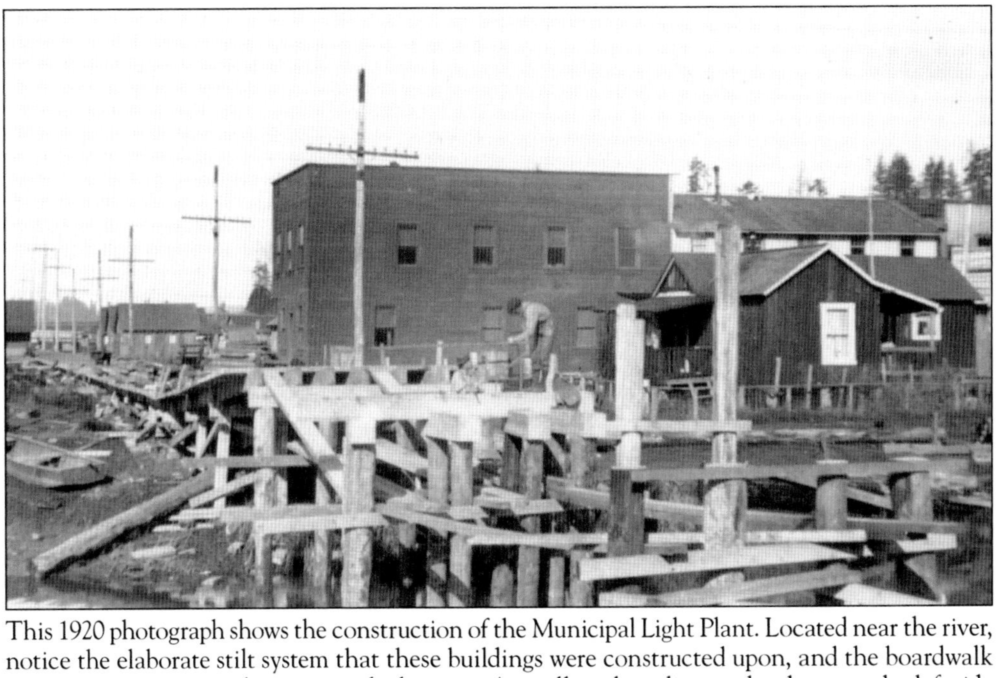

This 1920 photograph shows the construction of the Municipal Light Plant. Located near the river, notice the elaborate stilt system that these buildings were constructed upon, and the boardwalk structure as it goes northeast towards the river. A small rowboat lies on the shore on the left side of the image. (Courtesy of Sunnie Heddon.)

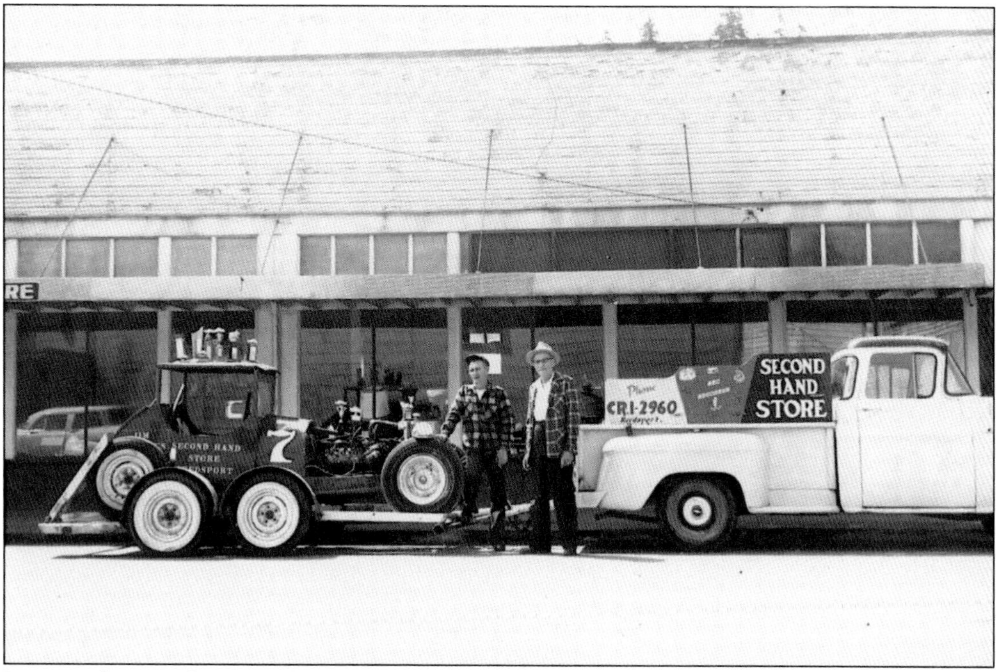

In 1940, this was the Second Hand Store, located on the corner of Fourth Street and Greenwood Avenue, next to the Rainbow Café. Jim Shanelecs, pictured on the right with his hand on the fender of his publicity car, was the owner. Anything from tools to pots and pans could be purchased here. (Courtesy of Bob Huebner.)

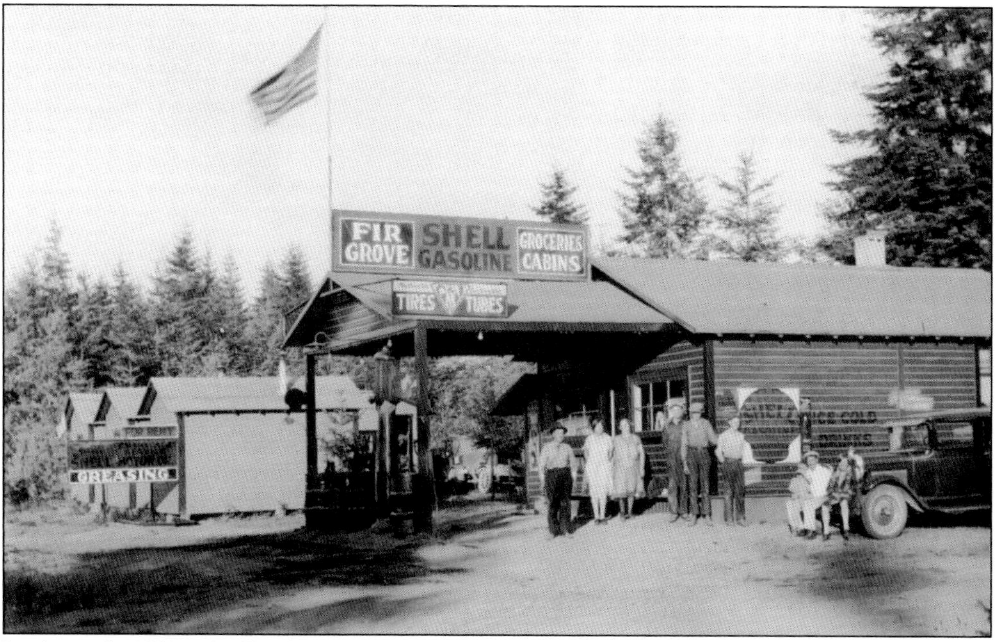

In the early 1930s, the Fir Grove Gas Station was located on the south end of town. This later became the Fir Grove Motel, on the corner of Highway 101 and Eighteenth Street. When the motel was constructed, the small cabins to the left in the image were moved to the other side of Highway 101. (Courtesy of Bob North.)

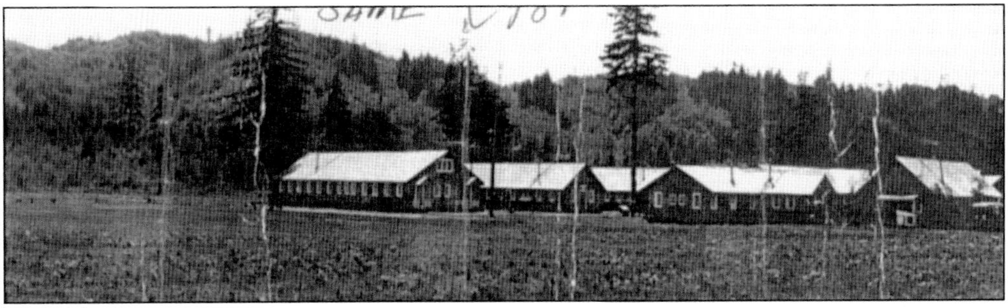

National Civilian Conservation Corps Camp Reedsport Co. No. 981 is pictured in the late 1930s. The camp and others like it hosted young men to work on conservation projects in national forests and national parks from 1933 to 1941. They constructed forest roads and trails, planted trees, fought forest fires, and fought floodwaters. This experience shaped their personal work habits and moral and psychological character.

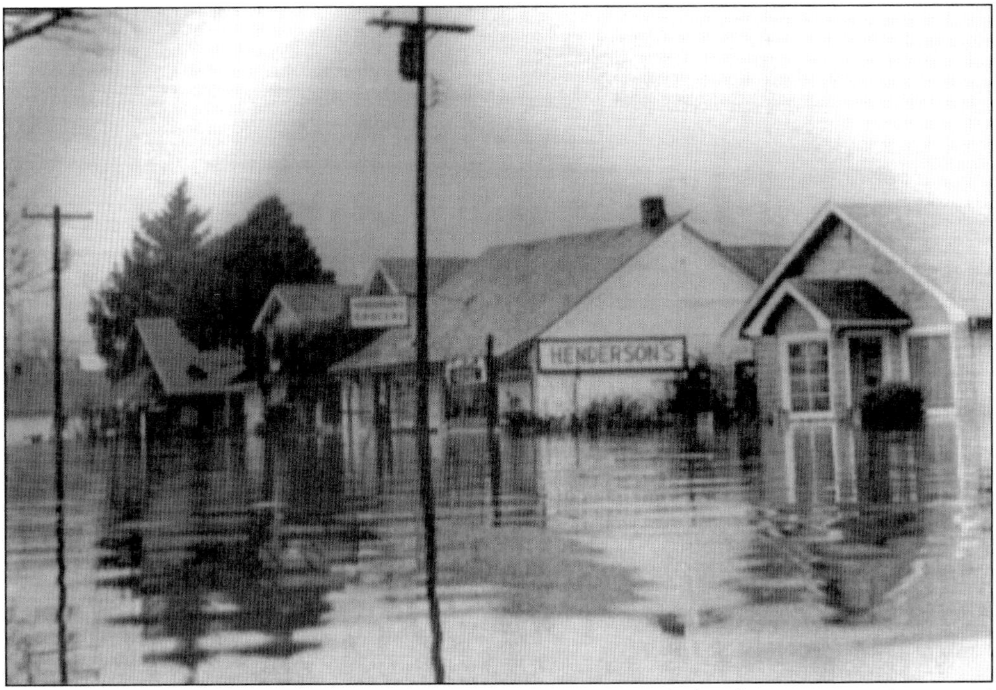

Roy Henderson, who once served as mayor of Reedsport, renovated Blanch's Grocery and reopened this store as Henderson's Grocery in 1931. The grocery store remained a business in Reedsport until 1980, when it finally closed its doors. The Henderson Grocery is pictured during the 1964 flood in Reedsport. (Courtesy of the Henderson family.)

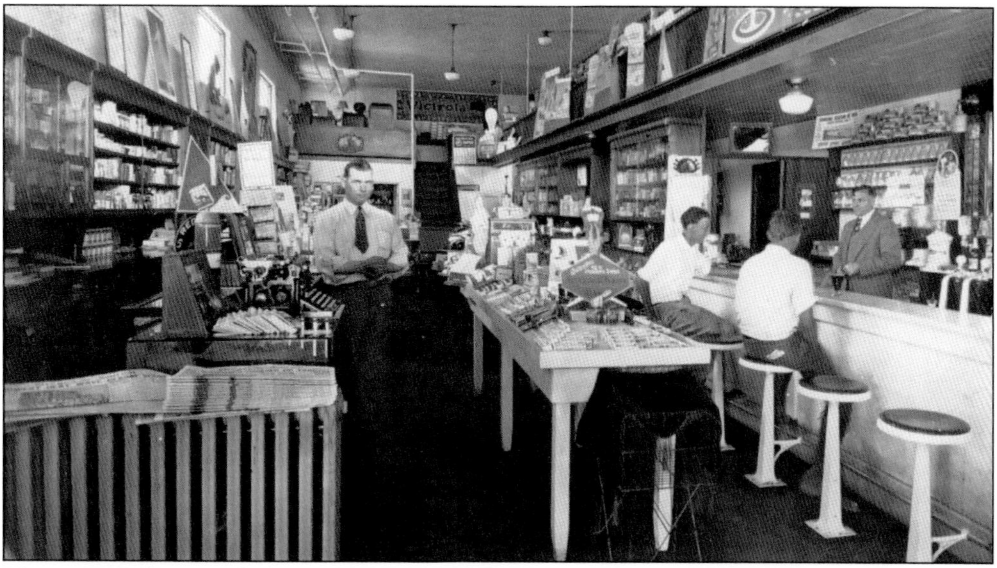

This c. 1935 photograph shows the interior of Burdick's Drug Store with Bill Burdick behind the counter, Mr. Frink, the pharmacist (left), and Jack Unger with an unidentified man at the counter. Located on the corner of Fourth Street and Fir Avenue, across the street from Dunn's Clothing Store, it was one of the few places in the area where prescriptions could be filled.

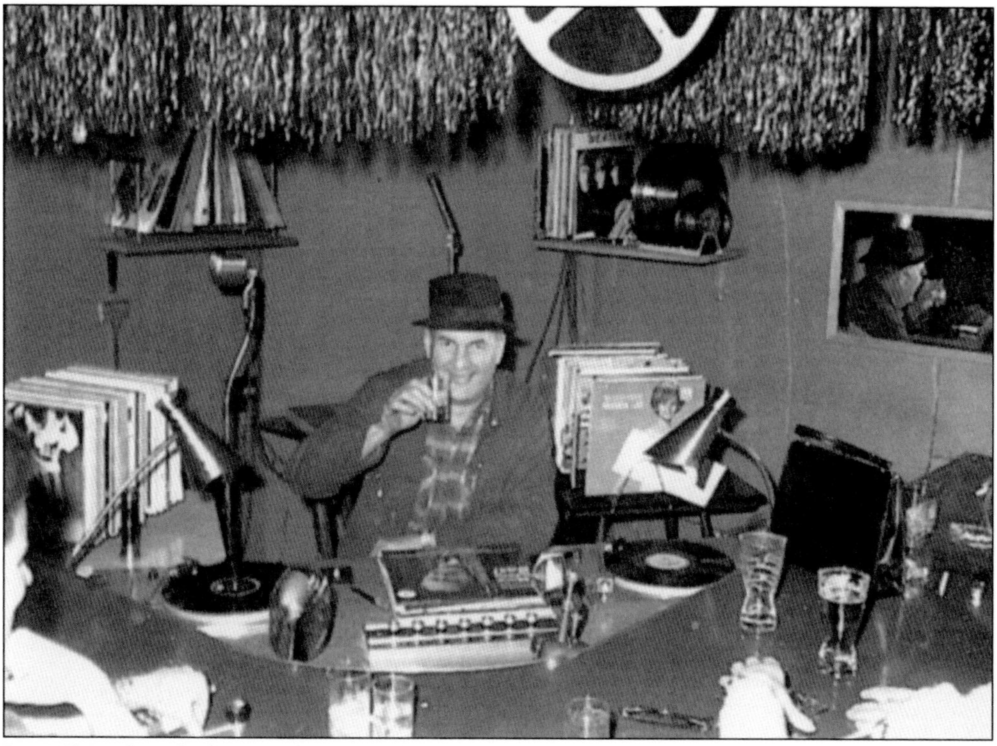

In 1965, Paul Hurlocker was the famous host of the "Scandahovian Hour" on Reedsport's first radio station, KRAF, owned by the Conoy's. His playlist always involved an abundance of accordion music, and he enjoyed a faithful following of local residents. This 1965 photograph shows Paul enjoying a drink while at work. (Courtesy of Bob Huebner.)

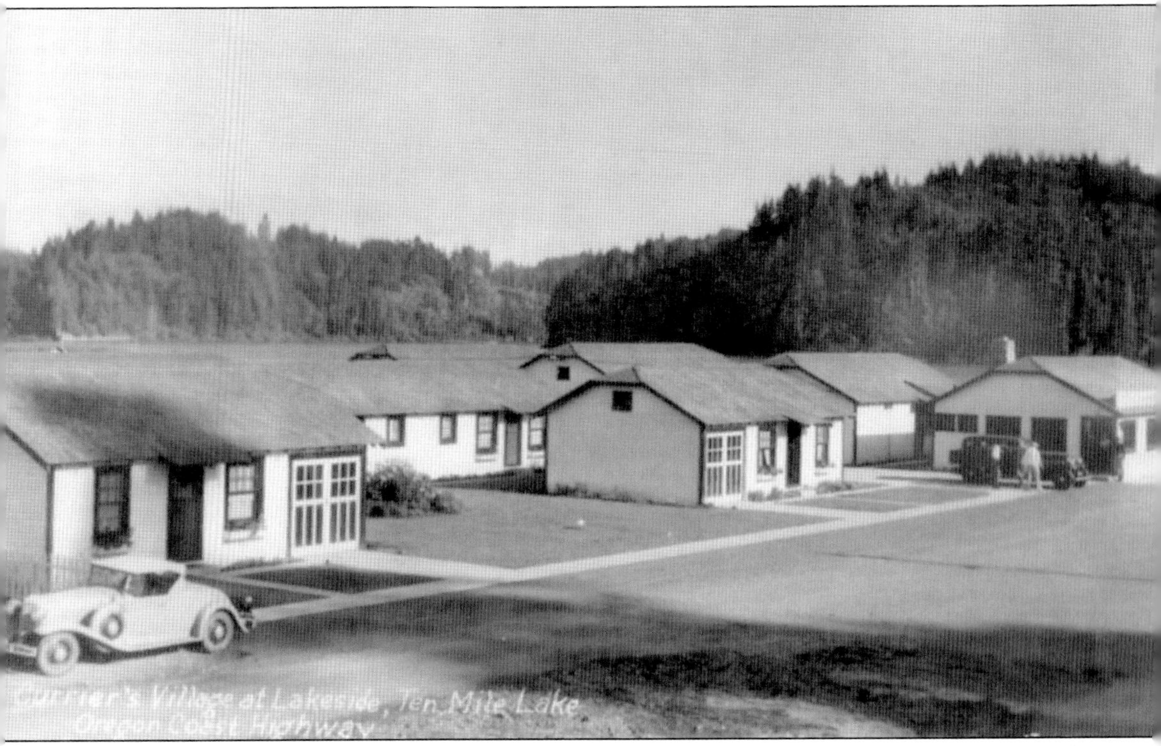

In 1937, a man named Currier bought property next to Tenmile Creek, with the intent to take over Lakeside and name it Currier's Village. He constructed Lakeshore Lodge and the adjoining property pictured here and named it Currier's Village. It was the area's first nightclub with a dance floor, large wall mirrors, and a beautiful bar with live music. It even had a velvet rope across the door when the place was full.

Four

Logging

By 1900, the Oregon timber industry lagged behind Washington and California, because cut timber was not easily accessible via available modes of transportation in Oregon. To combat this in the Reedsport area, railroad spurs were built up Scholfield Creek and near Winchester Bay. Splash dams were erected on Mill Creek and other small tributaries to the Umpqua River. But in many places, logging depended on the grinding pace of hand cutting timber and relying on bull teams and horse teams to pull timber on skid roads, and then roll the logs to the river. The Umpqua River was still the main transportation vehicle of the day. The Umpqua River and Smith River were just as important in transporting logs as the railroad.

Living in logging camps for months at a time, these workers were up at 4:00 a.m. and in the woods by 6:00 a.m. Lunch was at noon, and work ended at 4:00 p.m. After dinner, lights were out at 9:00 p.m., and a new cycle of work began. Men lived in close proximity to each other in bunkhouses or work cabins, and the ability to get along was as important as the everyday logging routine.

Logging at the turn of the century was backbreaking, dangerous work. At most, 8 to 10 trees were cut each day, while loggers fought poison oak, brutally steep terrain, trees splitting as they were cut or falling, and dangerous jobs—from breaking up log jams to maneuvering log rafts down the river at the convenience of the tide. Job titles were distinctive and powerful: bull buck, woods boss, peelers, sawyers, whistle punks, choppers, choker setters, rigging slingers, hook tenders, timber fallers, high climbers, and bull whackers. All evoke a strong tie to the past days of men in the woods—a huge part of Reedsport's legacy.

Early loggers in the area were Bill Esselstrom, Ben and Jack Baldridge, Ben Henderson, Warren Waggoner, John Waggoner, Mick Rose, Harold Dick, Dick Bangs, Asa Henderson, Stan Furman, and Ed Seabloom.

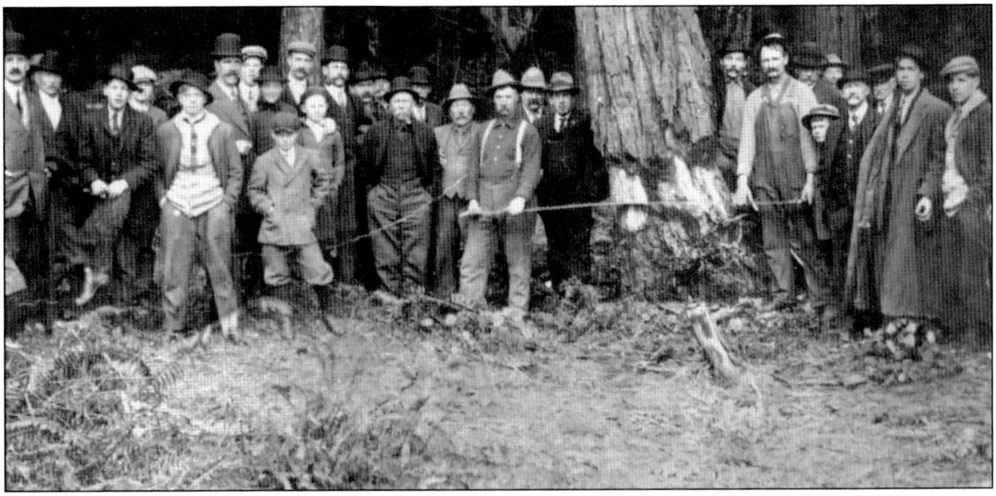

In 1912, Reedsport loggers began to cut the final trees to allow the Pacific Great Western Railway access to the Umpqua River and the crossing to Reedsport. This 1914 photograph shows the logging crew that began cutting on Bolon Island and crossed to the swamp on Schofield Slough. This ultimately led to the construction of the Railroad Bridge and the entrance to Reedsport.

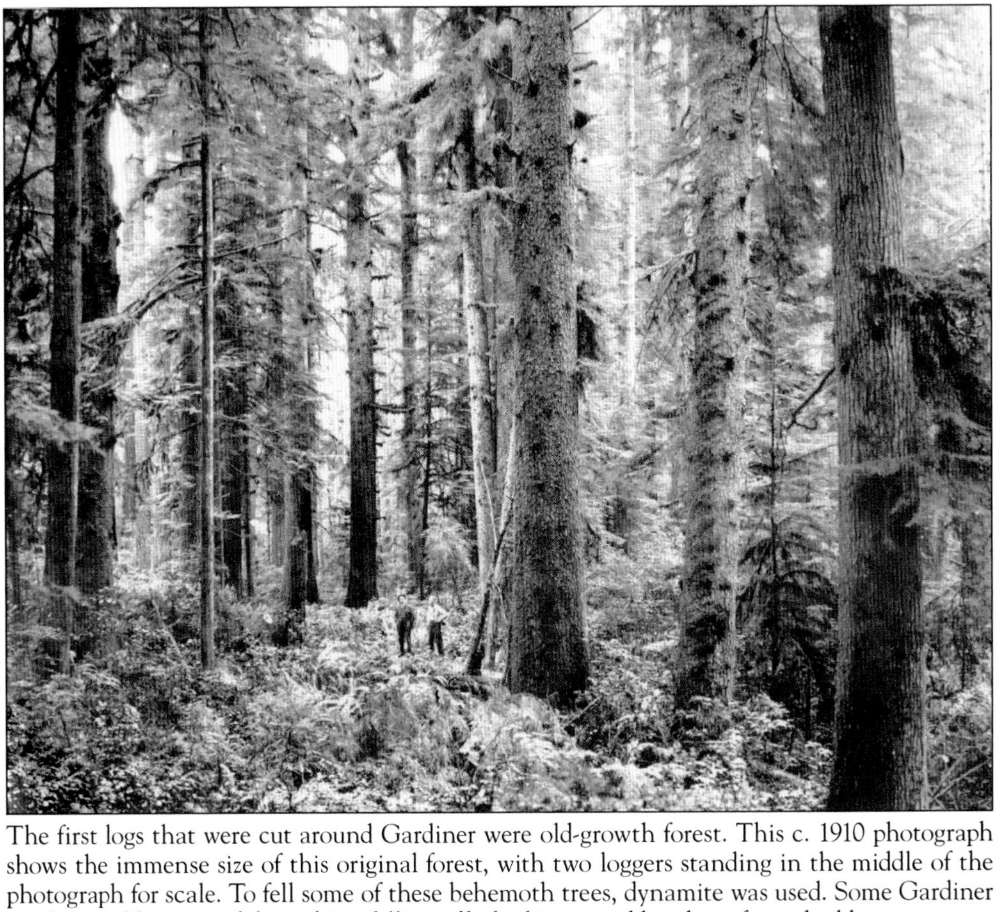

The first logs that were cut around Gardiner were old-growth forest. This c. 1910 photograph shows the immense size of this original forest, with two loggers standing in the middle of the photograph for scale. To fell some of these behemoth trees, dynamite was used. Some Gardiner residents told stories of their china falling off of cabinets and breaking from the blasts.

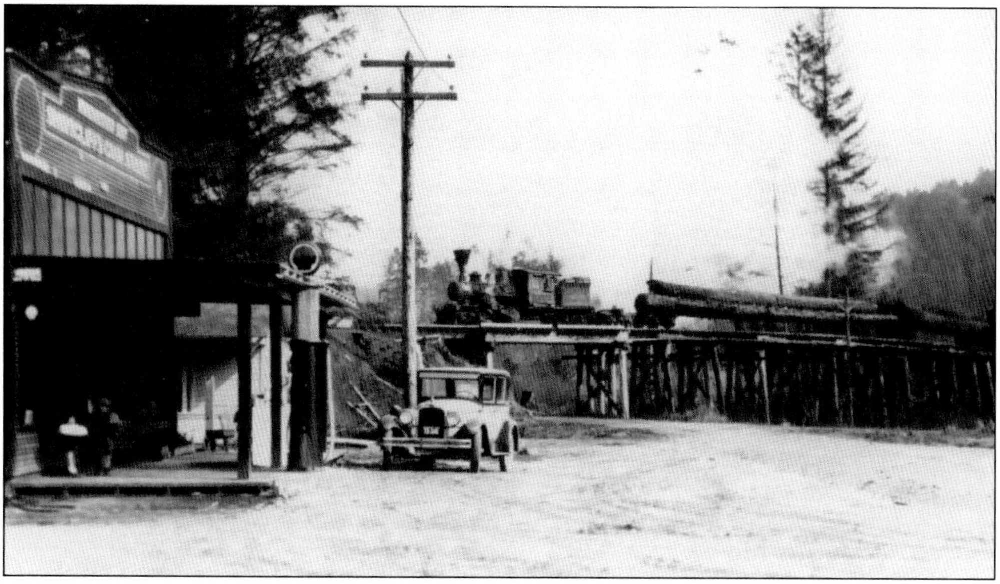

The railroad took logs from the Winchester Creek area and traveled spurs to inlets like Macey Cove. It was one of several of the bays on the Umpqua River where the logs were dumped into the Umpqua for their trip to the mills in Gardiner and Reedsport. The Winchester Bay Railroad Camp in 1915 was located where the Winchester Bay Inn now sits in Winchester Bay. This 1927 photograph of Winchester Bay shows the railroad track just behind where the Winchester Bay Store now stands. The Pontiac was owned by Bill Esselstrom. This explosion of lumber resources made shipping by water even more important and spurred the development of the jetties. As the *Port Umpqua Courier* wrote on December 31, 1926, "Industry, which has suffered by the handicap of the shallow bar, will be able to compete with other coastal mills. It will give a margin of profit which is now lost to them. The improvement of the harbor channel, the completion of the North Jetty, and the dredging of the channel and with the prospects of a south jetty, Reedsport is able to make tremendous strides within the coming few years."

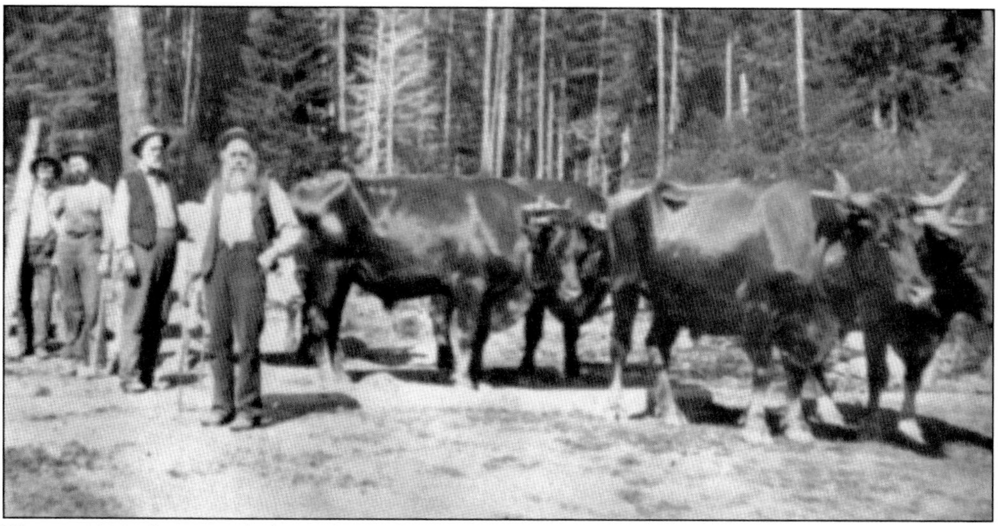

This c. 1890 photograph shows boss Chris Hacker on the right with his bull team on a skid road near Scottsburg. Oxen were much preferred when hauling logs on a skid road because they were much more powerful than their horse counterparts. Oxen also proved to be easier to manage.

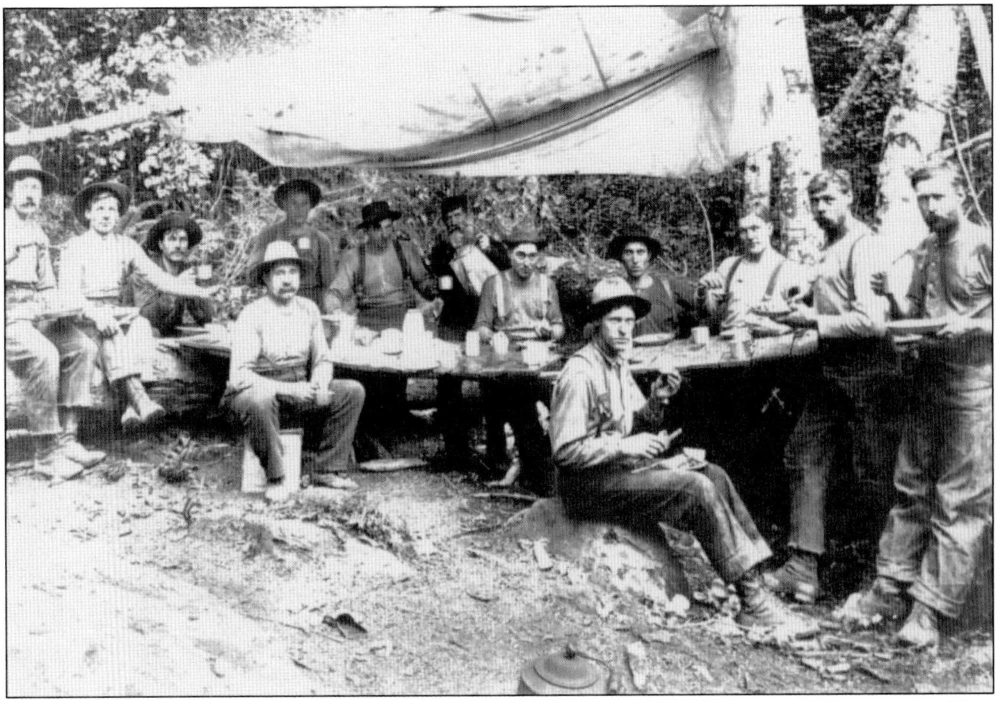

Camp 7 was located just east of Hudson Slough on Smith River at the turn of the century. This was a typical logging camp up the Smith River where loggers slept in small buildings and shared a communal mess hall. These camps traditionally had 20 to 25 men. Between 1890 and 1900, they earned an average of $1 a day. This c. 1900 photograph shows the work crew having a meal during their day.

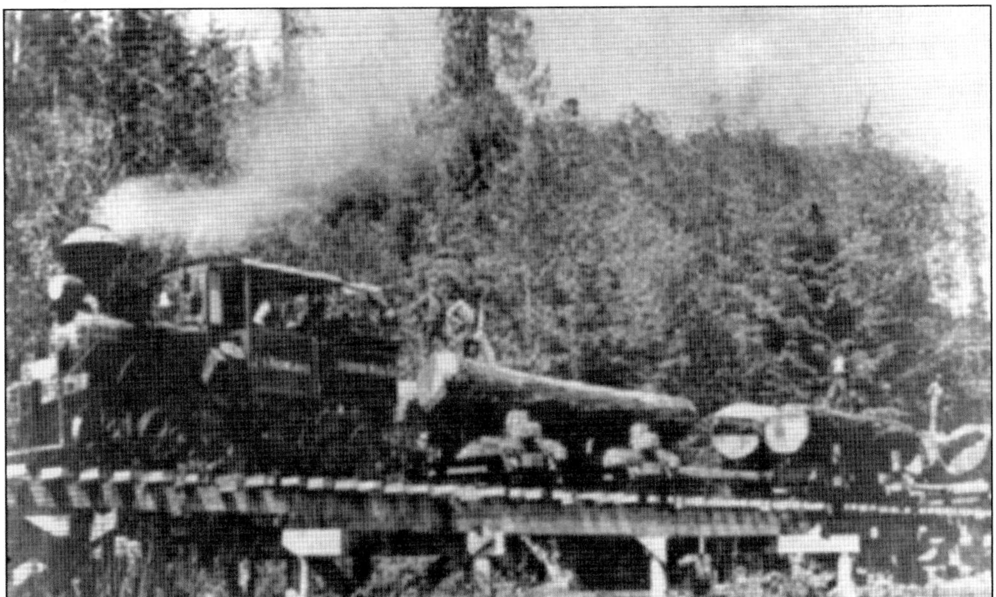

This is a c. 1902 photograph of the Jos. Knowland train on Scholfield Creek, taking a load of logs from the woods up the Scholfield Creek to dump in the Umpqua River. At other times, these trains would take students to schools or passengers to farms up the creek on its way to work.

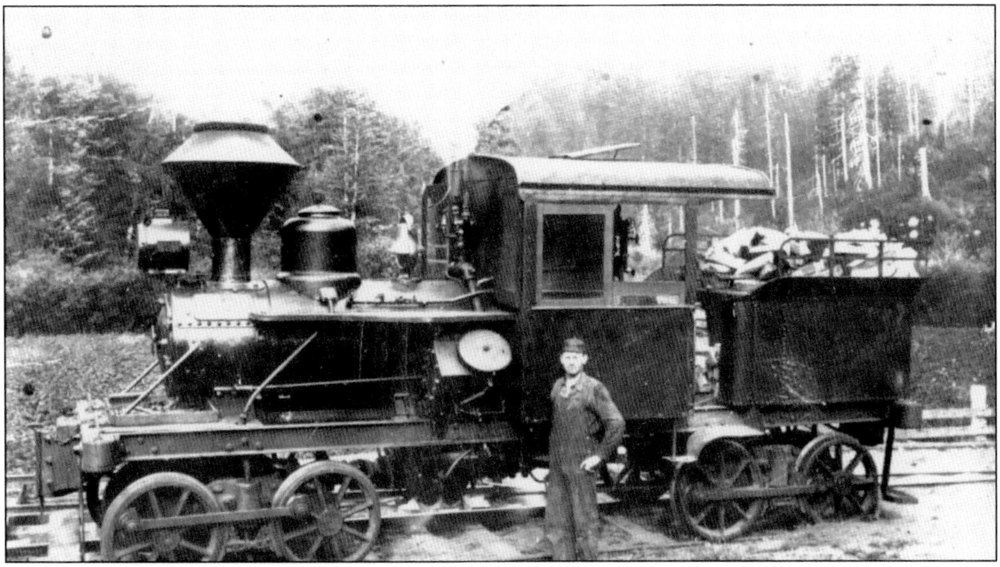

In this c. 1900 photograph, the Jos. Knowland can be seen in closer quarters. Powered by a Heisler- type motor, trains like this were invaluable to the logging industry in getting timber from the forest to the rivers or to the mills for processing. This advance in technology soon outdated the use of chutes and bull teams for transporting timber.

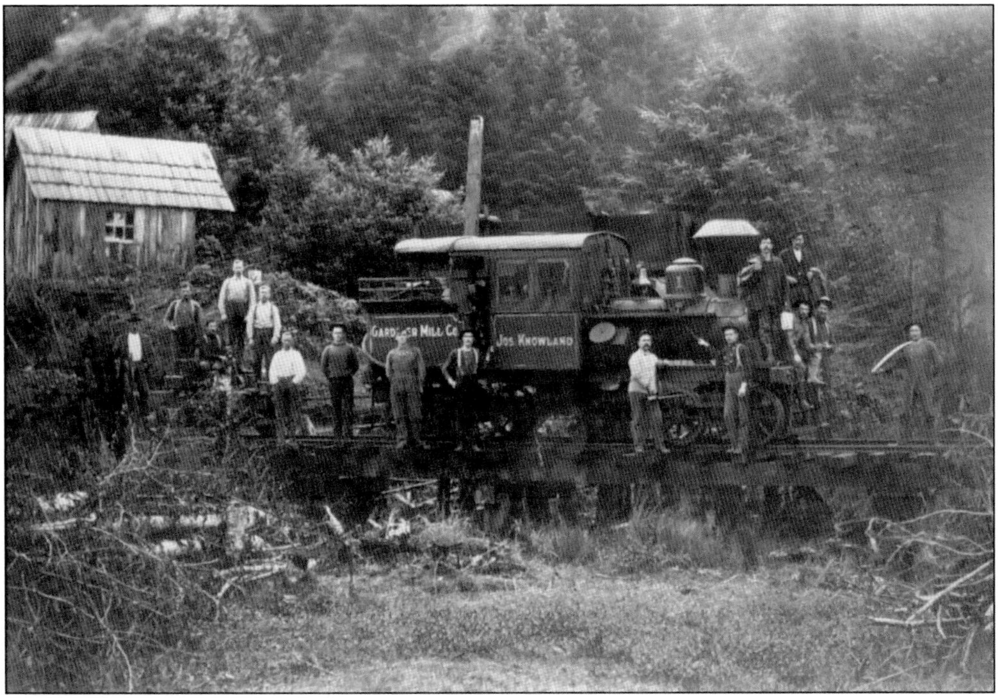

The Gardiner Mill Company owned the Jos. Knowland and several other locomotives that plied the woods on spurs constructed throughout the Lower Umpqua River area. Crews such as this were dependent on these trains for transportation, supplies, and being able to move their product.

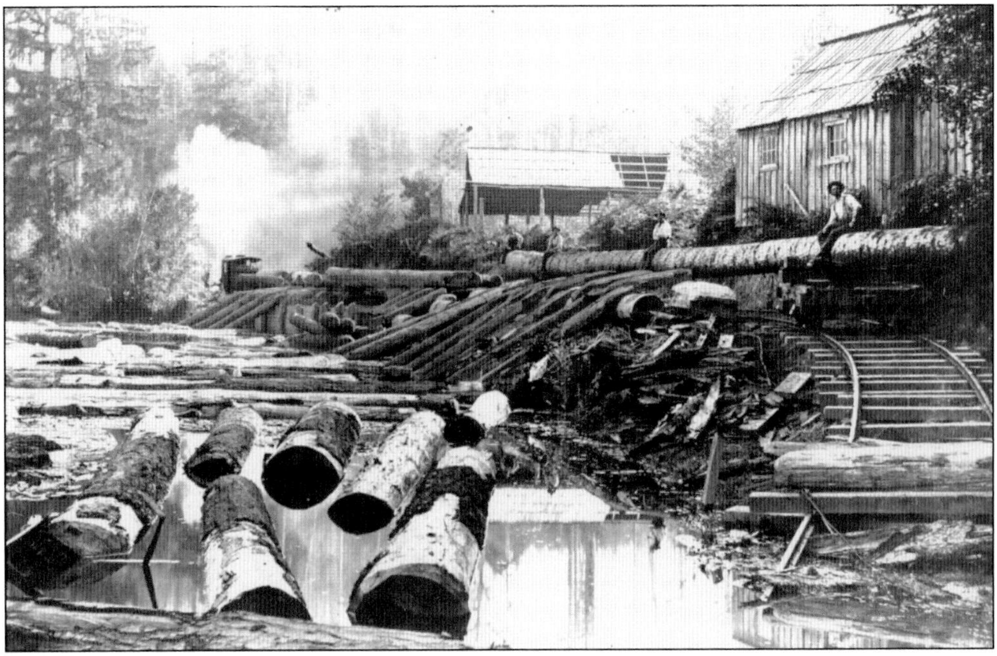

Trains were able to dump logs into holding ponds near mills, as is shown in this c. 1910 photograph. The railroad made this process much more efficient than floating logs down the river, and was much preferred to the maintenance of log booms.

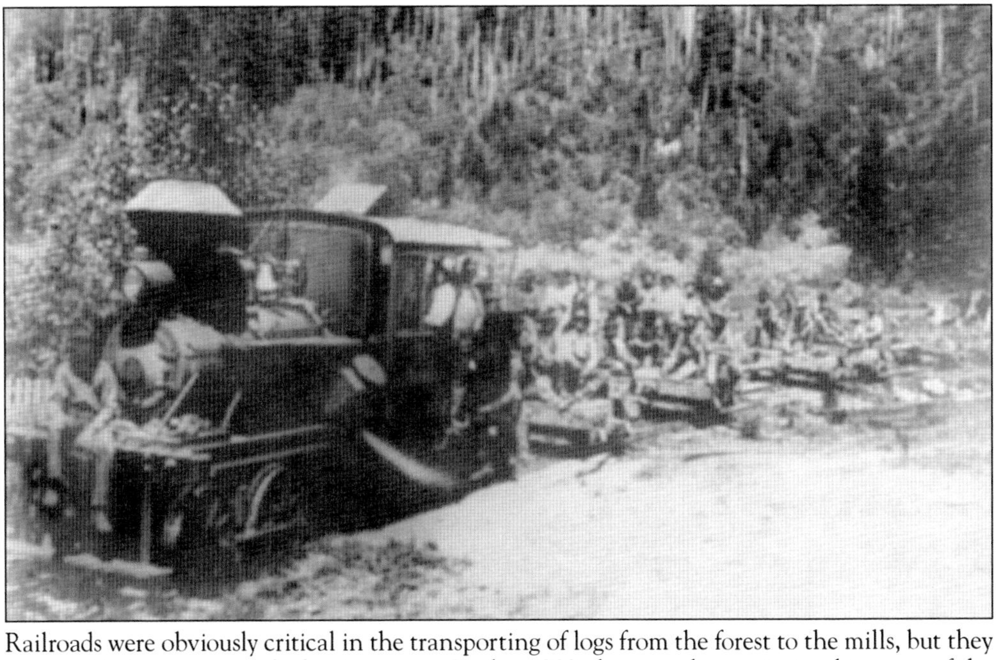

Railroads were obviously critical in the transporting of logs from the forest to the mills, but they also doubled as transport for logging crews. In this 1902 photograph, a train is taking one of the Gardiner Mill logging crews up Scholfield Creek to their logging site. Note the loggers on top of logs on train cars pulled by the locomotive.

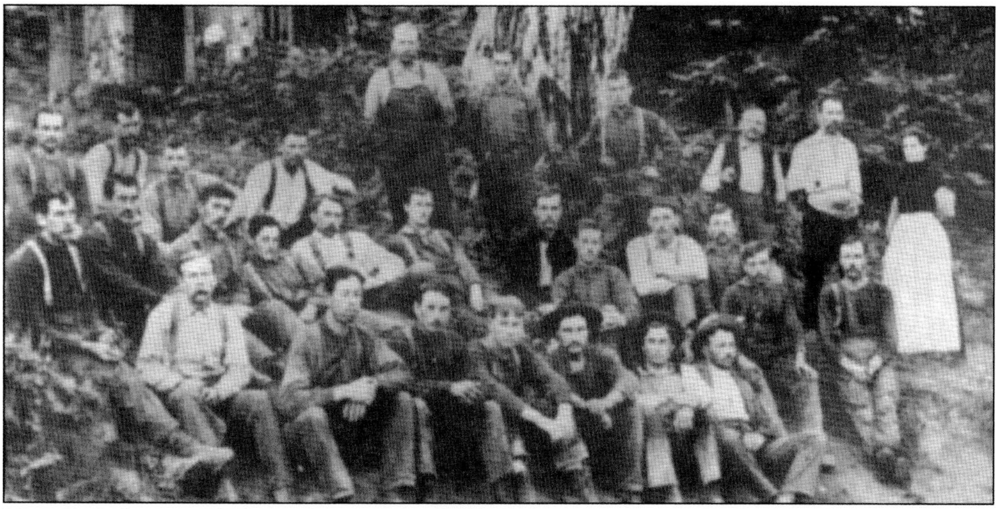

This 1902 photograph shows the Gardiner Mill logging crew that worked up the Scholfield Creek. From left to right are (first row) Matt Vister, Roy Van Curen, William Hanson, Joe Floyd, Fred Miller, Maudi Miller, and "Bulldog"; (second row) Frank Sanford, Charles Leggitt, Pearly Orr, Eugene Terry, boss Grant Balderee, Noah Black, Otto Lindros, Ernest Everttson, Walter Lewis, unidentified, Sammy Webb, and unidentified; (third row) Arti Everttson, Frank Terry, and Leo McCurdy; (fourth row) engineer Virgil White, Charles Morris, Matt Lectee, Rudolph Garrish, cook Will Chamberlain, and cook Jenny Chamberlain.

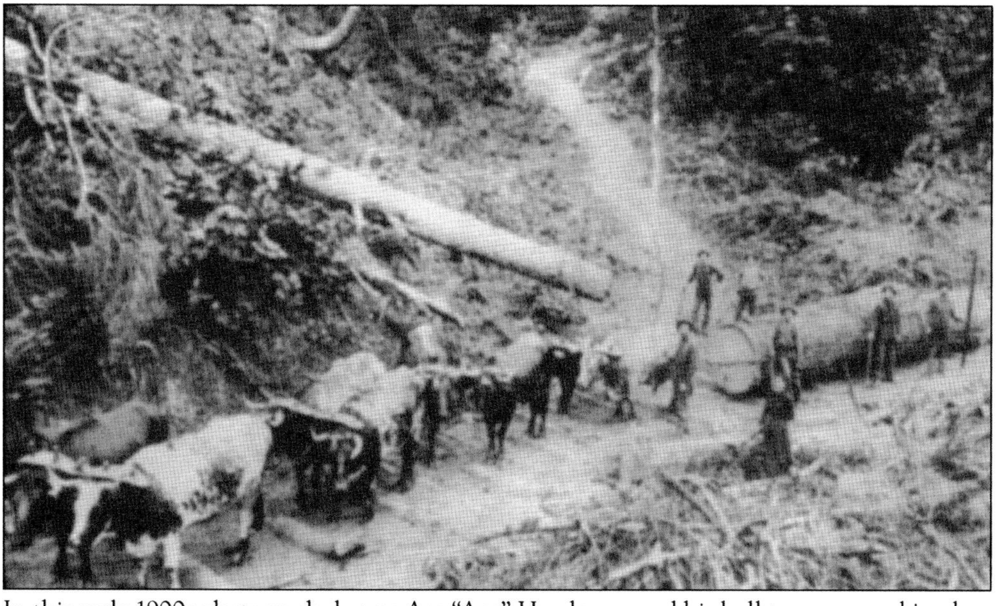

In this early 1900s photograph, logger Asa "Ace" Henderson and his bull team are snaking logs over a skid road to Slemmons Slough. A road of horizontal logs would be laid to drag larger logs that had their bark removed to allow them to be pulled more efficiently. Children would be hired to grease the skids with barrels of beef tallow that was kept handy. (Courtesy of Gary Waggoner.)

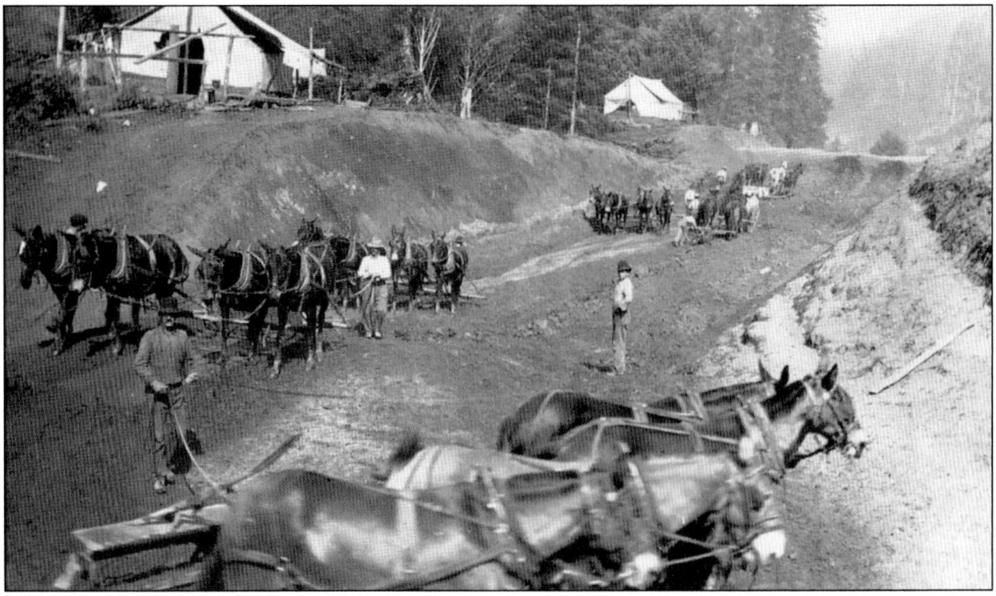

Both horses and oxen were used to haul logs over skid roads. In this c. 1910 photograph, teams of horses are being used to move supplies and wood products in an existing lumber camp on Smith River. The strain of this kind of labor made teams of four horses invaluable in this work.

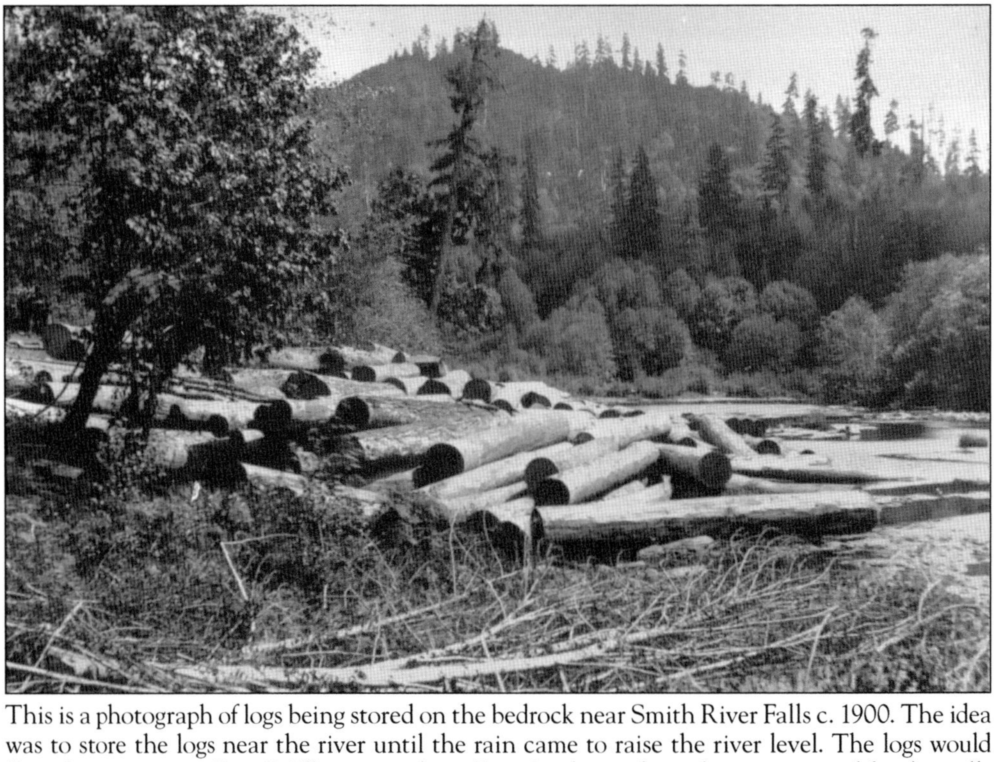

This is a photograph of logs being stored on the bedrock near Smith River Falls c. 1900. The idea was to store the logs near the river until the rain came to raise the river level. The logs would float downstream to Devil's Elbow, just above East Gardiner where they were stored for the mills that operated in Reedsport and Gardiner.

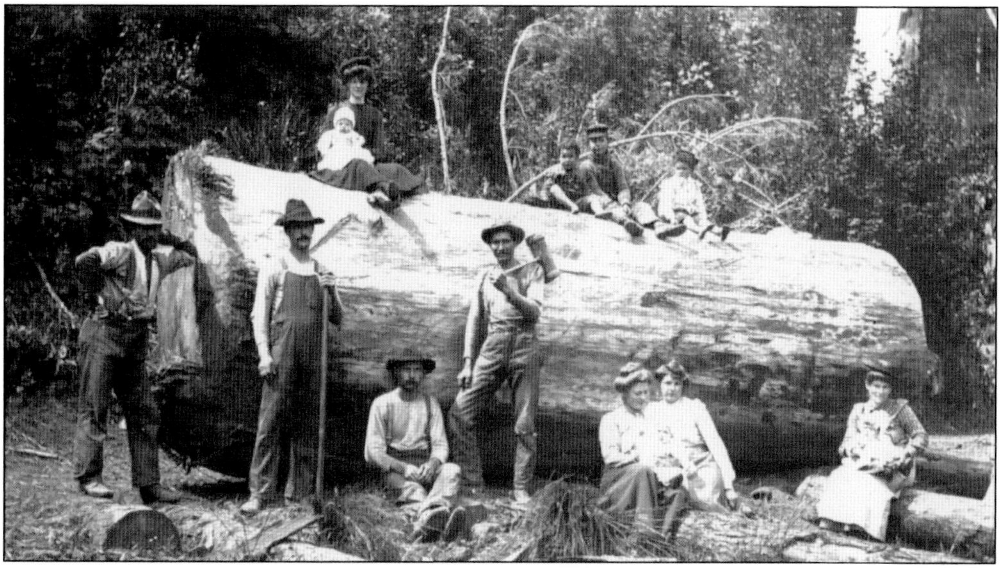

This is a 1902 photograph on Fingerboard Slough at the Wroe property on Smith River, near the mouth of Noel Creek. Pictured from left to right are (in front of log) Bill Judd, Glen Noel, Leigh Noel, Jesse Abbott, the Birch girls, Arilla Abbott, and Clarence Abbot; (on log) Jean Abbott and her baby, Doug Abbott, Lloyd Noel, and Everett Abbott. (Courtesy of Gary Waggoner.)

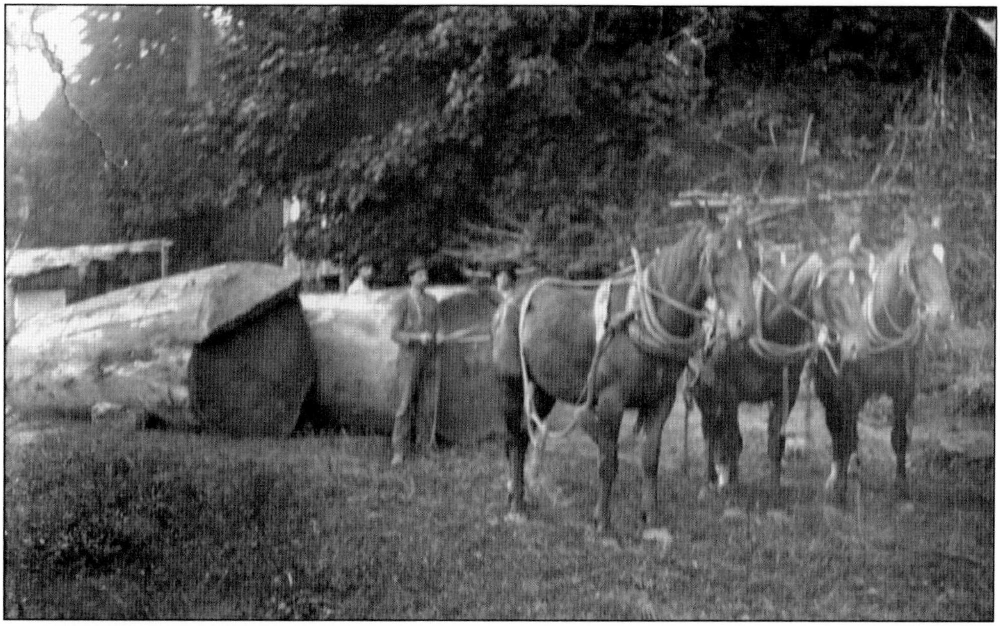

This 1902 photograph shows the size of the old-growth logs harvested from the surrounding forest. This photograph was taken at the Ashworth property on the Smith River. In the photograph are, from left to right, Bill Judd, Glen Noel, and Aldon Leach. Instead of a team of oxen, three horses are used to move the logs from the forest to tributaries. Splash dams were then constructed on tributaries running into the Umpqua River to prevent logs from floating down the creeks unintentionally. When enough logs had been stopped by the splash dam, the gates were opened and the collection of logs floated through on their way to the Umpqua River. (Courtesy of Gary Waggoner.)

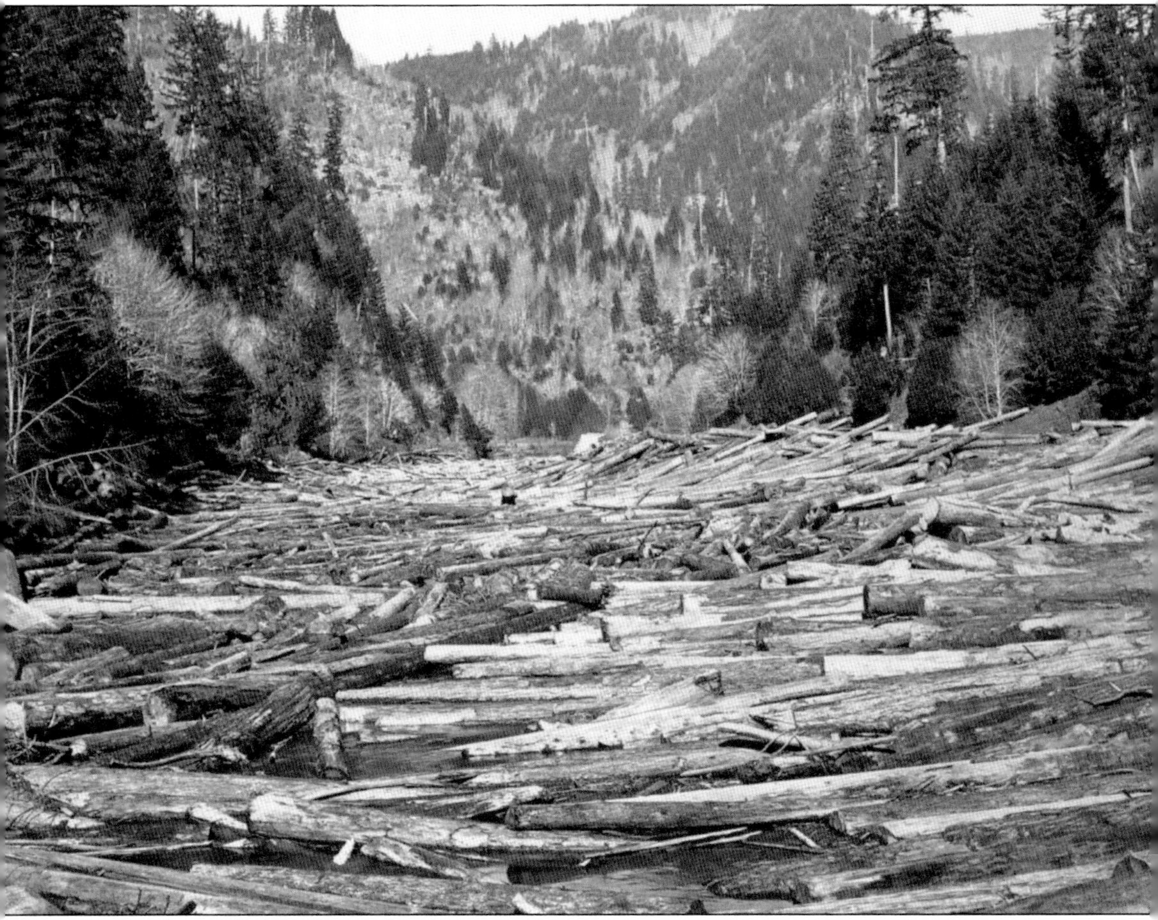

Harvested logs in 1905 were deposited in Mill Creek. Logs were put in tributaries of the Umpqua River like Mill Creek when the water was low. As the water rose from rain or splash dams, these logs would float to the Umpqua River, where they would float to various mills downstream. At this time, logs sold for $4.50 per thousand board feet.

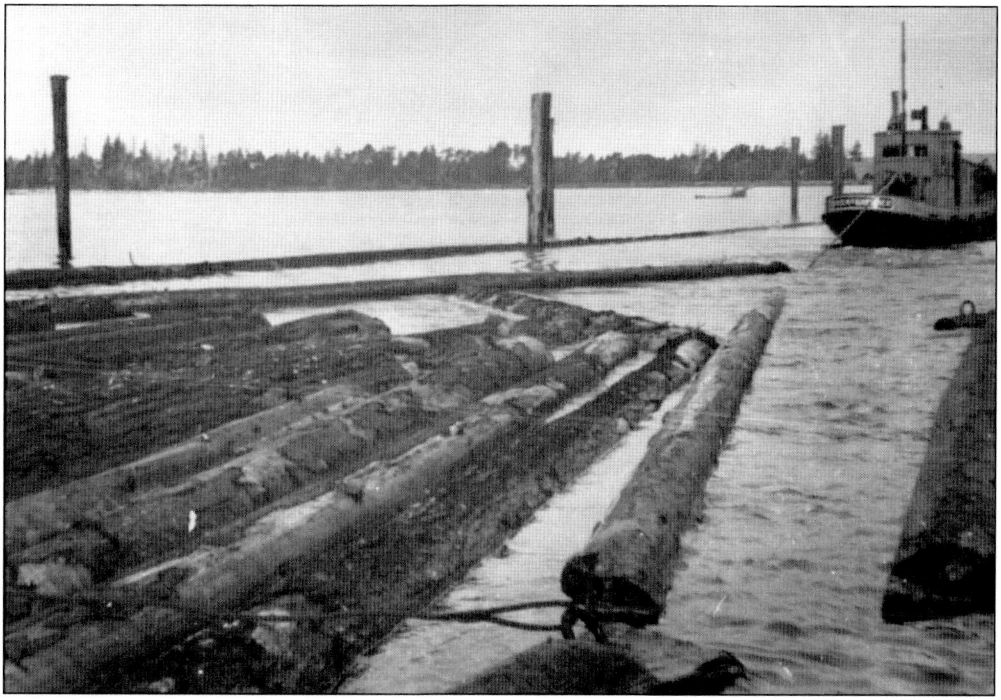

Once logs reached the Umpqua River, they were gathered in log booms and taken down the river to the mills. This 1912 photograph shows the steam tugboat *Queen of Gardiner* hauling logs on the Umpqua River. Before being taken to their final destination, log booms were tethered to pilings in the river until enough booms were collected to make a final run.

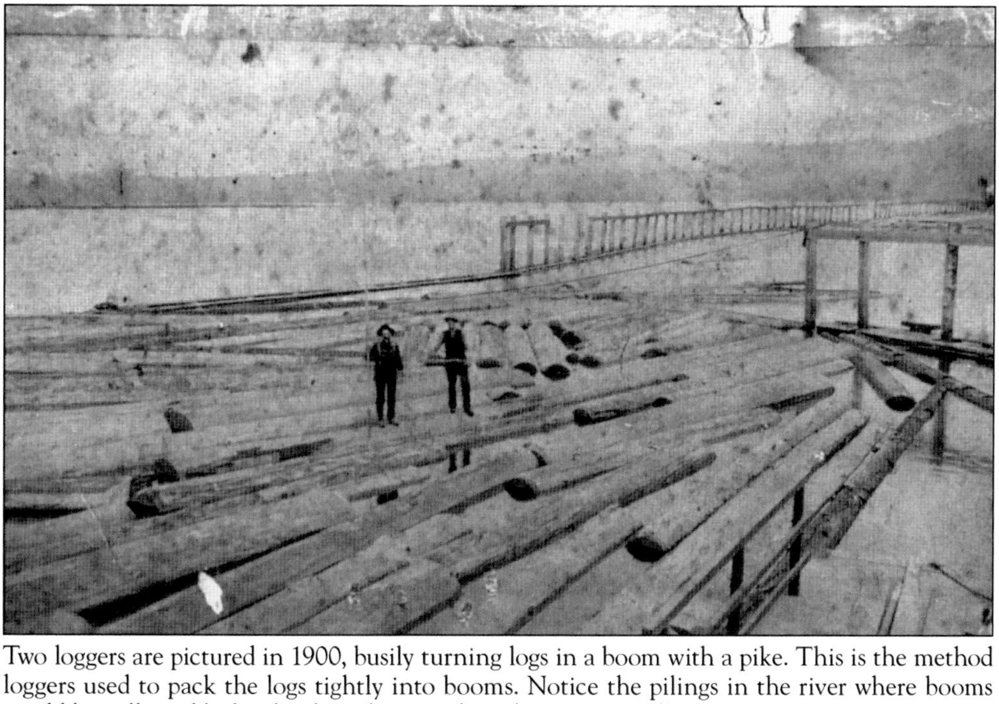

Two loggers are pictured in 1900, busily turning logs in a boom with a pike. This is the method loggers used to pack the logs tightly into booms. Notice the pilings in the river where booms would be collected before hauling them to their destination mills.

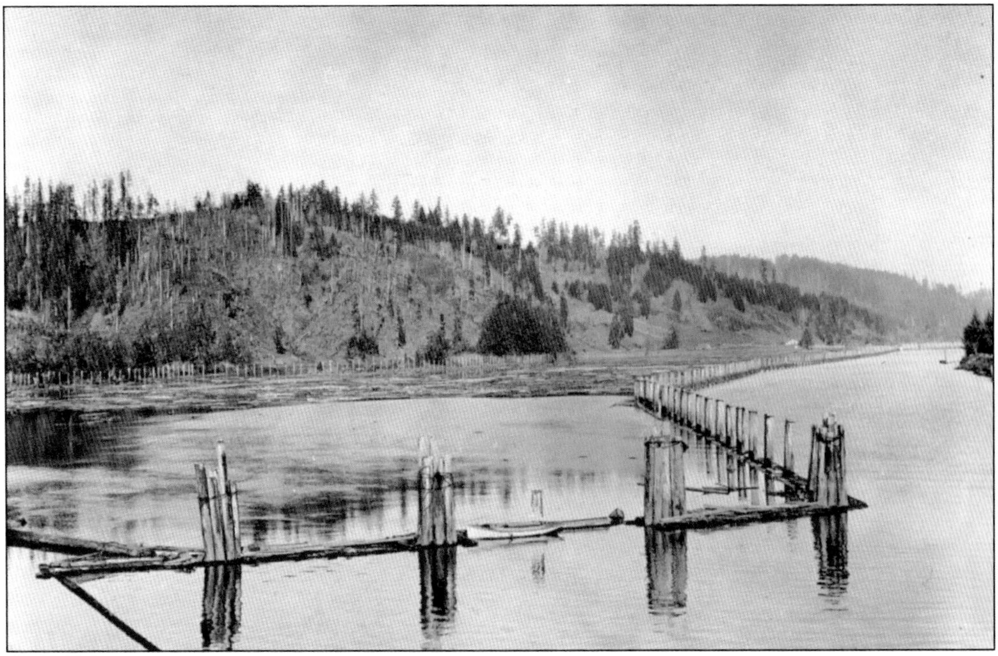

Log booms and the pilings that hold them stretch up the Smith River from Reedsport in this c. 1910 photograph. The booms would be stored behind these pilings until enough logs were collected to float them to the mills in Reedsport and Gardiner. This was done on both the Smith River and the Umpqua River.

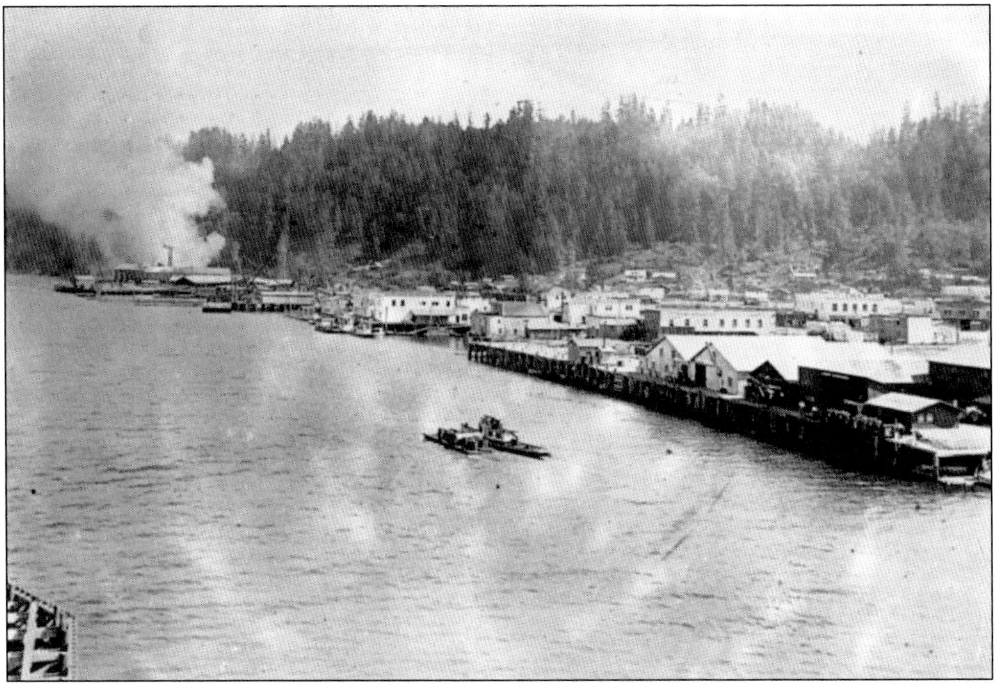

This is a view of the Reedsport waterfront taken from the Southern Pacific Railroad Bridge. The Rainbow Slough inlet is in the middle, with the canneries lining the right bank. Reedsport's Hubbard's Mill is on the left in the photograph. A barge carrying fish is in the middle of the river.

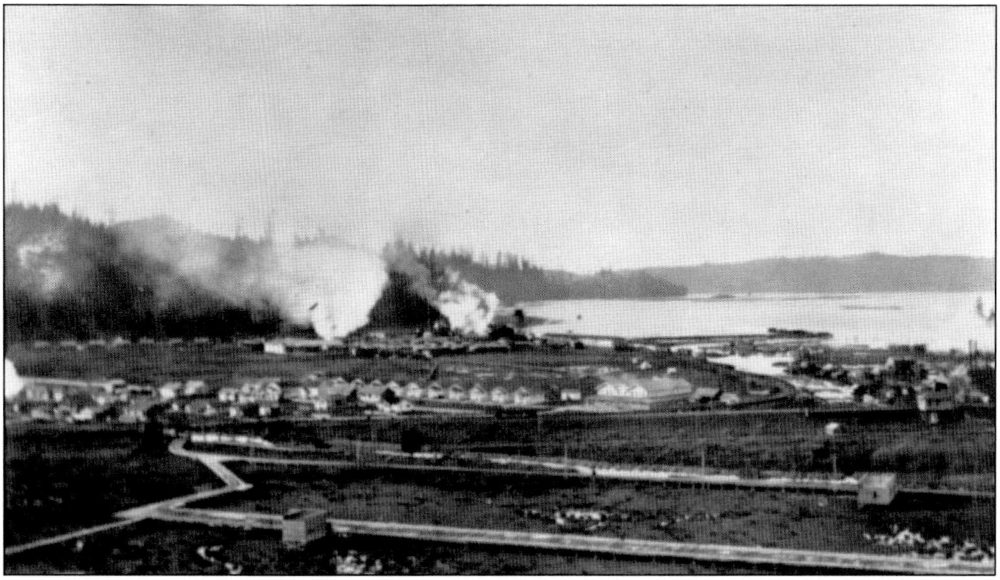

Another mill in town was the Winchester Bay Mill, located on the old International Paper Log Dump near Champion Park. Because of the housing shortage in Reedsport, the mill constructed a hotel for men with 68 rooms and a dining hall. The photograph shows the additional company housing that was available on Mill Street.

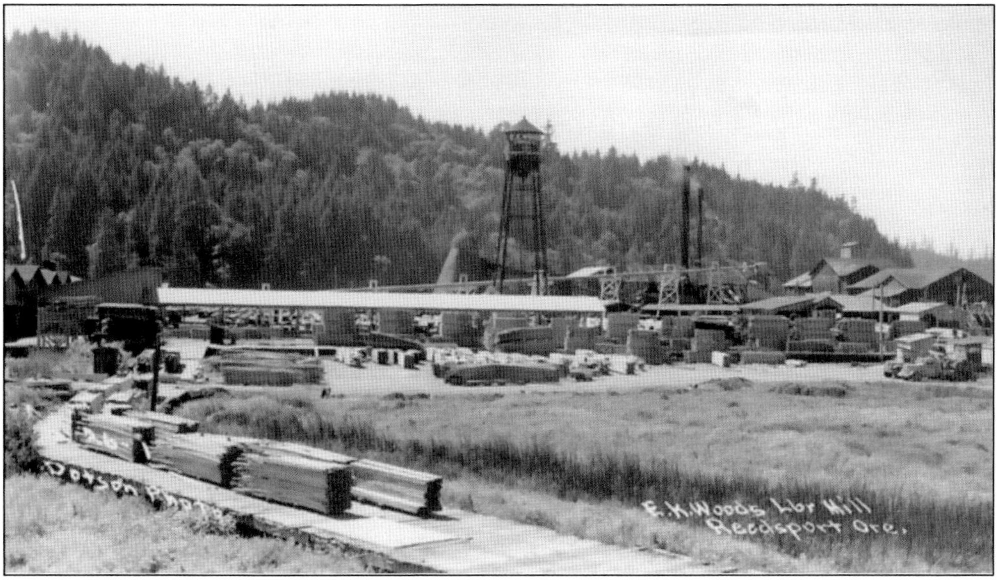

This late-1920s photograph shows the E.K. Woods Mill, previously the Winchester Bay Mill. The mill had its own ship to transport lumber to California. Among other things, the E.K. Woods Mill manufactured single-log booms that were used by oil rigs in Texas, before the widespread use of iron. The mill manager was Ed Seddoom, and their motto was "Goods of the Woods."

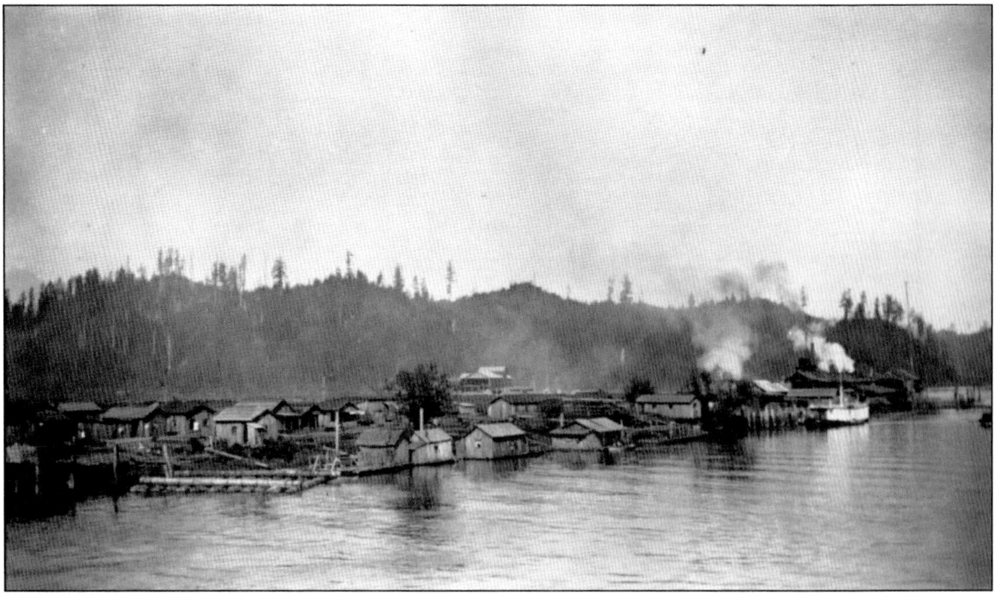

At the west end of Reedsport, this c. 1910 photograph shows the Bridge Mill to the far right. This mill was so named because it sat near the Railroad Bridge that spanned the Umpqua. Float houses can be seen all along the riverfront. Housing was short in Reedsport that these shanty houseboats often offered the only housing available.

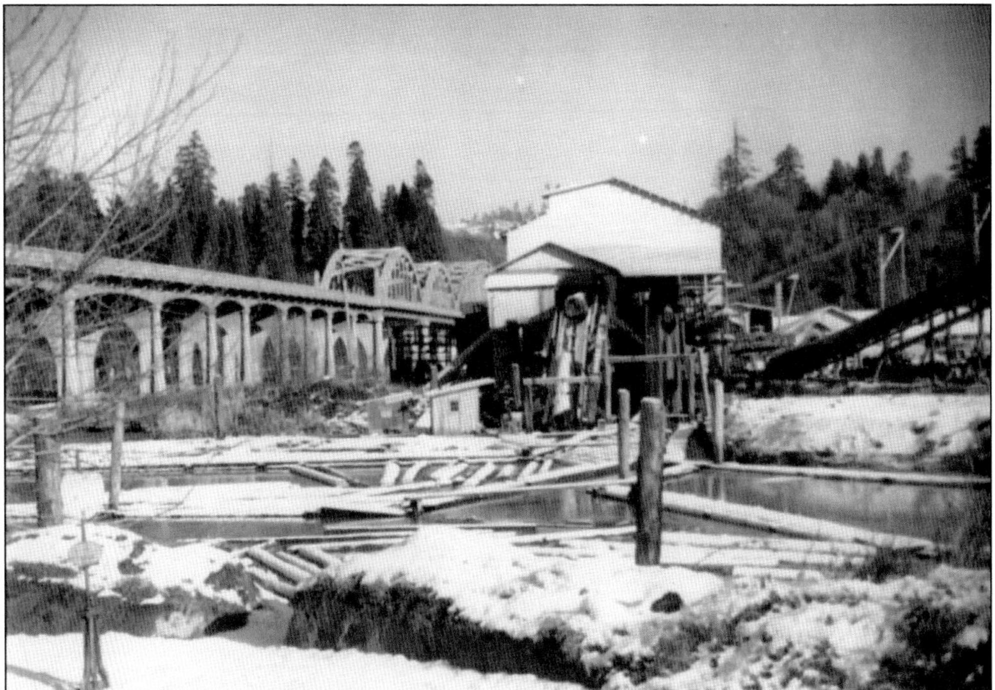

This 1949 photograph of the Bridge Mill Pond was taken after a freak snowstorm dumped a foot of snow on the area. Logs that were delivered to the millponds sat until enough were collected to warrant being milled into timber products. Note the Conde McCullough Umpqua River Bridge to the left. (Courtesy of Nan Hansen.)

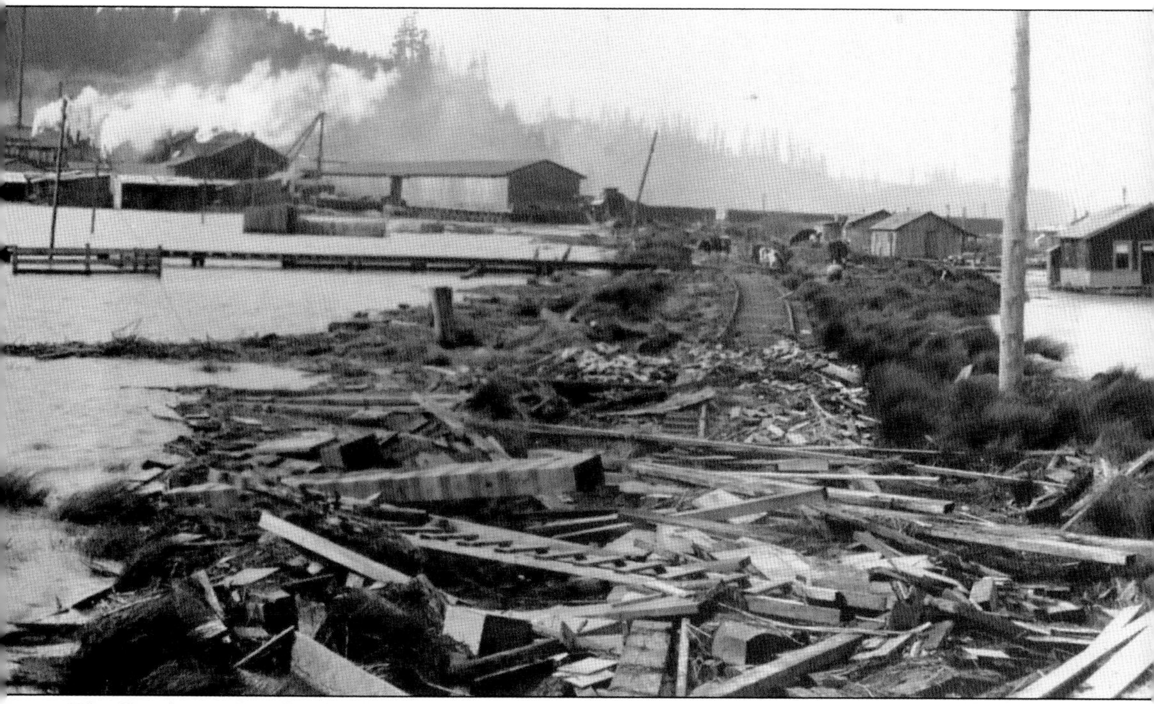

The Reedsport Lumber Mill was another mill in town that was located near where the River Bend community in Reedsport now exists. In this 1922 photograph of floodwaters, debris from the Umpqua River has piled up on the railroad track going through town. On the far left, the Reedsport Lumber Mill is visible.

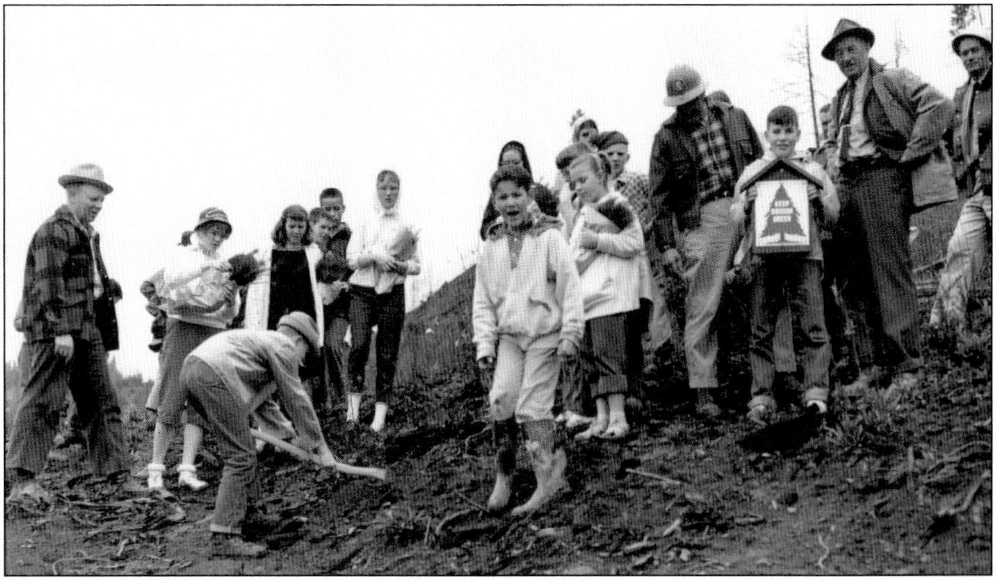

In 1946, John Skaaluren, one of the managers at E.K. Woods Mill, began the tradition of children in the Lower Umpqua area schools planting trees every spring to help replenish trees being cut in the lumber trade. Above is a photograph of the 1962 tree plant. Note the young man digging a hole for a tree with some of his classmates carrying seedlings to the plant. Below is a 1962 photograph of students from schools in the Lower Umpqua area planting trees on a recently harvested hillside. Students worked in groups where they were given bundles of seedlings to plant in established areas. A number of student groups participated in the event and can be seen in the distance. (Courtesy of Doris Hedges.)

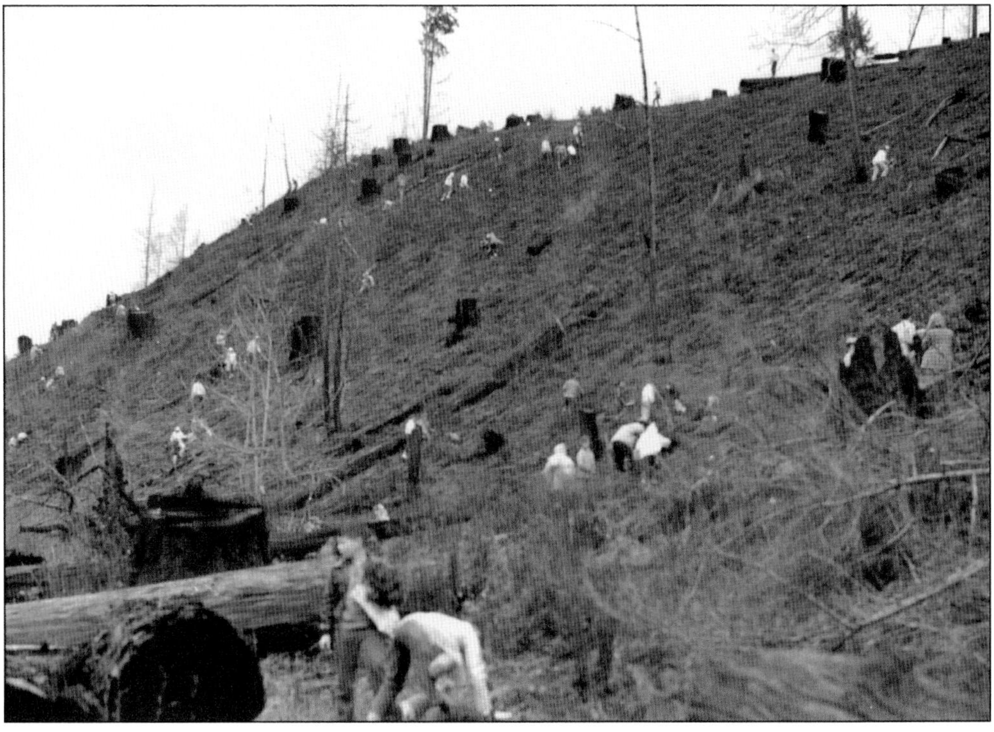

Five

Entertainment and Leisure

Entertainment was sometimes hard to come by in early Reedsport, but citizens managed to create a variety of events that kept life interesting. The most prominent social events were dances held up and down the river, most of them on barges that were floating in the river. Since they had to be careful of the tide when rowing to and from such an event, the evening could easily last all night. Local lodges also hosted dances for the public.

The earliest entertainment events in Reedsport were held on Wade's Flat, the southern part of town that was above Scholfield Creek and the marshes below. Picnics, baseball games, and even the occasional fistfight were all part of the day's entertainment. The largest Reedsport event was the Fourth of July celebration at the Pajari Ranch up the Scholfield Creek. Partygoers had to take the 5:00 a.m. train to Scholfield Creek and then walk to the orchard. Games included rolling-pin throwing, and Grace Bartow always performed "Casey at the Bat." There was also an annual Labor Day Salmon Bake.

The community sponsored a community band and there were a variety of lodges that each provided their own varied entertainments. There were the Odd Fellows and the Rebekahs. The Masonic Lodge had the Masons, the Eastern Star, and the Rainbow Girls all under its roof. There were even log-rolling events held at Tahkenitch Lake. Taverns also had their own clientele throughout the community.

Perhaps the most common social events centered around athletics. Each small school on the river had a basketball team, and it was a common sentiment that it was always good to beat Reedsport. Smith River and Gardiner were particularly proud of their athletic heritage, and the rivalry with Reedsport was deep-seated. As Reedsport grew, its athletic teams became more and more a part of the fabric of the community. Sports were offered to both boys and girls, and they originally competed in the Star League, which was comprised of the local towns in the immediate vicinity.

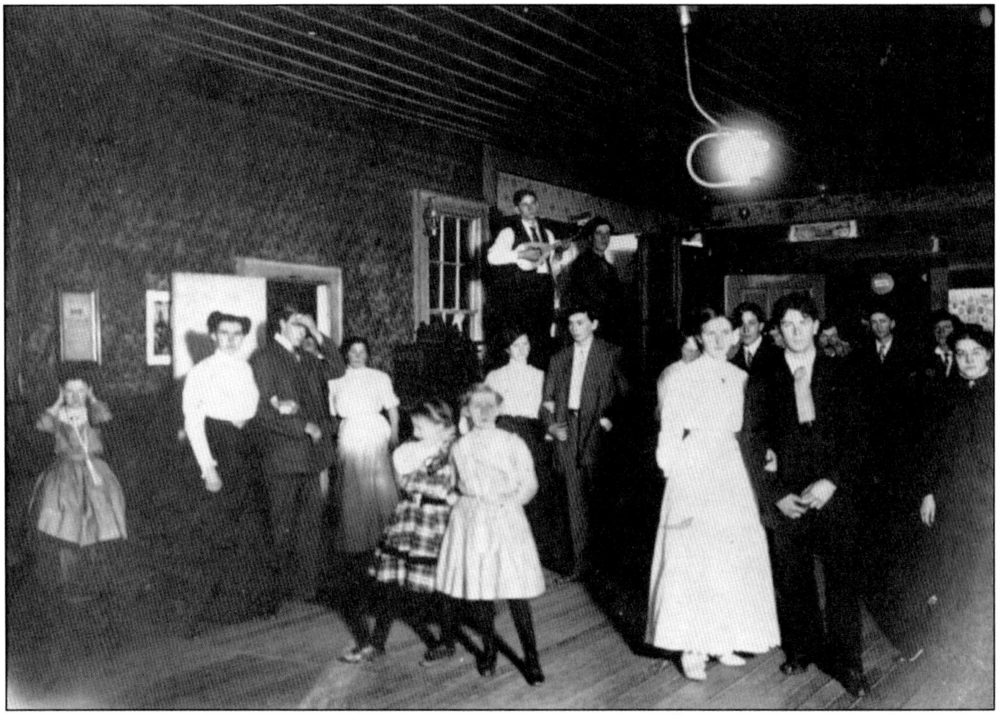

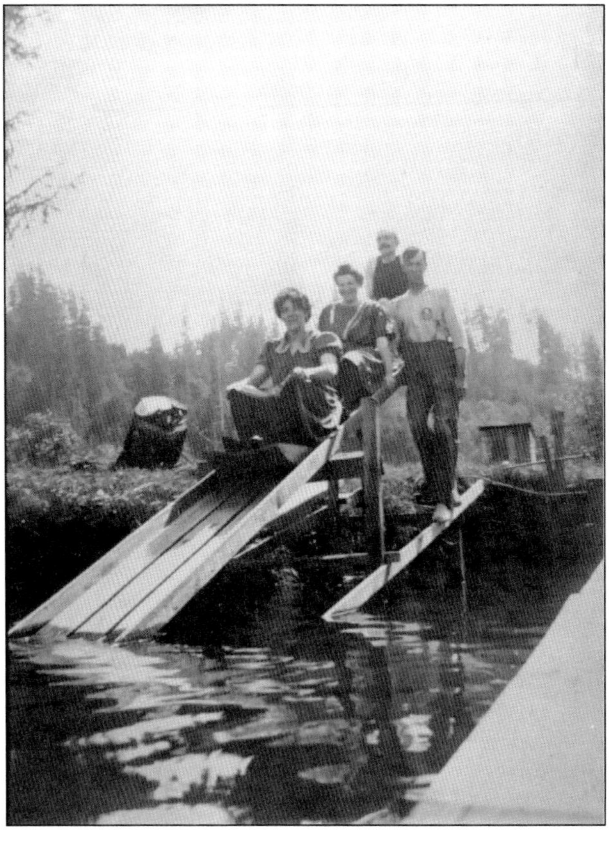

In the early days of Reedsport, dances were commonly held at the Masonic Lodge in Gardiner. No roads were yet available, so all dances at the lodges or on barges in the river were reached by boat. Dances were huge and held all over the rivers. It was not uncommon to walk to Lakeside or to row from Reedsport to Scottsburg for a dance. This is a c. 1900 photograph of a dance held in Scottsburg.

This is a photograph of Louise Seymour's chutes on the south side of the Umpqua River, just above the county dock in 1911. Pictured here are, from left to right, Janet Davidson, Nora Seymour, Louis Seymour, and Bert Melvin. These were the first chutes Louis Seymour constructed as a way to enjoy playing in the Umpqua River.

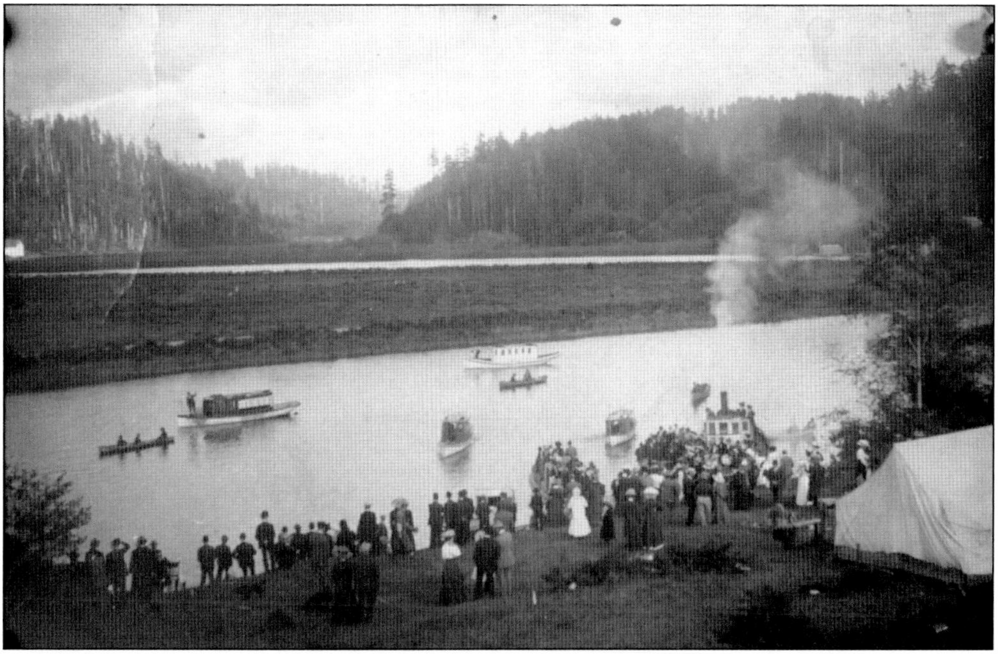

The forested section above Scholfield Creek's swamp was referred to as Wade's Flat. This 1915 photograph shows people who have rowed over from Gardiner to have picnics on the flat. They were limited in how far they could travel by boat, and this was the extent of where they could comfortably row. Decker Point farm is in the background.

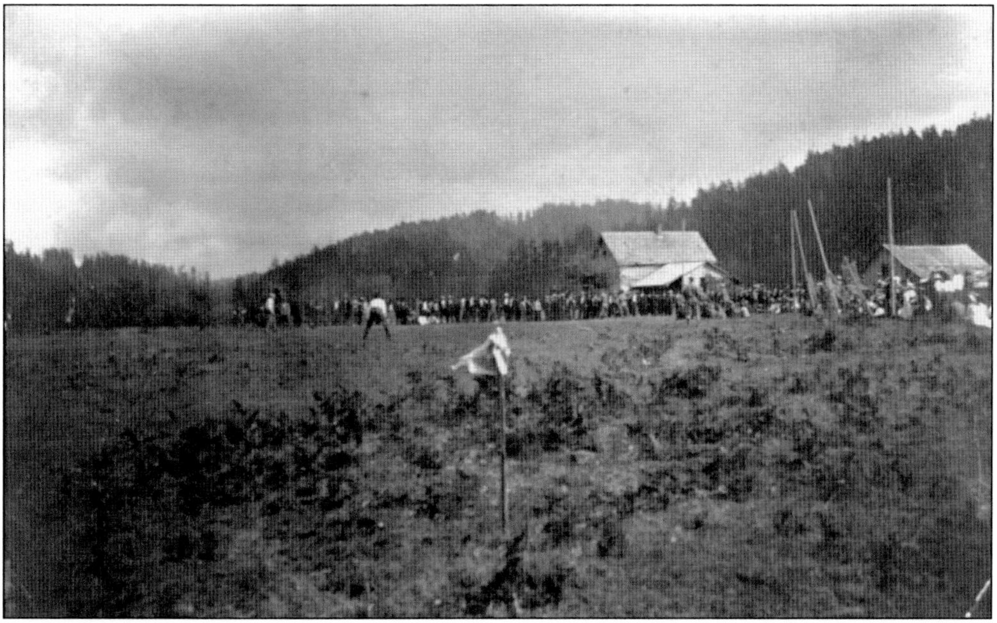

This 1915 photograph captures one of the many baseball games played at Wade's Flat. Summer baseball was a huge entertainment up and down the Oregon Coast. Communities from Florence to Bandon had town teams that traveled the area, playing games against other towns. Several of the local players considered trying professional baseball, but they decided they made too much money in the woods.

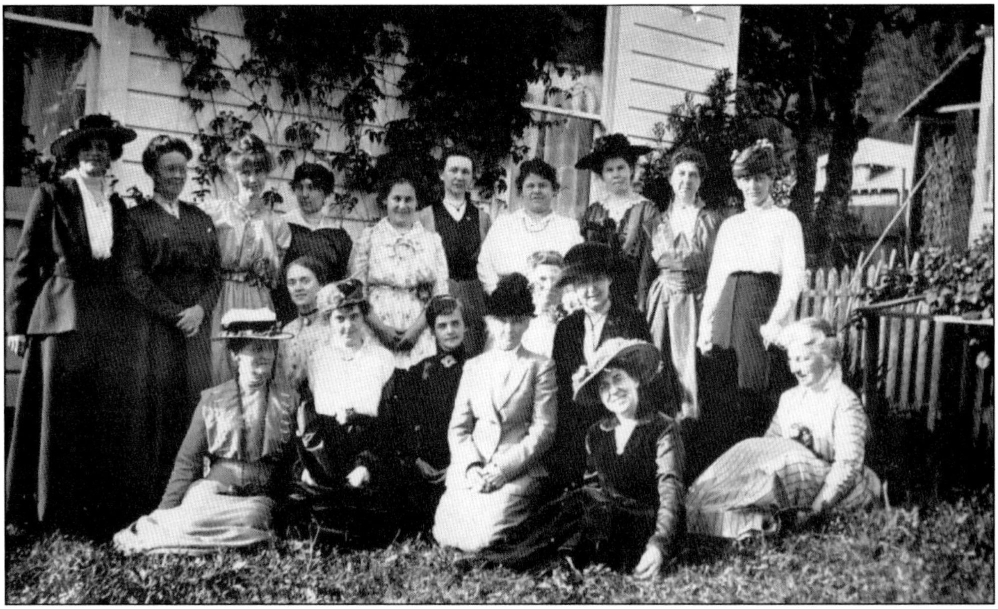

This is a photograph of the original Gardiner Literary Society, a group that still exists today. The members are, from left to right, (first row) Julia Perkins, Liz Wade, Eva Cornwall, and Mary Jewett; (second row) Mrs. Myrick, Margie Reed, Fannie Westerdale, Mrs. Riggs, and Maude Corwall; (third row) Annie Perkins, Jennie Brownell, Reita Edmunds, Mrs. Burdick, Mrs. Warren, Mae Fields, unidentified, Mrs. Janelle, Mrs. Cornwall, and Belle Wade.

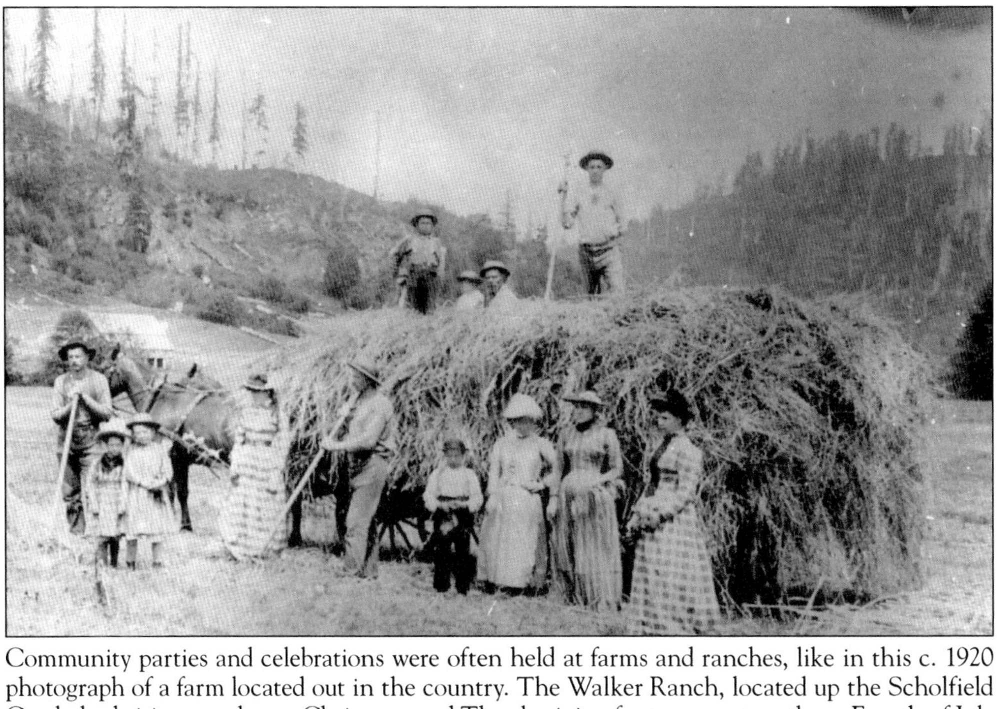

Community parties and celebrations were often held at farms and ranches, like in this c. 1920 photograph of a farm located out in the country. The Walker Ranch, located up the Scholfield Creek, had citizens gather at Christmas and Thanksgiving for town get-togethers. Fourth of July celebrations were held at the Pajari family ranch up Scholfield. Visitors had to take a 5:00 a.m. train and walk to the Pajari orchard.

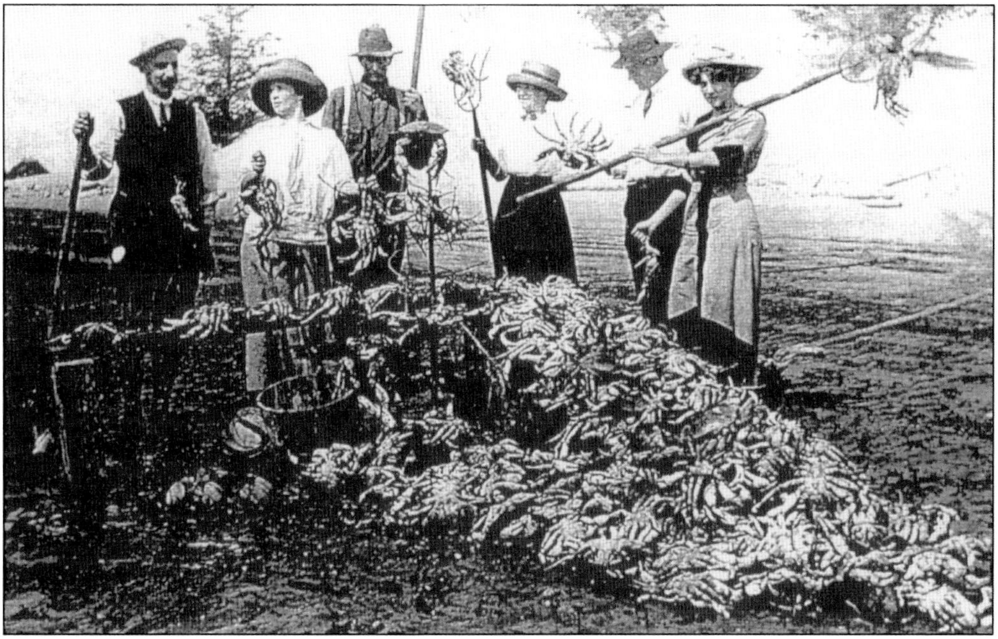

This c. 1900 photograph demonstrates how prolific crabbing was in the Umpqua River at the turn of the century. Instead of using crab pots and boats, recreational crabbers would make a trip to the ocean for a picnic and to collect crab in the river. It was important to make the trip at low tide so that crab could be gathered in the fissures of bedrock in the river with shovels and rakes. This bounty of seafood was a common addition to meals for local residents. Many would bring iron kettles and boil the crab at the beach after they had been gathered. Clamming also had its followers, and a bounty of clams was available for those who chose to dig for them. Like most inhabitants of the Lower Umpqua River, the tide dictated many outings.

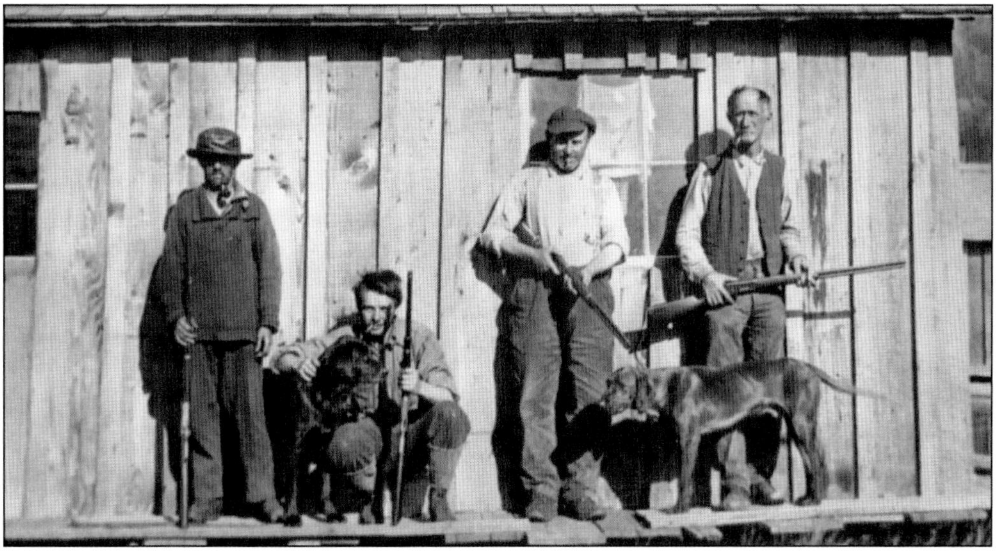

Hunting had always been a means of providing food for families, and with an abundance of deer, elk, bear, and waterfowl, natural resources provided a great deal for local hunters like these pictured c. 1930. As early as 1880, pelters worked in the area, working only for the hides. Others would hunt deer commercially and send the fresh meat and jerky to the Willamette Valley.

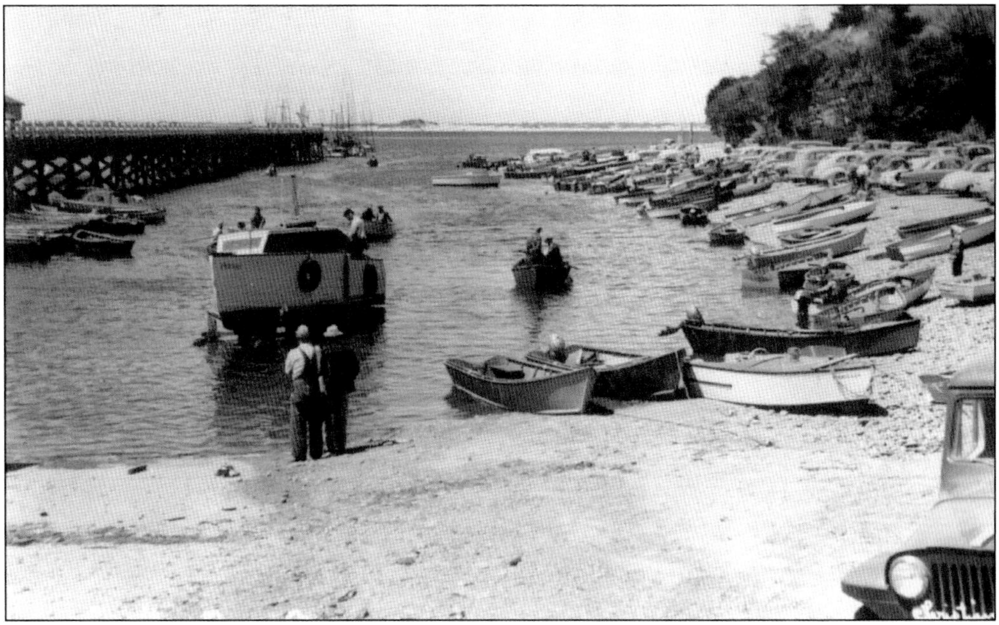

Winchester Bay was a favorite recreational fishing area. Before improvements to Salmon Harbor, people still flocked to the area. On July 4, 1951, it was reported that 2,160 cars arrived at the docks, many with trailers. It was estimated that 750 tons of salmon and 650 tons of crab annually would be landed at Winchester Bay if suitable moorings were provided. The Oregon State Game Commission decided that the average cost of catching a salmon on sport tackle was $63 a fish. It came out to $6.75 a pound.

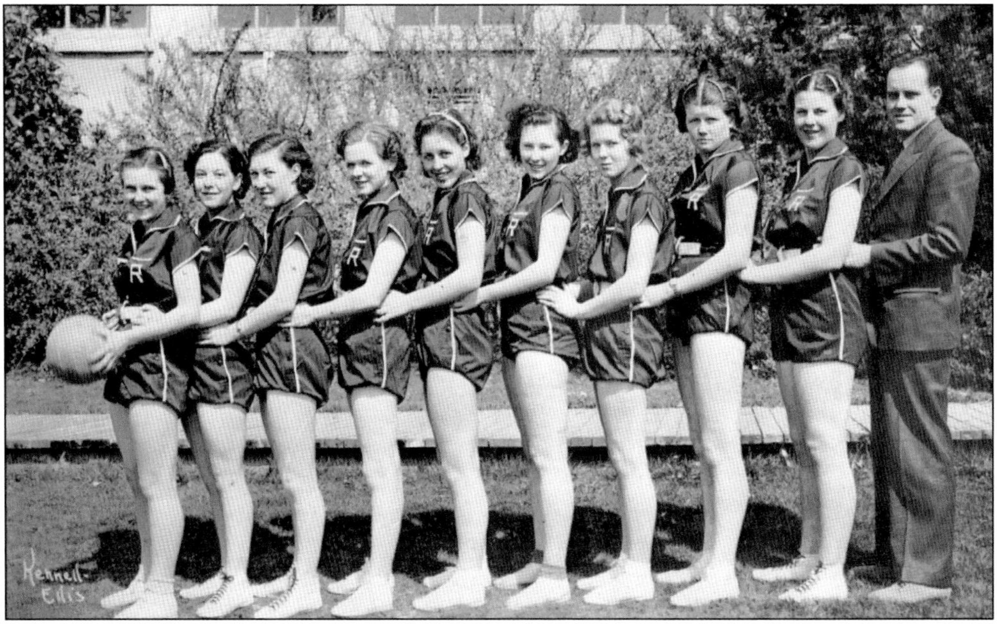

This is a photograph of the 1934 volleyball squad at Reedsport High School. Girls had opportunities to compete in volleyball, basketball, and track. Pictured from left to right are Genevieve Hudson, Melba DeVelbiss, Jean Neumens, Lorraine Rosier, Cristine Carlson, Mildred Holman, Margie Waggoner, Eveline Leach, Olga Jacobs, and Mr. Hegdahl. (Courtesy of the 1934 Reedsport Annual.)

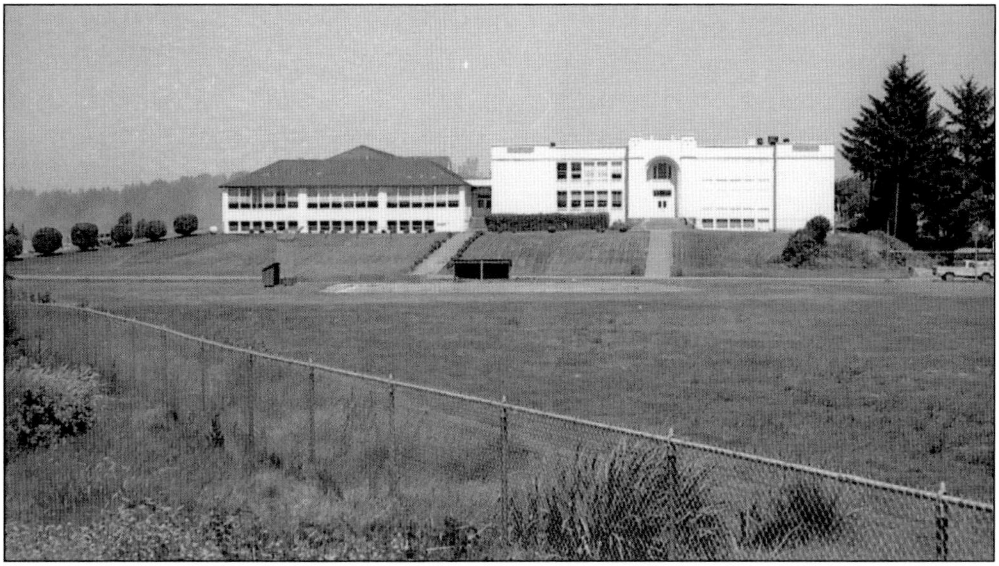

In the 1920s, the Reedsport football field sat just below the school. The field itself was basically dirt, and in late fall could turn into a mud field. It was close enough to Scholfield Creek that when the tide was high, the football field was further inundated by water. There are stories of salmon being found on the field after games.

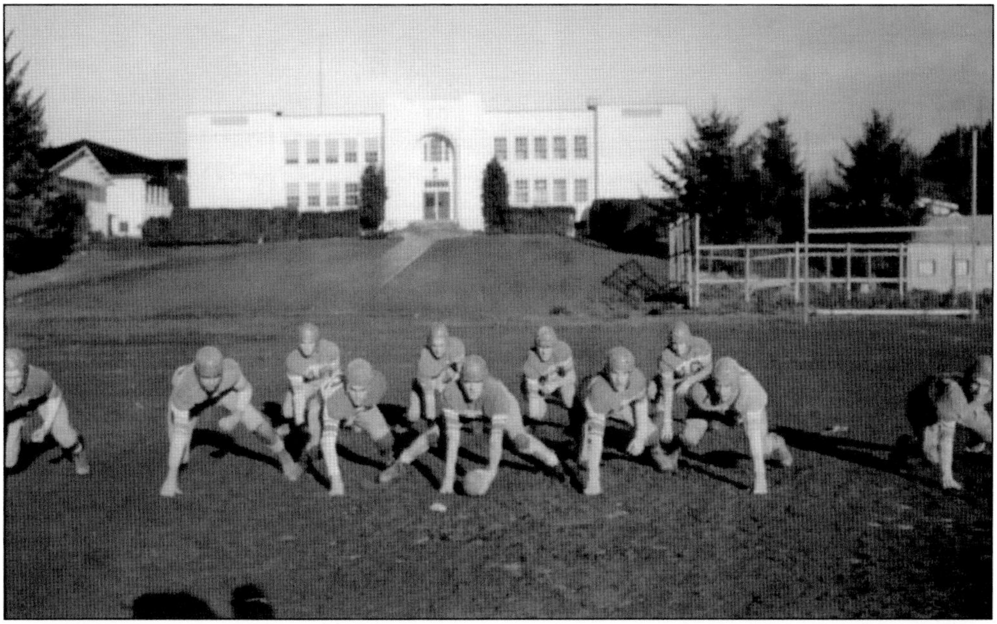

The 1946 Reedsport High School football team was the state champion for schools with less than a 150-student population by defeating Moro 27 to 0. Their record was 9 and 2, under coach Jack Flug, with losses only to larger schools, including Roseburg and Springfield. The championship game was played in Oregon City that year, because the Portland location was too wet. Clyde Dewitt scored on a 57-yard touchdown run in the first quarter and caught a 33-yard touchdown pass from Dick Mooney. Jack Diehl scored two touchdowns, one on a pass and one on a run. At the halftime of the championship game, the Moro coach asked Mr. Flug to take it easy on his boys in the second half.

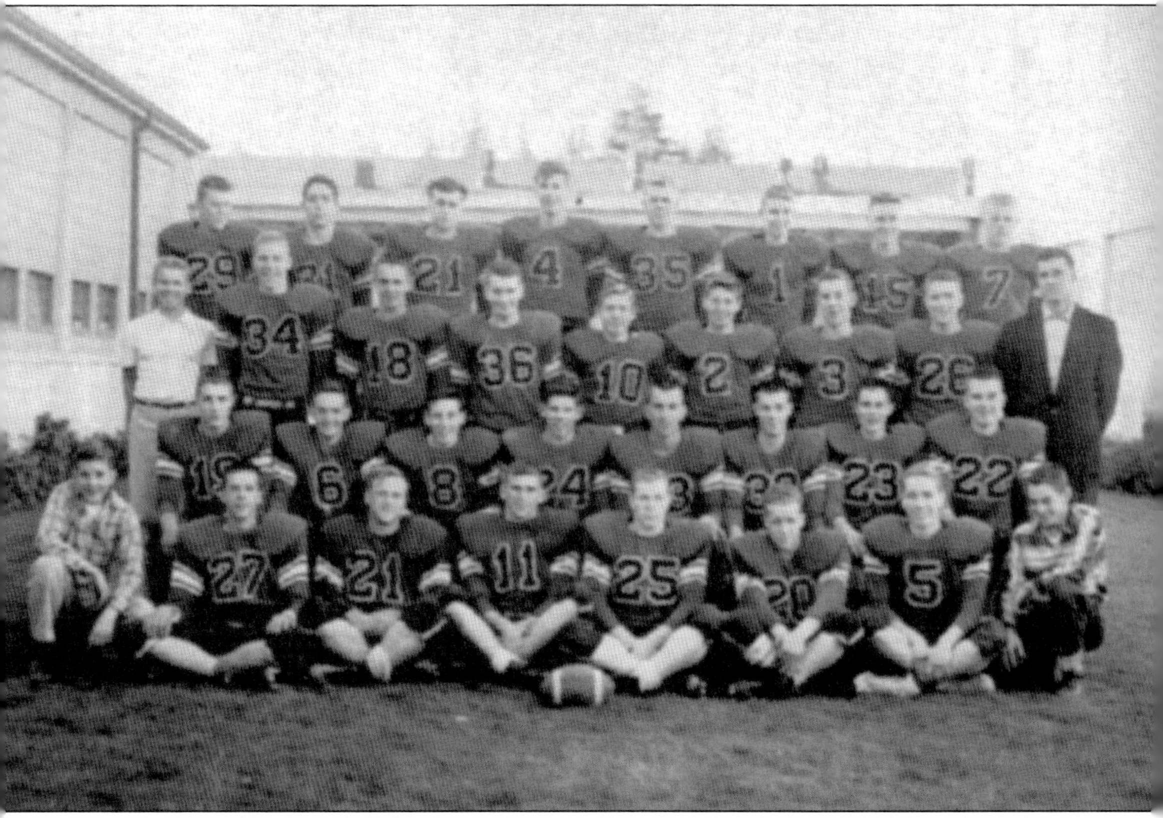

In 1957, Reedsport High School won the state championship under Rudy Ruppe by defeating Silverton High School 7 to 6, after putting together an 11 and 1 season. This was an upset, in that Silverton had won 20 straight games and had not lost in two straight years. They outweighed the Reedsport squad on an average of 20 pounds a man. Members of that squad are, from left to right, (first row) manager Joe Reeves, David Brooks, Dan Baker, Allen Leach, Roy Burns, Glen Tompkins, Clayton Ladd, and manager Jerry Evans; (second row) Francis Tresler, Leland Koepke, Leon Fenner, Jack Hickman, Jerry Friese, Hubert Baker, Arthur Smith, and Ken Husko; (third row) manager Bobby Strickler, Herb Ladd, Bill Karcher, David Burling, Alvin Urie, Gary Waggoner, Jerry Abbott, Mike Henderson, and Coach Ruppe; (fourth row) Burk Rowe, Harold Forbes, Gary Sharp, Maurice Hedges, Tom Gorman, Sam Young, James Blakey, and Gary Olson.

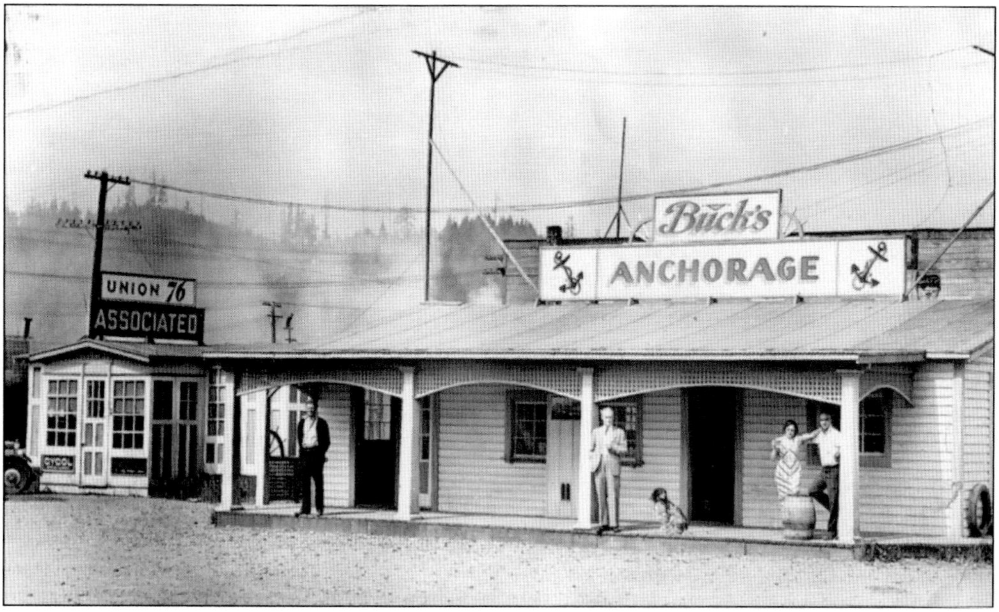

Taverns also played a role in Reedsport's entertainment. Drinking was so heavy at one point that Ripley published an article describing Reedsport as the town with the most per capita consumption of alcohol in Oregon. Pictured here around 1935 is Buck's Anchorage. In later years, this became the Waterfront. In the 1930s, Buck's and the Rainbow served hard liquor, while the Reedsport Tavern and the Silver Moon served beer, and Ward's had beer and a pool table. The picture below, c. 1940, is the inside of the Waterfront Tavern with the shuffleboard table to the right that was the scene of many weekend tournaments and occasional fights. The Waterfront was sold to Jim and Bunny DeWitt in 1949, and was open from 7:00 a.m. to 2:30 a.m., seven days a week. (Courtesy of Bob Huebner.)

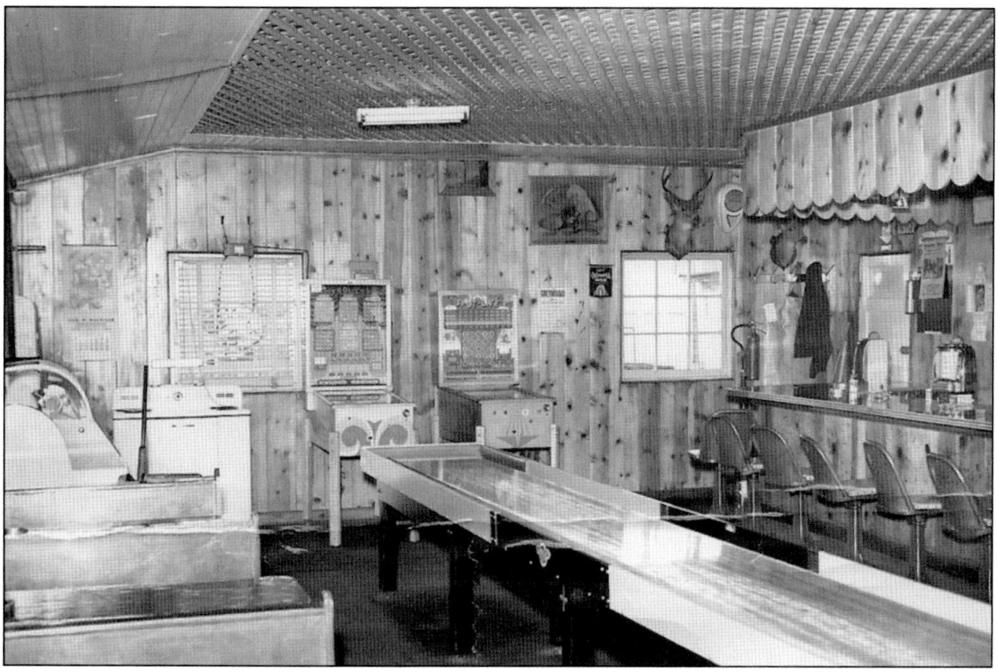

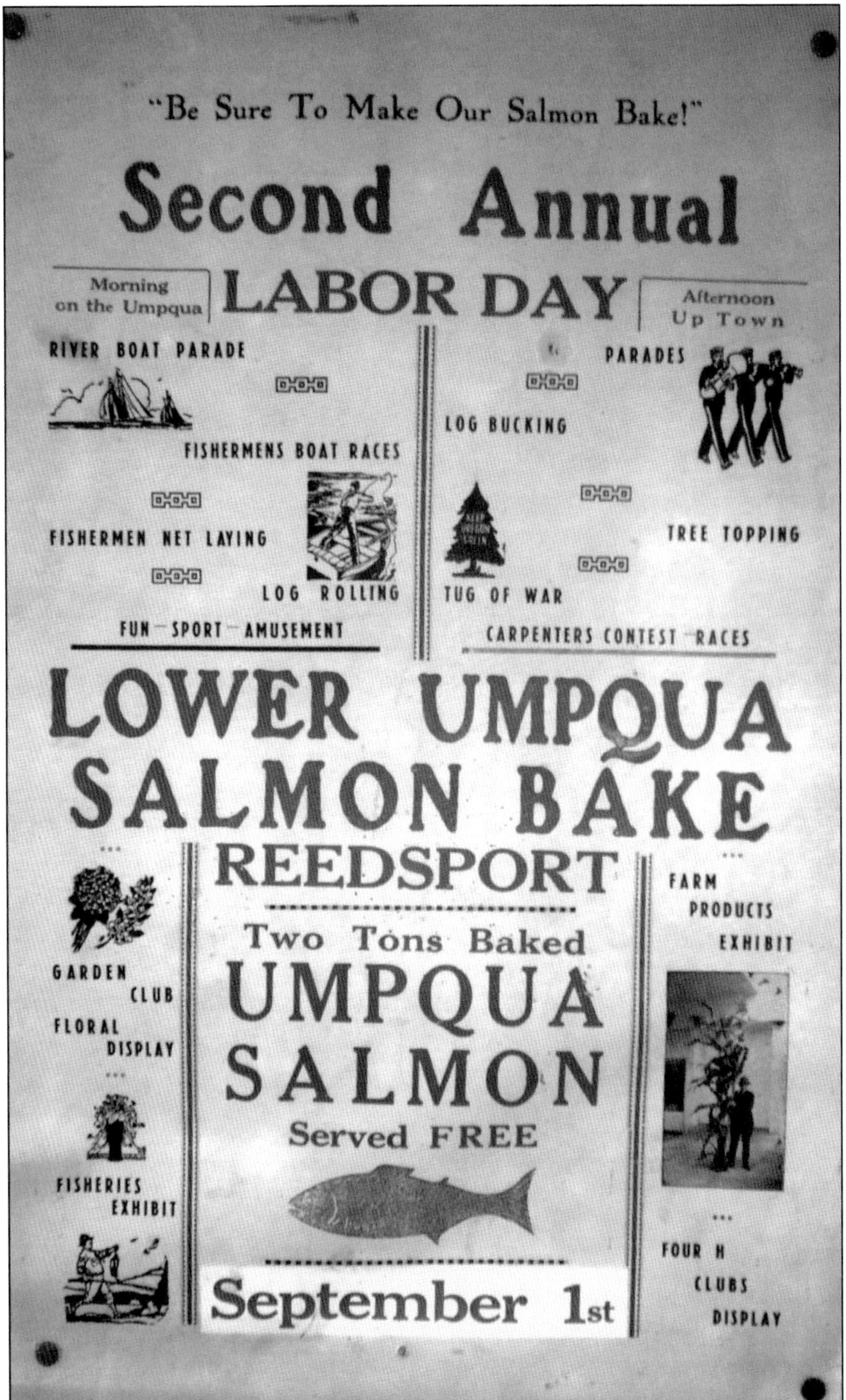

The community held its second-annual Lower Umpqua Salmon Bake over Labor Day in 1941. This celebration was held in Dunn's Department Store during the first celebration because of torrential rain. In later years, the Gardiner Reedsport Lions Club had a salmon bake during every Fleet Days Celebration in July.

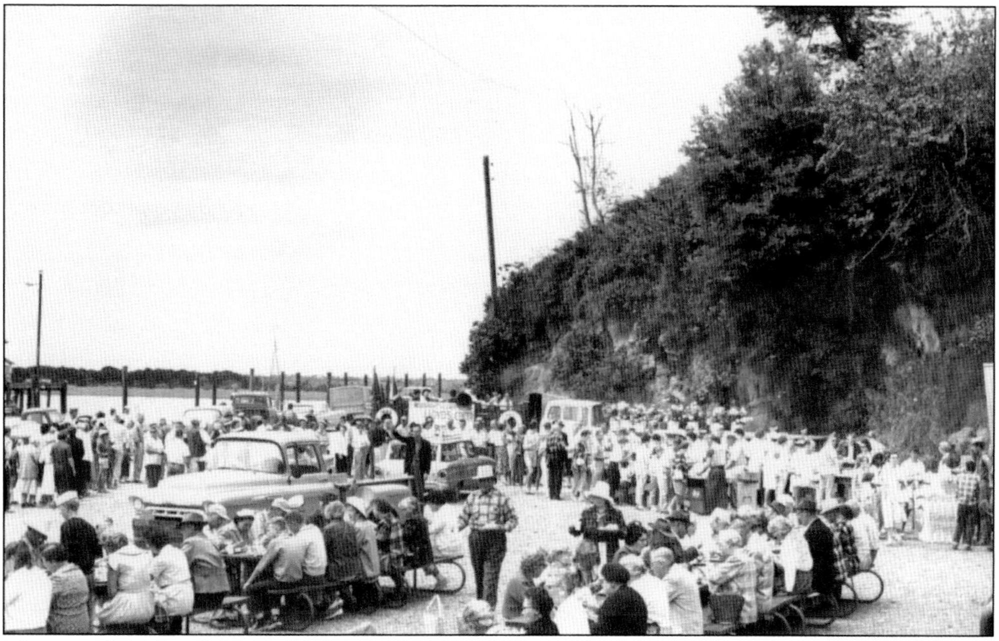

This is a photograph of the 1965 Salmon Bake sponsored by the Gardiner-Reedsport Lions Club. In 1966, the Lions served over 2,000 salmon dinners at this event. The dinner always occurred at Fleet Days, an annual summer festival that drew huge crowds to Winchester Bay and Reedsport. (Courtesy of Gary Waggoner.)

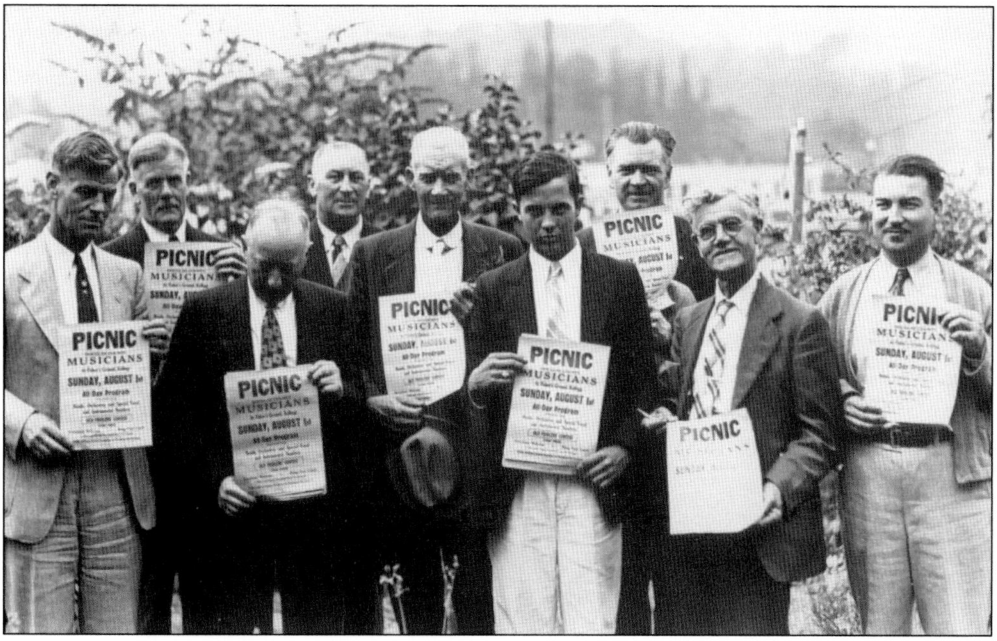

This is 1937 photograph shows a group of Douglas County volunteers advertising the Musicians Picnic event held at Fisher's Cove on August 1, 1937. Pictured here are, from left to right, J.D. Gilmore, Martin Homme, William "Billy" Ott, Charles Hartley, Lee Kennedy, Eldon Fisher, Charles Arundel, and Clyde Carstens. Since Reedsport and Winchester Bay are Douglas County's only ocean access, these events were popular throughout the county.

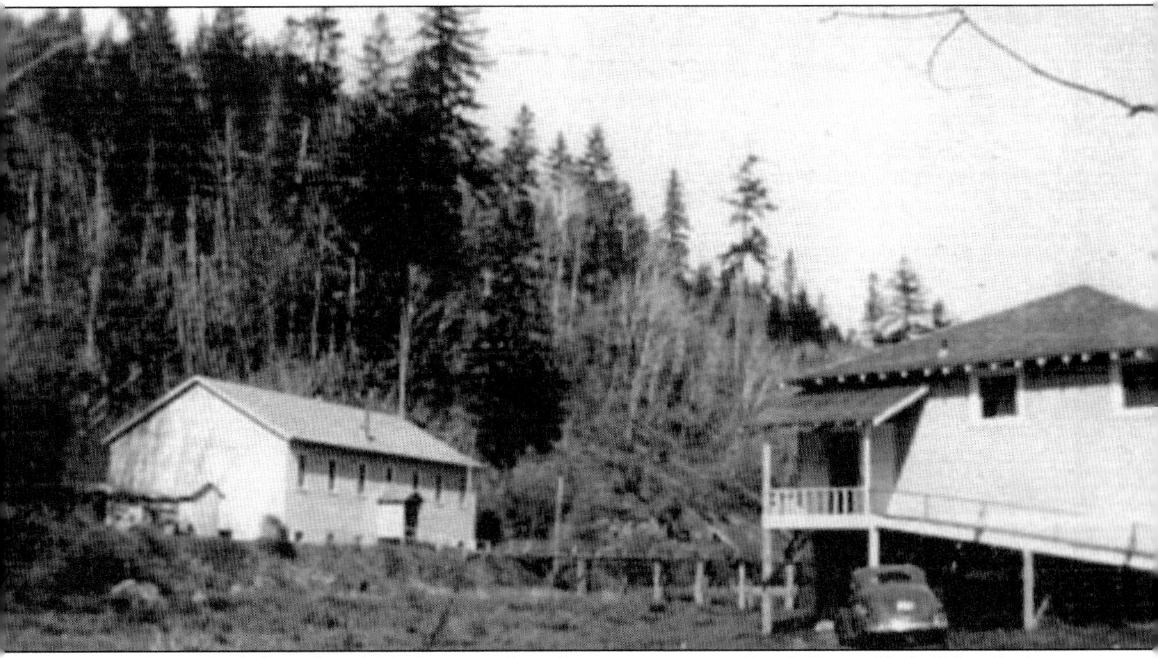

Sitting to the left in this 1938 photograph is the gymnasium at Smith River High School, the site of many hotly contested basketball games played between schools up and down both Smith River and the Umpqua River. Basketball rivalries were serious with both Gardiner and Smith River having teams that delighted in defeating Reedsport. When Smith River High School closed in 1945 and students were sent to Reedsport for their education, local ranchers still greatly valued the tradition of Smith River basketball. A local rancher took this gymnasium apart, shipped it across Smith River, and reconstructed it at Eslick Creek.

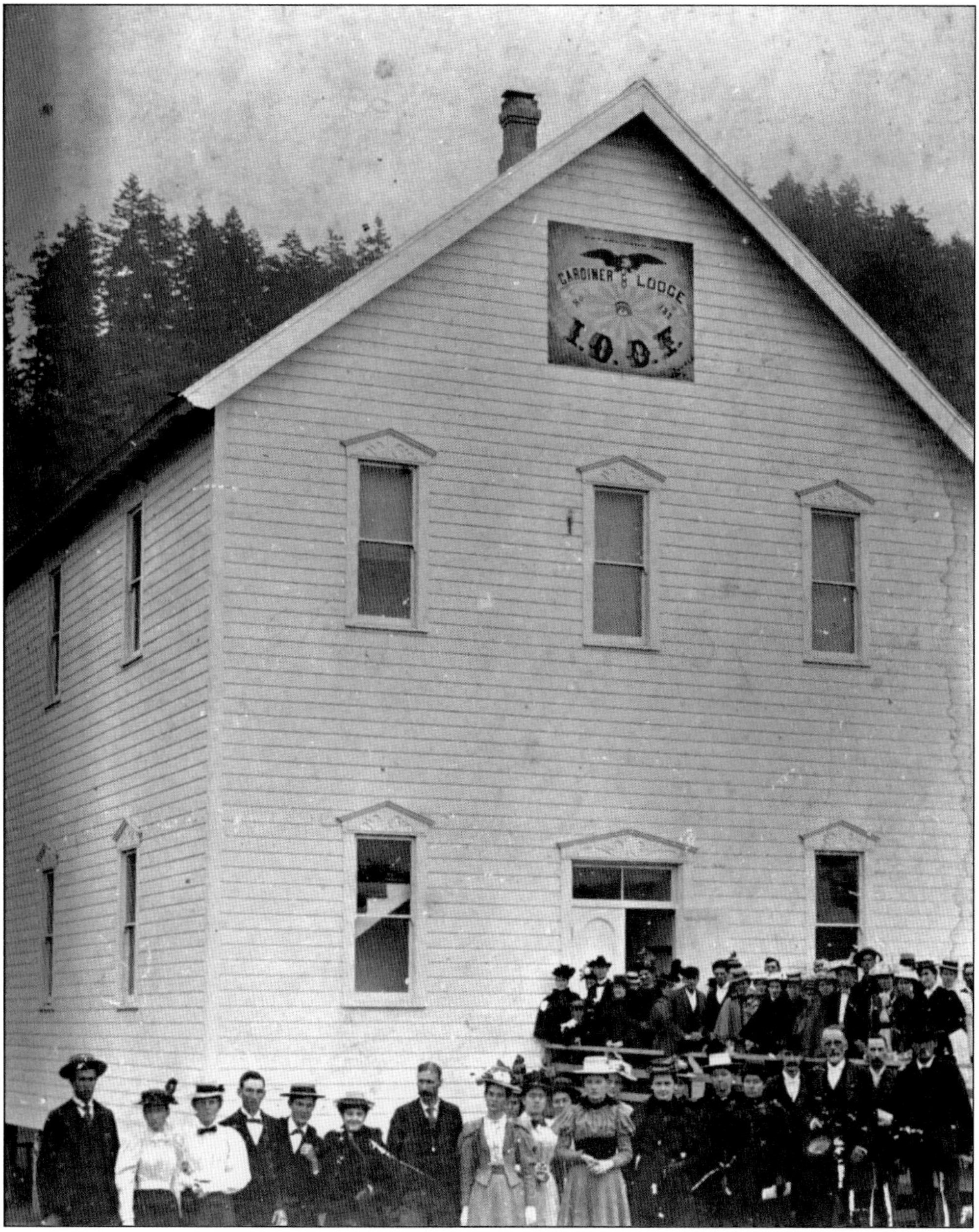

Lodges provided weekly entertainment for families. Potlucks, dances, meetings, and ceremonies all dominated the lodge scene. The Masons held their events on the first Saturday before the full moon, to allow folks to see by the light of the moon when trying to get home, which was often not before 2:00 a.m. The earliest meeting of the Aurora Lodge, pictured here, was held in Gardiner on December 14, 1872.

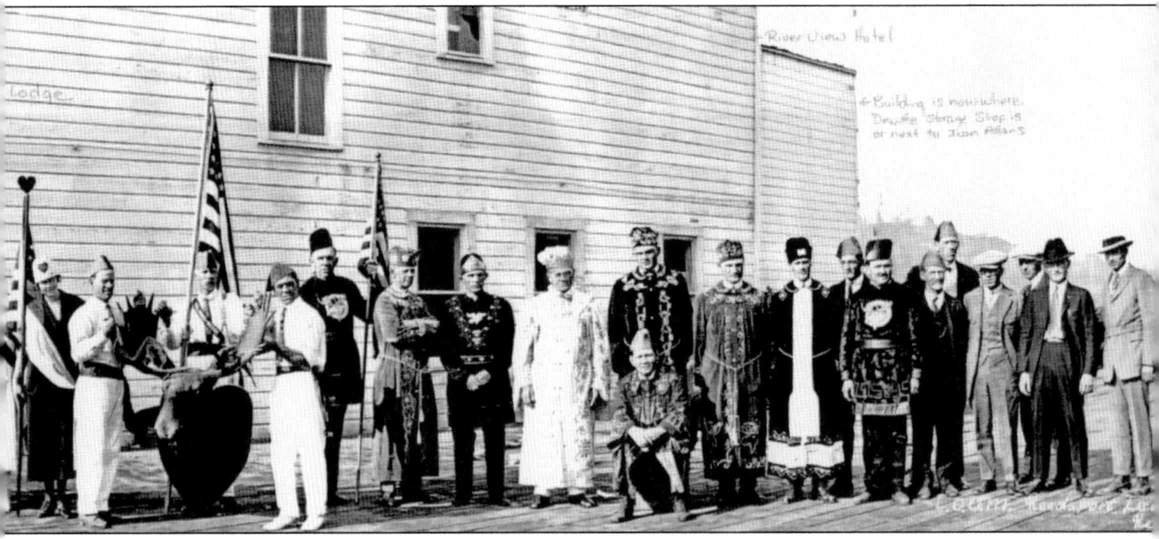

Reedsport's Moose Lodge formed in 1919 with 100 members. Pictured here to the right, Moose Lodge members are on the waterfront boardwalk, proudly displaying their lodge's moose head to the left. Other lodges included the Elks, Odd Fellows, and Eagles, as well as auxiliary groups of Eastern Star, Rebekahs, and the PEO. All of these groups reflected the values of these early years in Oregon. (Courtesy of Mindpower Gallery.)

Six

Schools

One-room schools proliferated the area in the early 1900s. Parents usually rowed the children to school, but steam-driven school boats later brought mail, supplies, and students up and down the length of the rivers. Schools on Smith River ran up the main branch and the North Fork. Along the Umpqua River were schools at Scottsburg, Ash Valley, which was up Mill Creek, Harvey Creek, Dean's Creek, and Scholfield Creek. Gardiner had its own school system that boasted the W.F. Jewett School and Ruby School at Five Mile on a road going north toward Ada. There were four different schools in Winchester Bay.

Reedsport's first school was at East Gardiner in 1894, but they had a terrible time keeping teachers because of the treacherous whims of the river. In 1911, a school tent on the river's edge was opened at the east end of Reedsport. At high tide, students had to put their feet on their desks because water would come up into the tent. In 1912, a school was opened at Rainbow Slough. This corresponded to the influx of population due to the railroad work. There were too many students for the building and some classes had to be held in the back room of the Kennedy and Brown Store and at the community church.

In 1919, a four-room school was constructed on the Orchard Tract. Six acres were owned by Warren Reed and was located at the southern part of town just north of Scholfield Creek. Three elementary classes and one high school class were held in this building. In 1920, additions were added, but in 1927, the entire building burned to the ground. Classes were held in the play shed and at the community church until the new school was completed in 1928.

School administrators such as Jack Flug, Homer Dixon, Orville Bailey, and Tom Huebner shaped the community. Teachers such as Kay Keating and Rudy Ruppe were also instrumental in influencing the character of the town.

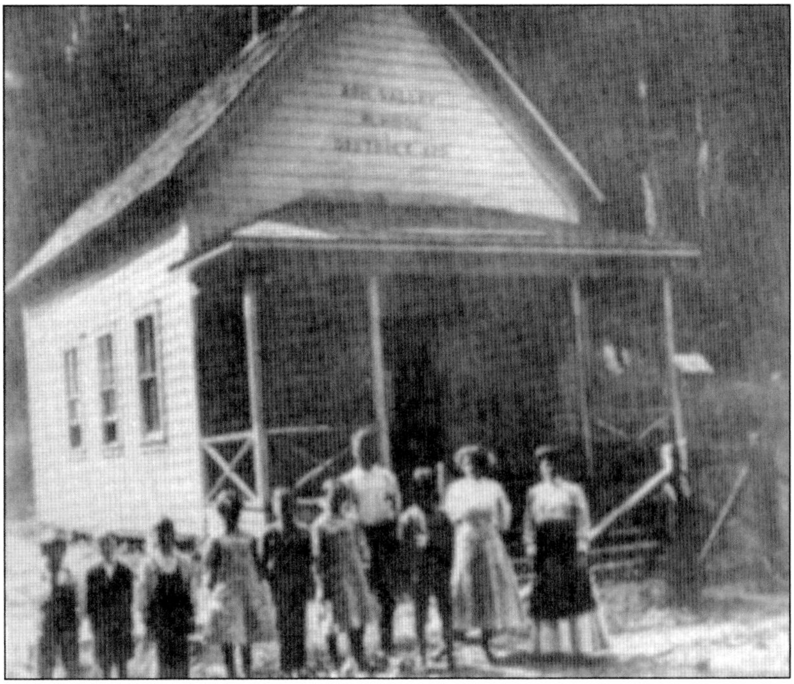

Located eight miles up Mill Creek, the first school in Ash Valley was established in 1894. In 1903, the school shifted to the Russell Snider home. In 1928, a third school was constructed. This is a 1929 photograph of that structure. Ash Valley did not merge with Reedsport until June 30, 1995.

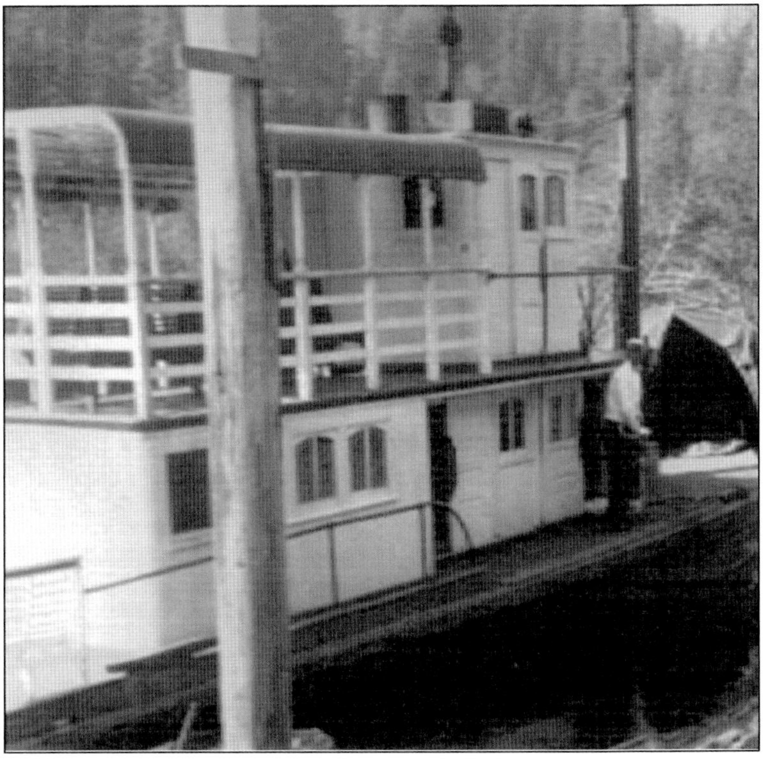

This is a 1922 photograph of the *Vulcan*, known as the waterbus, delivering students to schools up the Smith River. The school boats delivered mail, some goods, and students on a daily basis on their trek from Gardiner to Sulphur Springs, on the upper reaches of Smith River. Other boats that traveled the river were the *Bonita* and the *Minnie Mitchell*.

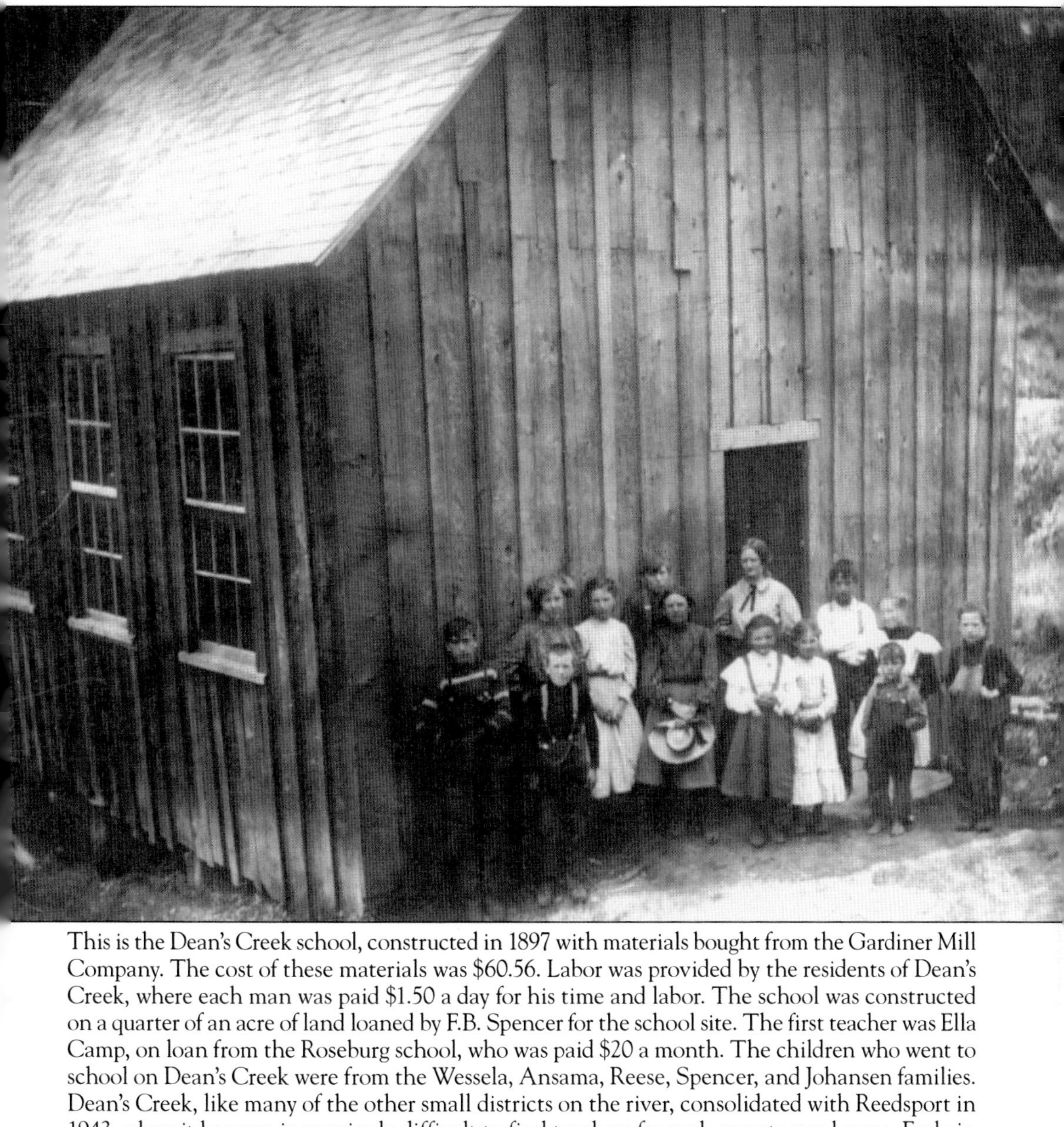

This is the Dean's Creek school, constructed in 1897 with materials bought from the Gardiner Mill Company. The cost of these materials was $60.56. Labor was provided by the residents of Dean's Creek, where each man was paid $1.50 a day for his time and labor. The school was constructed on a quarter of an acre of land loaned by F.B. Spencer for the school site. The first teacher was Ella Camp, on loan from the Roseburg school, who was paid $20 a month. The children who went to school on Dean's Creek were from the Wessela, Ansama, Reese, Spencer, and Johansen families. Dean's Creek, like many of the other small districts on the river, consolidated with Reedsport in 1943, when it became increasingly difficult to find teachers for such remote rural areas. Early in the century, many schools did not go beyond the eighth grade because it was believed that it was not necessary. An *Oregonian* editorial stated, "Give every child a good common school English education at public expense and then stop. There have been two presidents of the United States who have received less aid than this in their school education; if any want more, let those who dance pay the fiddler. This is the cure for drones."

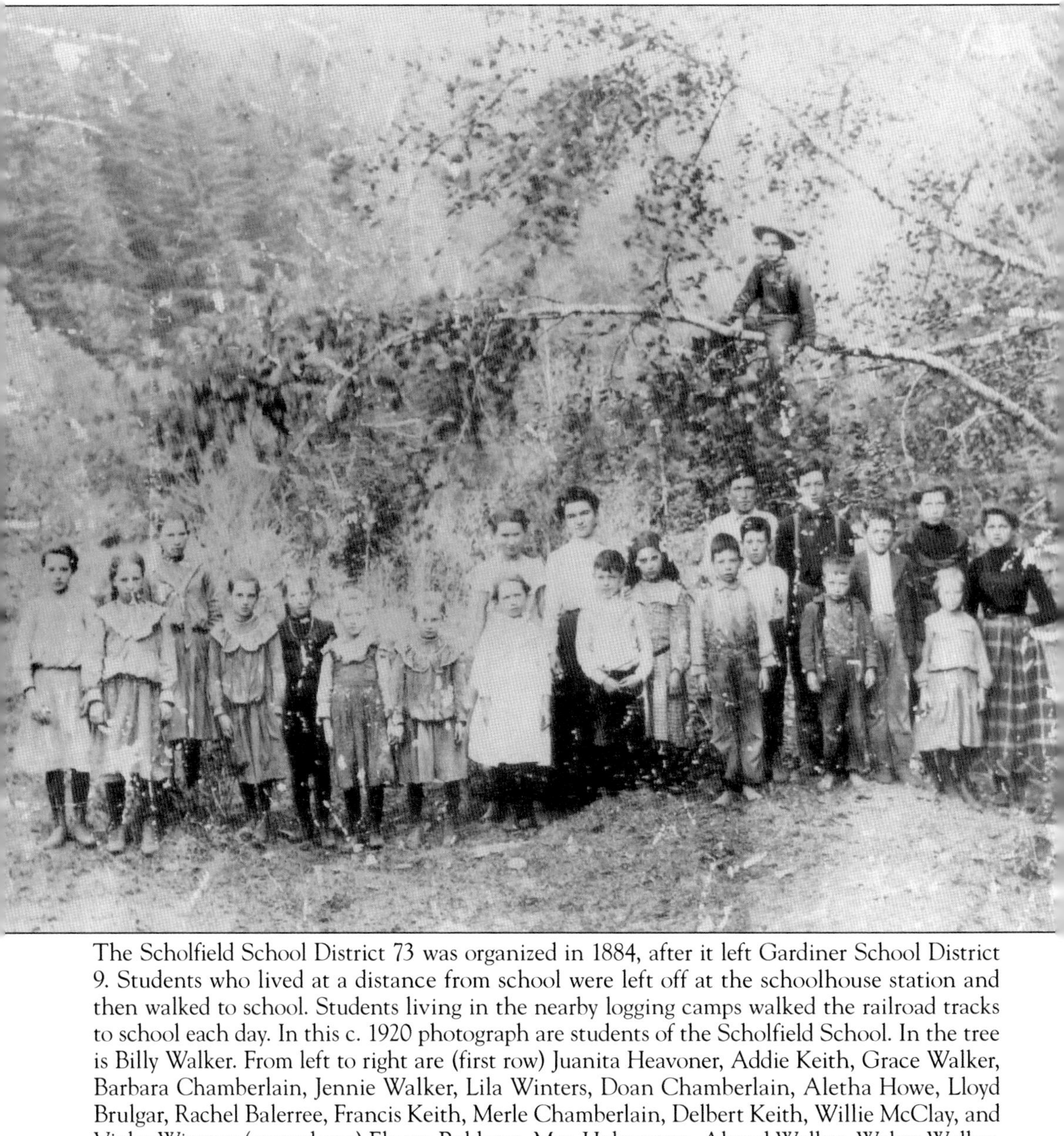

The Scholfield School District 73 was organized in 1884, after it left Gardiner School District 9. Students who lived at a distance from school were left off at the schoolhouse station and then walked to school. Students living in the nearby logging camps walked the railroad tracks to school each day. In this c. 1920 photograph are students of the Scholfield School. In the tree is Billy Walker. From left to right are (first row) Juanita Heavoner, Addie Keith, Grace Walker, Barbara Chamberlain, Jennie Walker, Lila Winters, Doan Chamberlain, Aletha Howe, Lloyd Brulgar, Rachel Balerree, Francis Keith, Merle Chamberlain, Delbert Keith, Willie McClay, and Violet Winters; (second row) Elnora Balderee, Mrs. Holmstrom, Alured Walker, Walter Walker, Quina Walker, and Elva Howe.

Schools were also found along Smith River. Long Reach School, in a 1918 photograph on the right, was the first school found on the north side of Smith River, traveling east from Reedsport. It handled students that lived between Otter Slough and Noel Creek. Students either had to row or walk to school each day. Pictured below is the school population in 1918. The students are, from left to right, (first row) Anita Wroe, Maxine Lyster, Glenva Lyster, Vivan Abbott, and Ruth Abbott; (second row) Pansy Andrews and Teresa Dolan; (third row) Luella Bernhardt, Verna Roberts, Rachel Smith, Mabel Wroe, Dulsie Andrews; (fourth row) Ellis Dolan, Harold Andrews, Bert Roberts, Everett Abbott, and George Roberts (hiding).

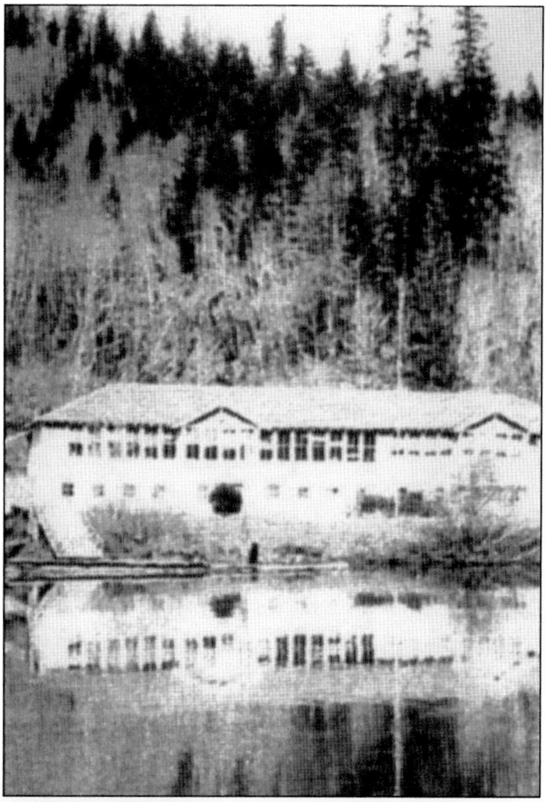

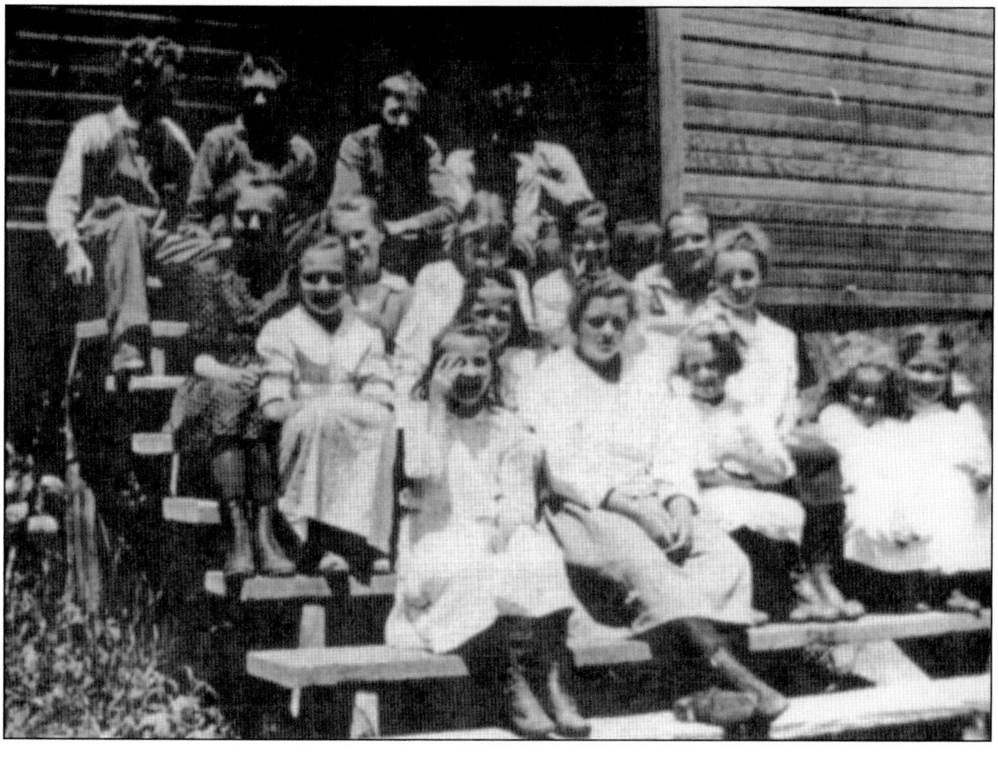

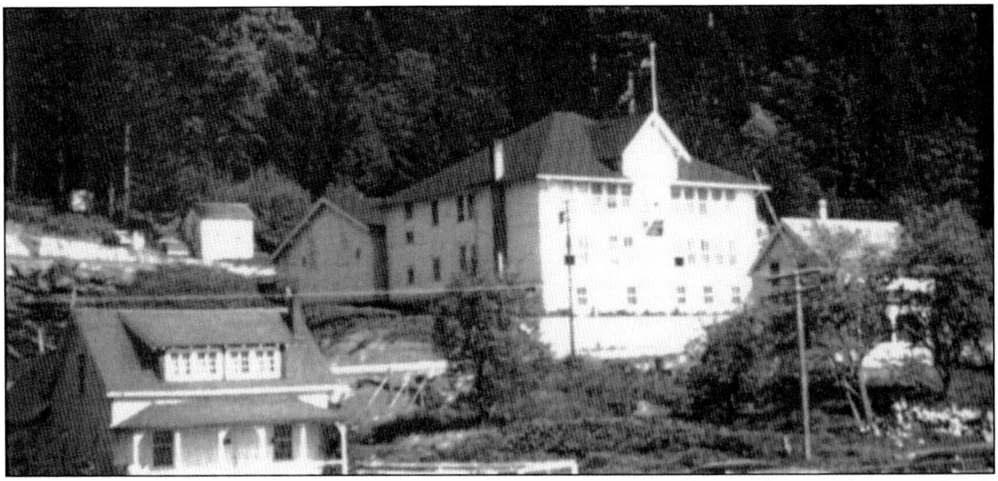

The Gardiner school system was the best in the area, with its jewel being the W.F. Jewett School, constructed in 1917. Originally, high school classes were held separately from the elementary classes, with the older students going to the Gardiner Mill House for school. When the building pictured here was finished, the elementary and the high school were housed in the same facility. There were eight classrooms on two floors. Grades 9 to 12 were upstairs, while the lower floor had elementary classes. Mrs. Jewett instituted a poetry recitation each year, where winning students were awarded silver dollars. This contest still takes place in the Reedsport school system. Gardiner combined school districts with Reedsport in 1968.

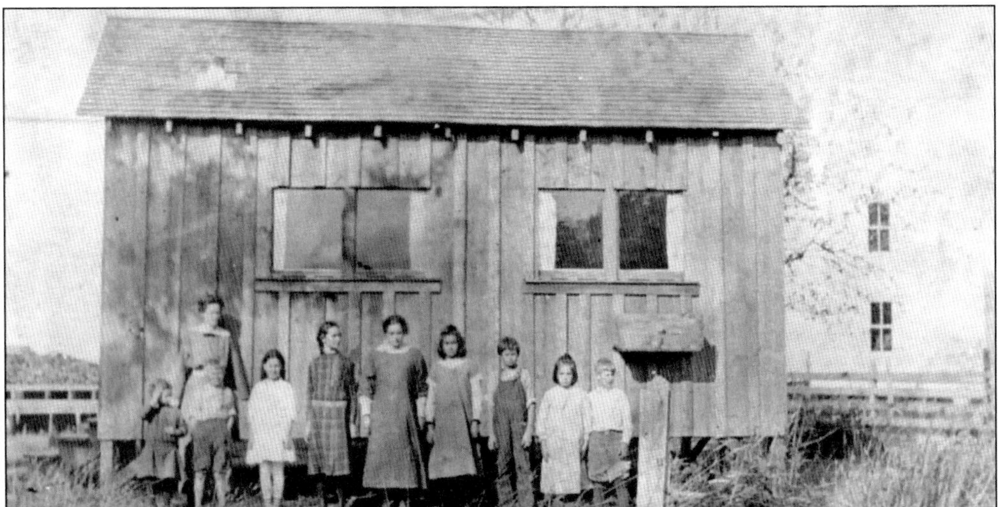

The first schoolhouse in Reedsport was only a tent on the riverfront and was open only six months out of the year. At high tide, the water would lap into the tent and students would have to put their feet on stools or benches to stay dry. In the winter, school rarely was convened because of high water and floods. This is a photograph of the 1912 Reedsport School on Rainbow Slough, the first school that was actually housed in a building. The students are, from left to right, June Roberts, Floyd Shebundy, Margaret Kennedy, Maybel Roberts, Krystal Hansen, Emma Hansen, Oscar Shebundy, Marion Hanson, and Francis Nelson. The teacher, Mary Melvin, is standing behind them. With the coming of the railroad, the school system quickly needed more space and moved classes to businesses in town. Several classes were held in the Reed Janelle Merchandise Store. (Courtesy of Leslie Chapman.)

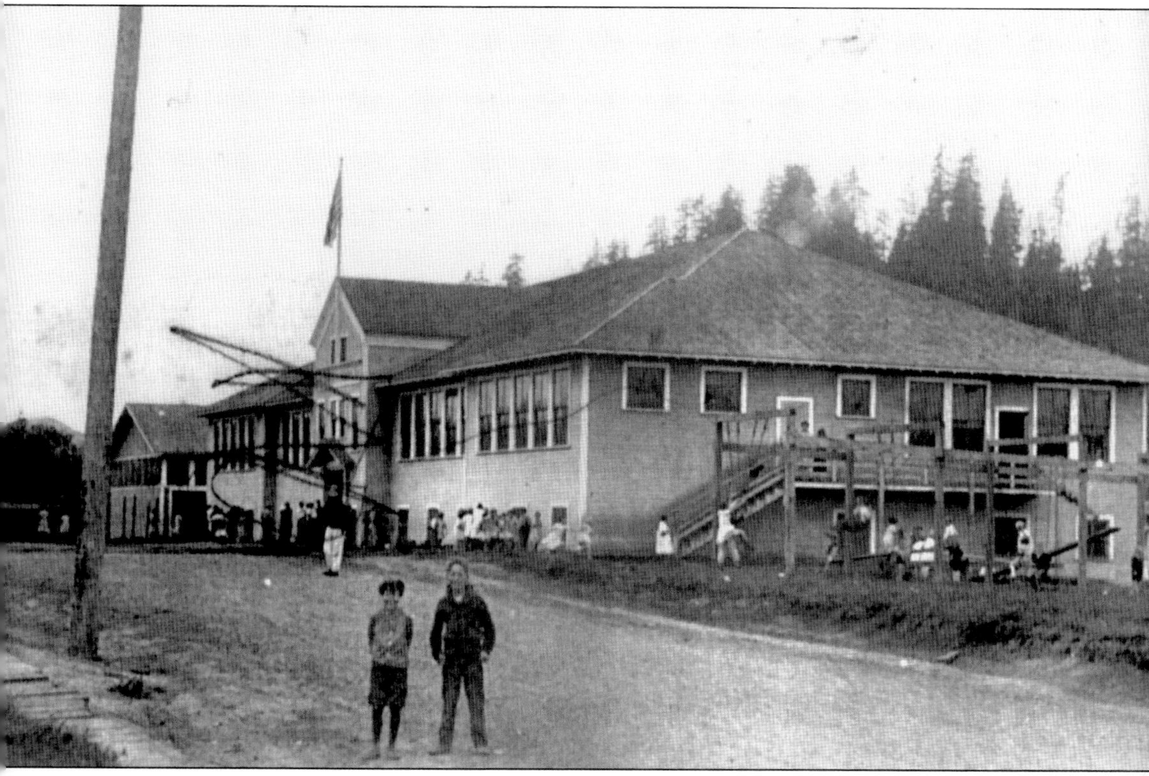

In 1919, a four-room school was completed on Warren Reed's Orchard Tract, located where Price and Pride now sits. There were four classrooms, with three of them being elementary classrooms and one being a high school classroom. In 1920, additions were added, with one becoming a wing of Pioneer School in later years. Most high school students were still sent to Gardiner or boarded in Eugene, Roseburg, or Portland. (Courtesy of Carole Plagmann.)

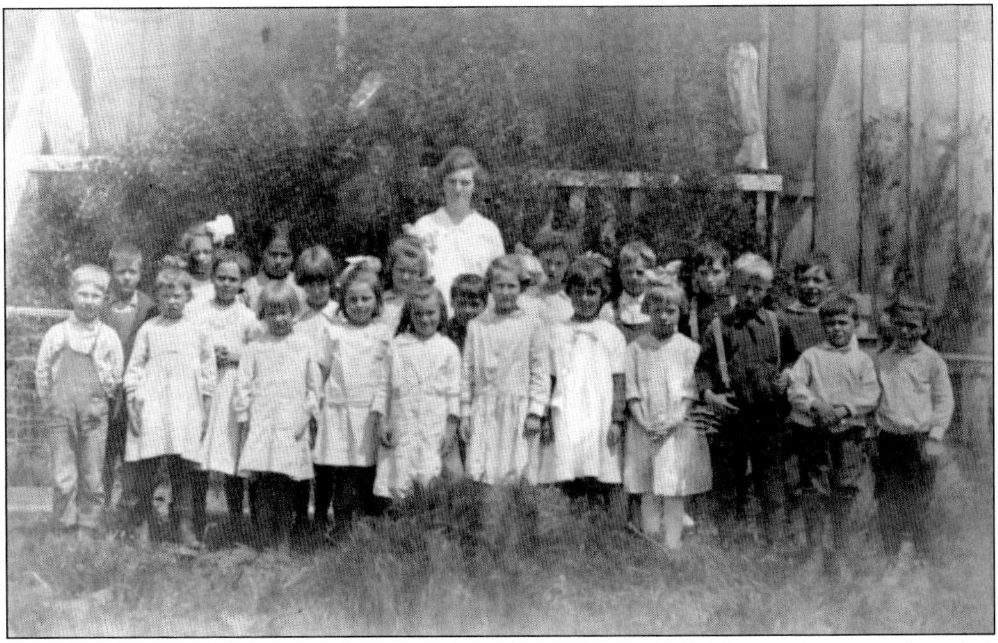

This is a photograph of the Reedsport students from 1918 to 1919. The students are, from left to right, (first row) Louis Smith, Lucil Johnson, Marie Tabor, Erros Drews, Lucil Lancelot, Ruth Smith, Dorothy Douglas, Virginia McDermott, Peter Krominga, Dudley Collins, and Dean Johnson; (second row) Wesley Balkema, Josphine Collins, Helen Tabor, and Franke Johnson; (third row) Eloise Davis, Odessa Johnson, Bonnie Walker, Echo Walker (teacher), Maxine Zachary, Fred Earl, Otis Rhodes, and Leonard Brown.

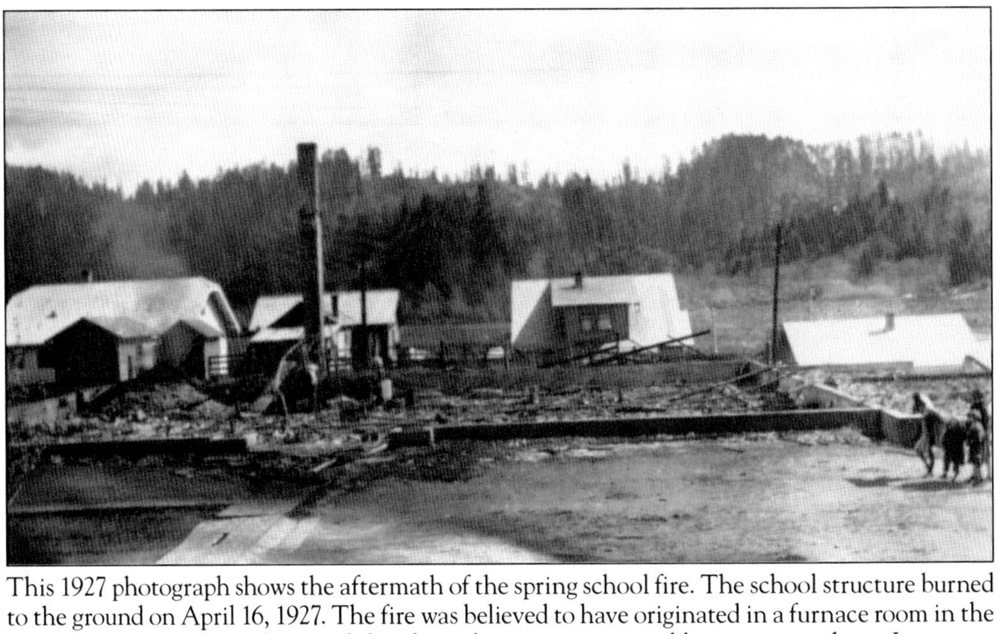

This 1927 photograph shows the aftermath of the spring school fire. The school structure burned to the ground on April 16, 1927. The fire was believed to have originated in a furnace room in the early morning and gained so much headway that it was not possible to save anything. Insurance covered 90 percent of the $36,000 loss.

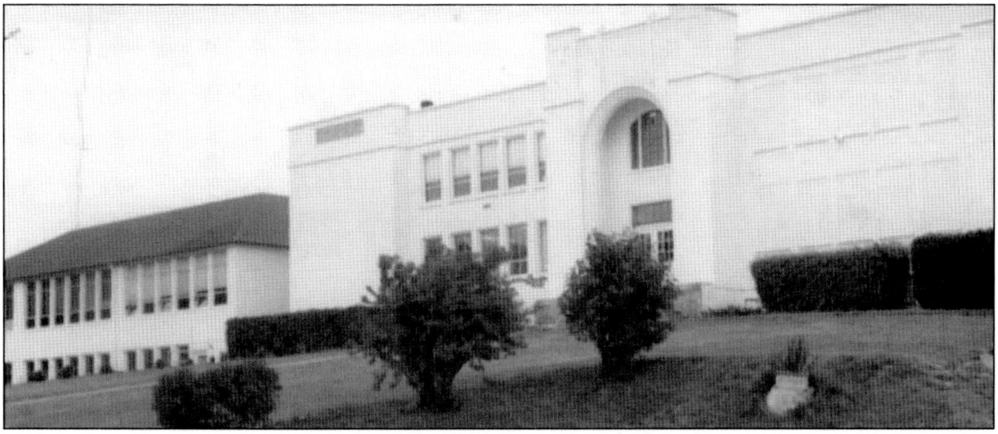

This is a 1929 photograph of the new high school that was constructed to replace the one destroyed in the fire. Until the new school was completed in 1928, classes were held in the play shed that doubled as a gymnasium and at the community church. Four more classrooms were added in 1947, and the high school was replaced in 1949 at a new location at the far south end of town.

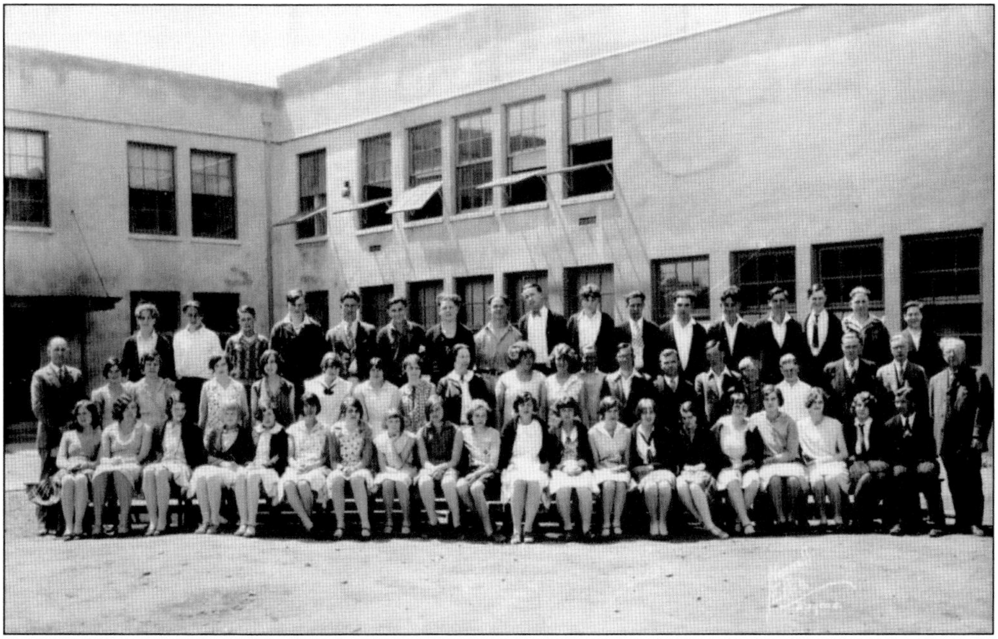

In 1928, the new school was being completed. This is a photograph of the 1929 Reedsport High School student body. The students are, from left to right, (first row) Vivian Eastland, Norma Henry, Thelma Ricker, Ellen Knutson, Georgia McHayne, Vesta Andrews, Mildred Bowman, Margaret Hanson, Isabel Wilson, Margery McClay, Alice Chambers, Alice Plaep, Lucile Chapin, Dorothy Drylan, Bonnie Walker, Ruth Borrevik, Helen Knutsen, and Harold Johnson; (second row) Mr. Gorrel, Va Barnes, Juanita Harrison, Elsie Foster, Gladys Foster, Doris Shirtcliff, Pete DeVelbins, Barbara Stinebaugh, Willa Mather, Glenva Lyster, Carl Dodson, ? Barnes, Walter Pagani, Jess Hoagland, Norman Smiley, Arnie Pagani, Clarence Doan, and Mr. Gray; (third row) ? Vandy, Jake Reeder, unidentified, ? McLead, Stillman Wessela, Ralph Kerman, Claud Esselstrom, Don Douglas, Paul Godhard, Bill Zalor, Harold Penter, Hal Esselstrom, Kennth Mather, Raymond Petzoch, Bruce Johnson, ? McLead. This structure was used as the high school until 1950, when a new building was constructed on Longwood Drive.

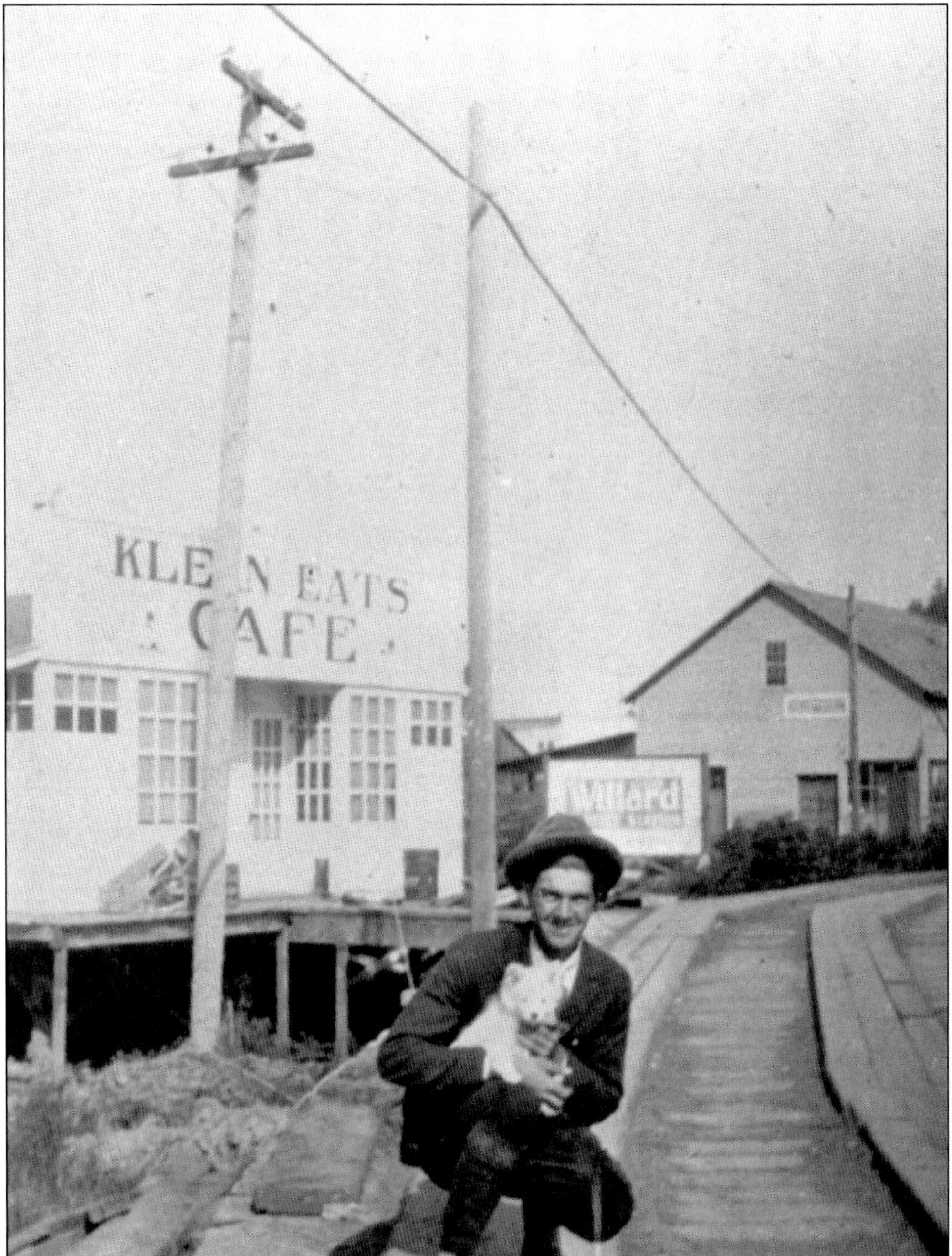

Although many students were transported to school by boat, those that lived in Reedsport often walked the boardwalk to get to and from school. This 1925 photograph of a man kneeling on the boardwalk in front of the Klean Eats Café shows the streets that were constructed 6 feet off the ground and 12 feet wide to accommodate wagon traffic. Students walking the boardwalk had to share it with commercial vehicles, totes of fish products, and a variety of lumber products.

Seven

TRANSPORTATION

At the beginning of the 20th century, the Umpqua River was the highway that connected people in the Umpqua Valley. Travel by boat was paramount for successful business people, timber barons, ranchers, and fishermen to ship supplies in and to send products out. The river was the king.

There was a stage line that ran from Drain to Scottsburg, delivering supplies and passengers, but to go any lower on the river, steamships were critical. They could carry goods and people to Gardiner and then to the ocean where other stage lines could transport them north or south to Coos Bay. Ferries were also a critical part of getting across the Umpqua River. Before the Conde McCullough Bridge was completed in 1935, ferries still operated between Gardiner and Reedsport.

The railroad, of course, was the transportation system that spurred the growth of Reedsport. In 1912, the Southern Pacific Railroad wanted to construct the railroad via the Siuslaw River and the coast. The line turned south along the eastern shore of Siltcoos and Tahkenitch lakes and into northern Douglas County and Reedsport. It was speculated that W.F. Jewett prevented the railroad from going through Gardiner because of his love for steam vessels that transported his mill goods. In the race to Coos Bay, the Southern Pacific Railroad prevailed. This line stimulated local economies along the line as it led to the export of logs, lumber, and dairy products.

State and federal monies were used to create Highway 38 in the early 1920s, creating a reliable route from the Willamette Valley to the coast. Highway 101, also known as Roosevelt's Highway, was the last of the highways to be completed in the area. One exasperated traveler commented on the roads around Reedsport by saying, "How can there be any Christians where roads such as these exist?" But with the help of Civilian Conservation Corps workers, Highway 101 was completed. With the 1935 completion of the Umpqua River Bridge, a viable coastal route was created.

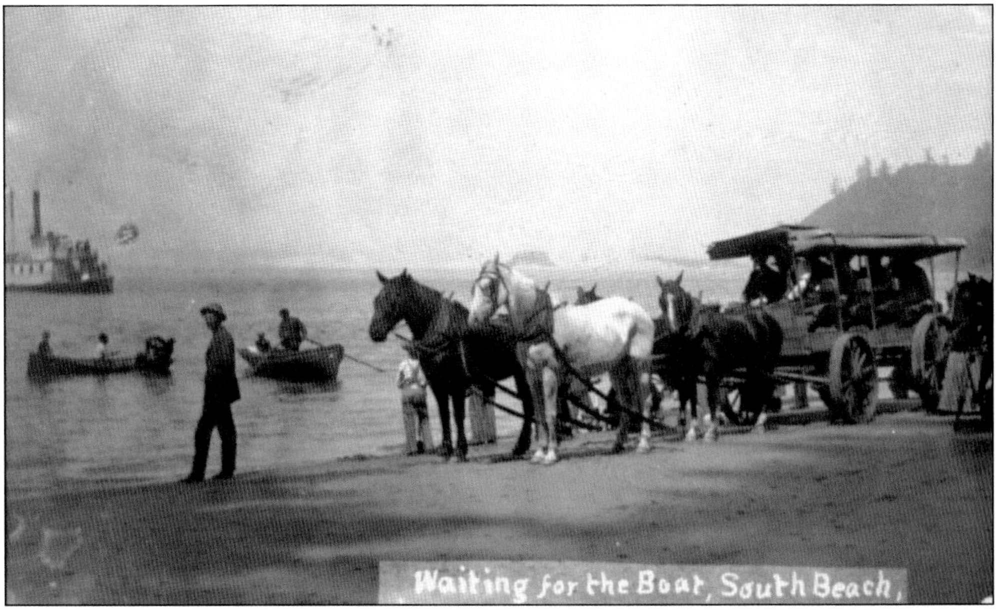

Steamships would travel to the coast carrying passengers and supplies. Passengers would have to transfer by smaller boat to reach the steamer in the bay. In this photograph, the steamer *Eva* is off the left, waiting for passengers transferring from the stage. If passengers had to walk down the beach for their transportation, they had to carry their own luggage.

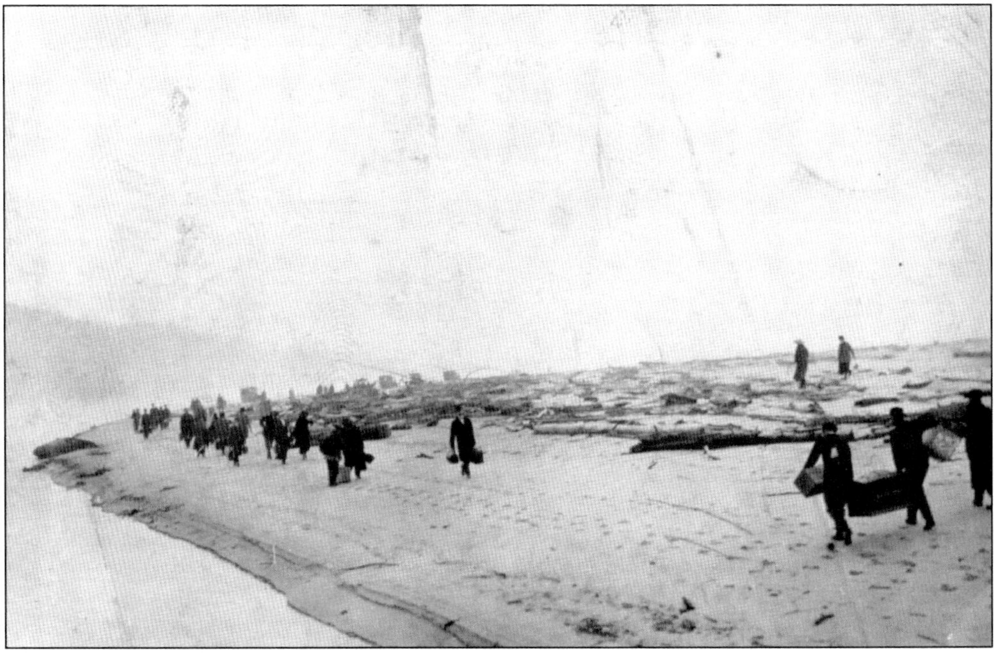

When passengers were dropped off on the beach, either by steamship or stagecoach, passengers were expected to carry their own luggage to their next form of transportation. In this c. 1910 photograph, passengers are going both ways on the beach. Some are carrying luggage to waiting steamships, and some are carrying luggage to their stagecoach.

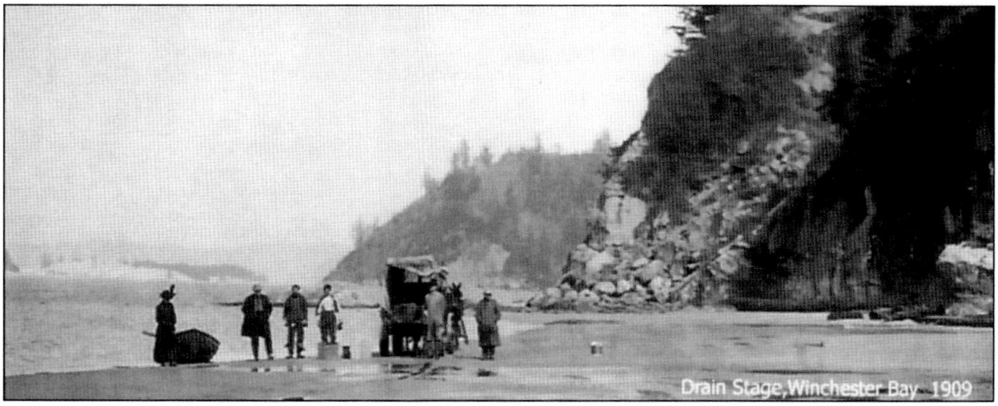

In 1909, the stagecoach that ran from Drain to Winchester Bay dropped off passengers that are waiting to board a steamship that plied the Umpqua River. Notice the small dory that is on the beach that these passengers would use to row to the steamship. These routes operated completely at the whim of the tides.

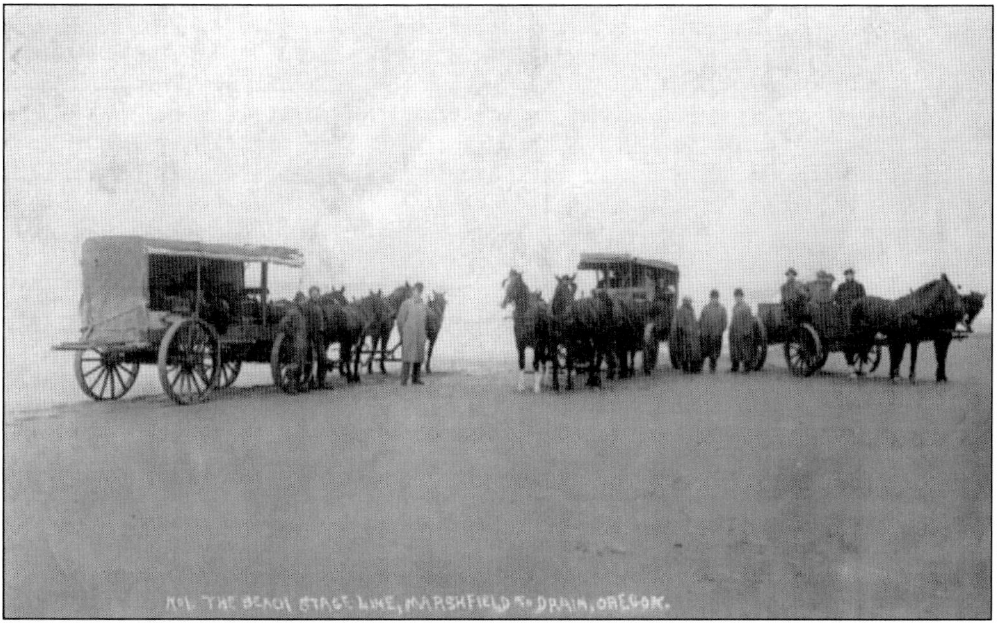

The stage routes ran north to Florence and south to Coos Bay on the ocean beaches. High tides and storms often caused delays, and each stage route had creeks to cross that flowed into the ocean. This is a c. 1910 photograph of the early stages, which operated between Marshfield and the mouth of the Umpqua River. (Courtesy of Joyce Brandon.)

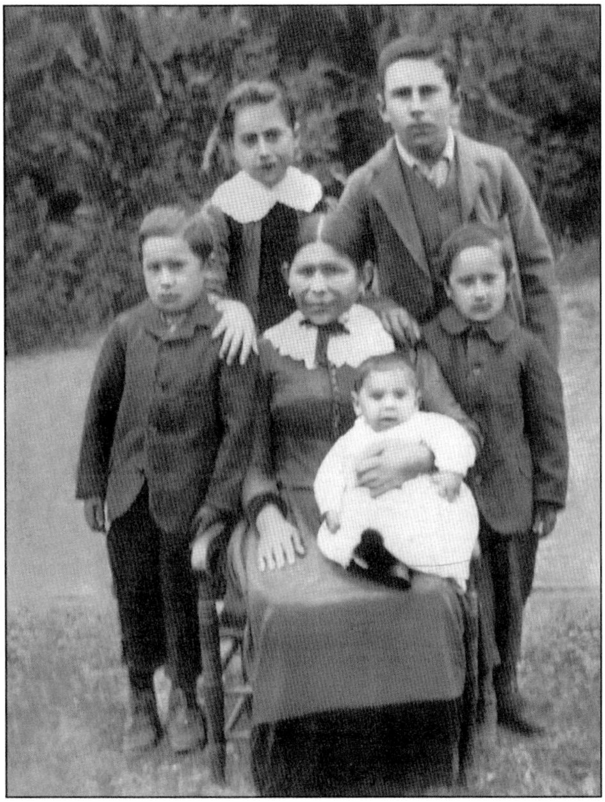

In the 1880s, Henry Hudson Barrett and his wife, Ellen, had a stage house and mail landing at a wharf, known as Barrett's Landing, which was just down the river from Gardiner. He ran a stage route to the beach and on to Florence. They had stage houses on the north bank of the Umpqua River and at the south bank of the Siuslaw River. Steamships plying the Umpqua would blow their whistle, summoning them to come with a dory for mail, supplies, and customers. At left is a 1895 photograph of Ellen Barrett holding Howard Barrett, while flanked by twins Logan and Blain. May and Clay are behind her. Below is a photograph of the beach stagecoach with Barrett standing next to his team. (Both, courtesy of Frank Barrett.)

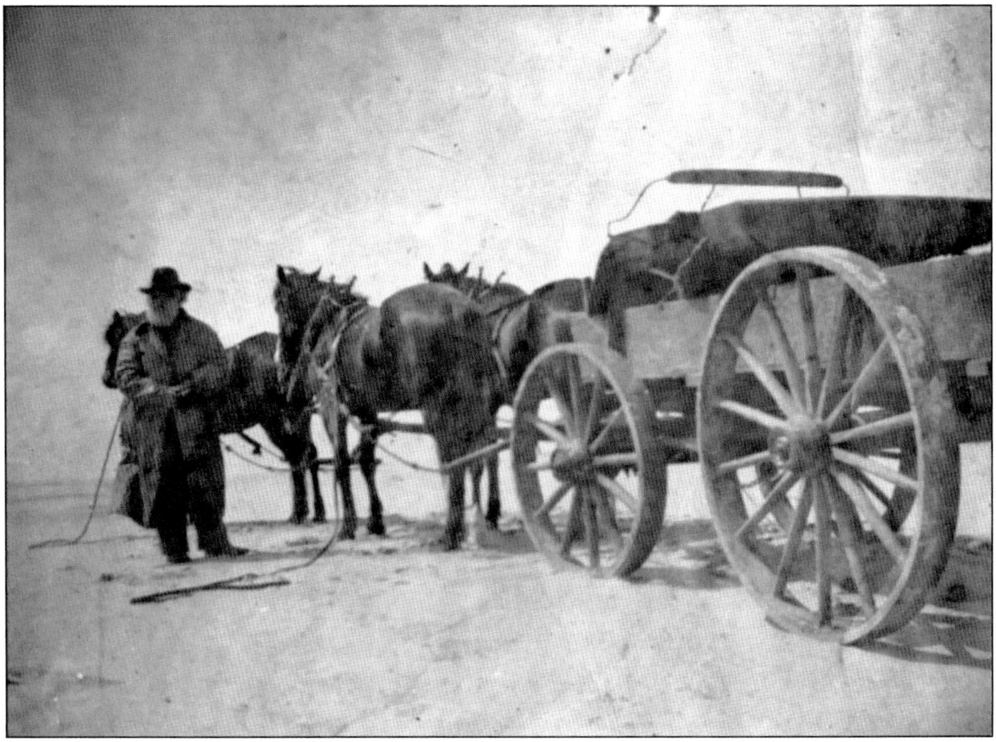

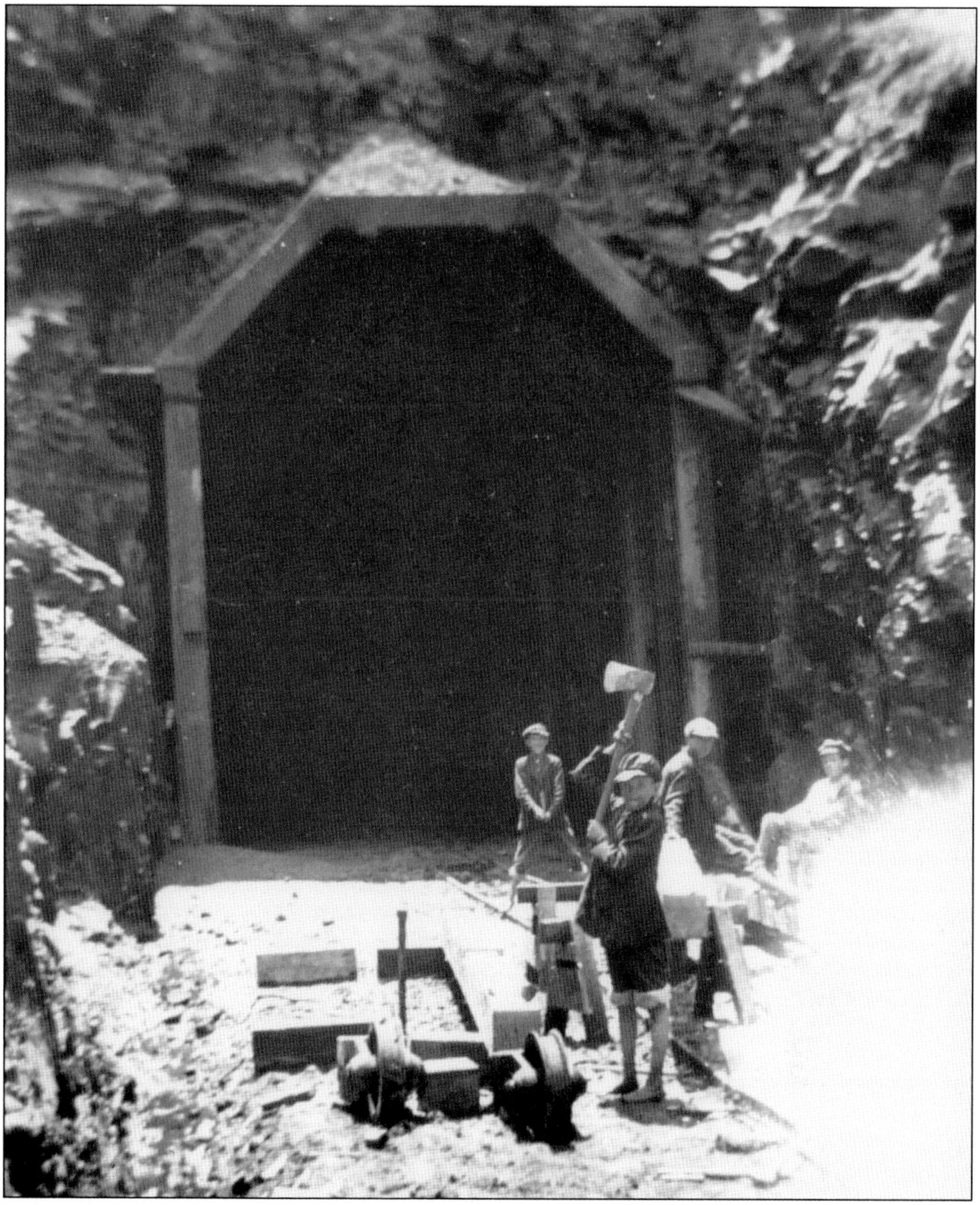

When the railroad came to Reedsport, spurs were constructed into the woods so that timber could be shipped by rail to the rivers. This 1917 photograph shows a tunnel being constructed on the Scholfield line to allow trains to run the length of the creek to help the logging camps find access to the Umpqua River. Blasting tunnels through the Coast Range for railroads to reach the coast from the Willamette Valley was a fairly common occurrence in the early 1900s. Highway 38 runs through an old railroad tunnel that was abandoned when the Eugene to Coos Bay Rail Line was constructed before the Roseburg to Coos Bay line could be completed. (Courtesy of Sunnie Heddon.)

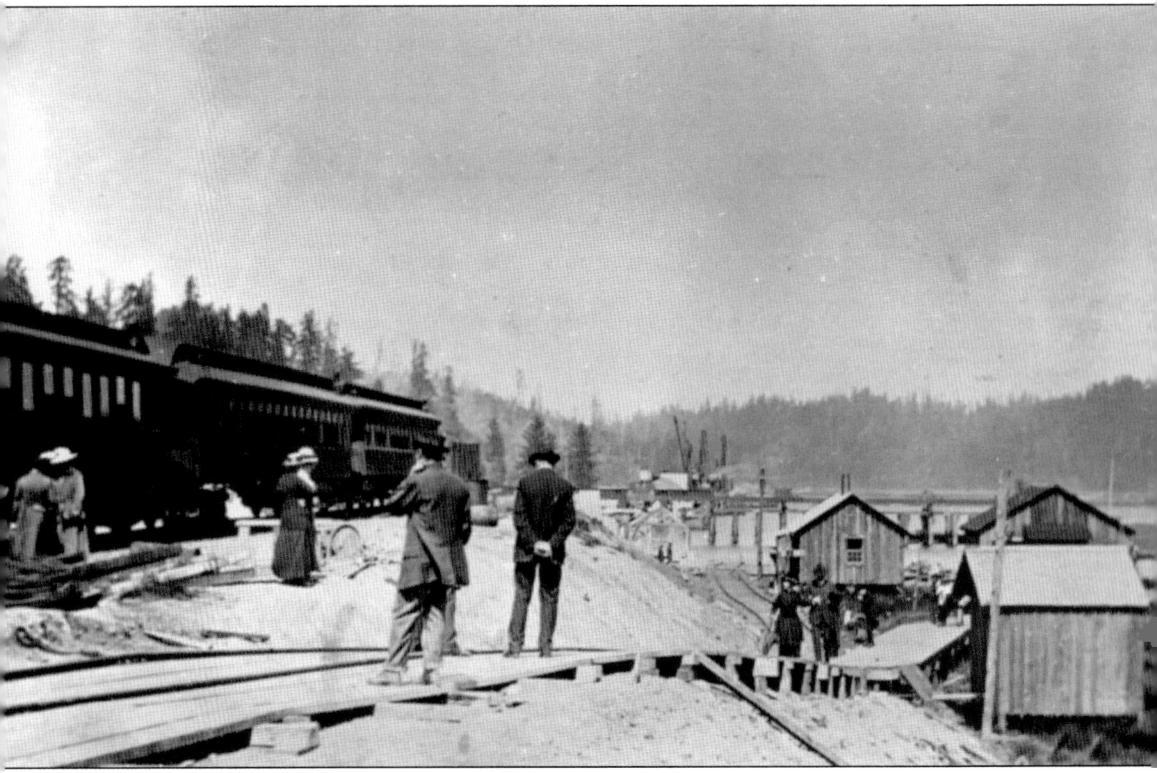

This c. 1925 photograph shows passengers walking up the boardwalk to join other passengers waiting for the train on the railroad right-of-way. In the distance, the dredge on the river is visible. When all the lumber mills in town were operating at the same time, the entire right-of-way would shake.

To the right is an 1858 map of the region in which the Southern Pacific Railroad constructed the first railroad line that went to Reedsport and on to Coos Bay. The line turned south along the eastern shore of Siltcoos and Tahkenitch lakes and came into northern Douglas County, east of Gardiner and across the river to Reedsport. Warren Reed owned key properties along the winding line as it came to the banks of Smith River, crossed Bolon Island, and entered the swampy margins of Scholfield Slough. Oscar Hinsdale, another local entrepreneur, wanted to construct a new town on the tidal flat at Dean Creek and felt that the route on which the railroad was constructed would lead to this construction. Below is a picture of the original railroad's right-of-way in Reedsport in 1919.

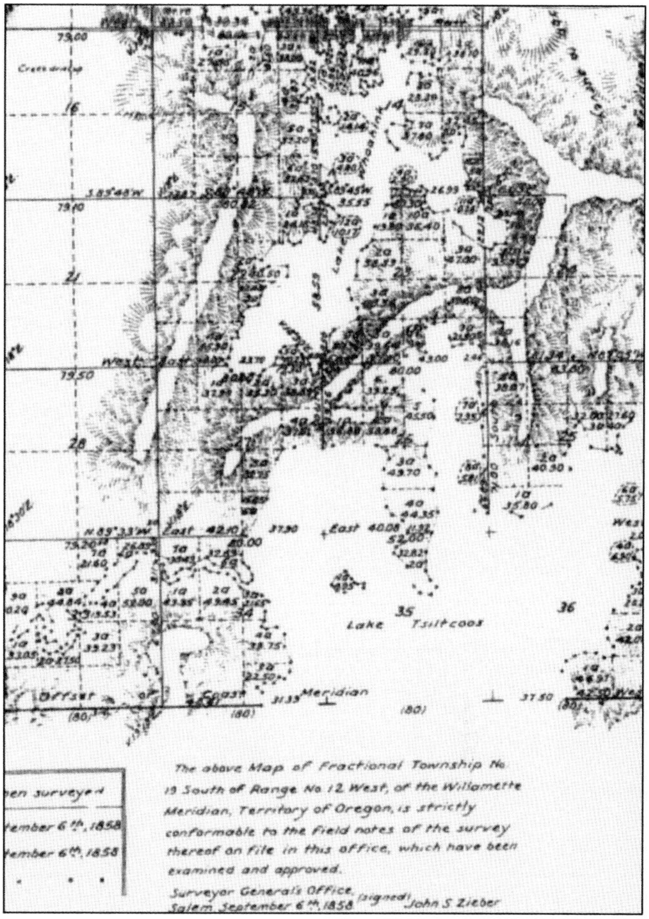

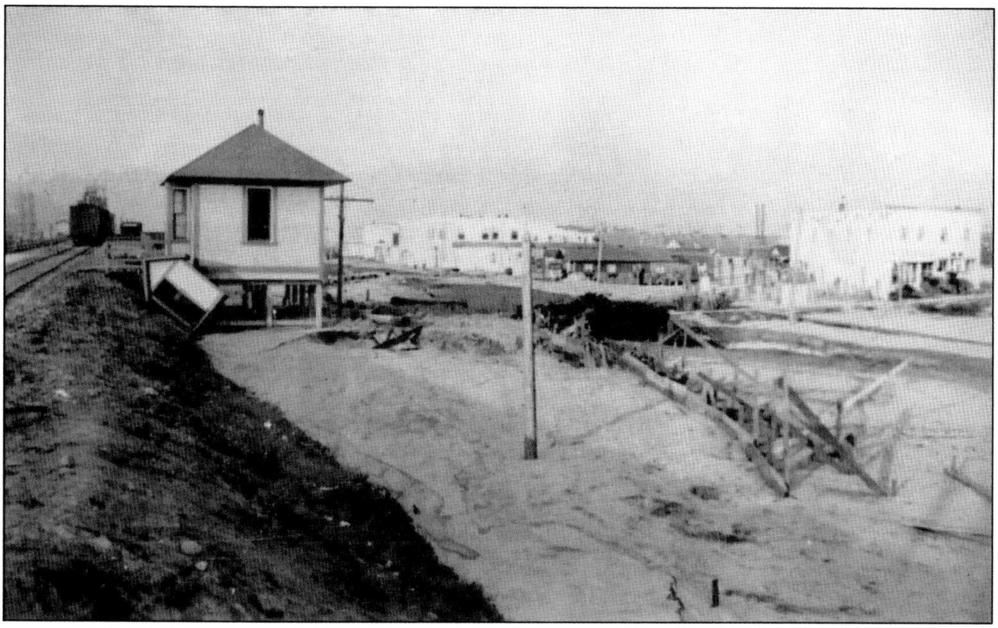

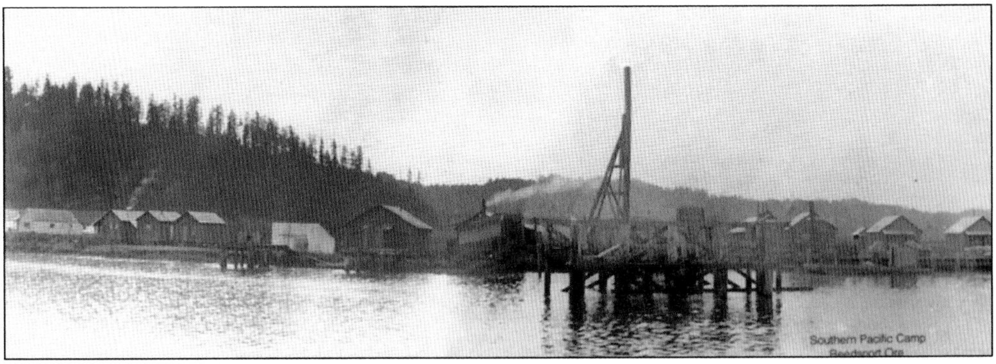

When the Copenhagen brothers brought in a steam shovel for grading on the railroad in 1913, 500 men were instantly employed to help construct the railroad. This is a photograph of the Southern Pacific Railroad camp on the banks of the Umpqua River. It was necessary to do this to house their workers, because there was not enough housing available in town.

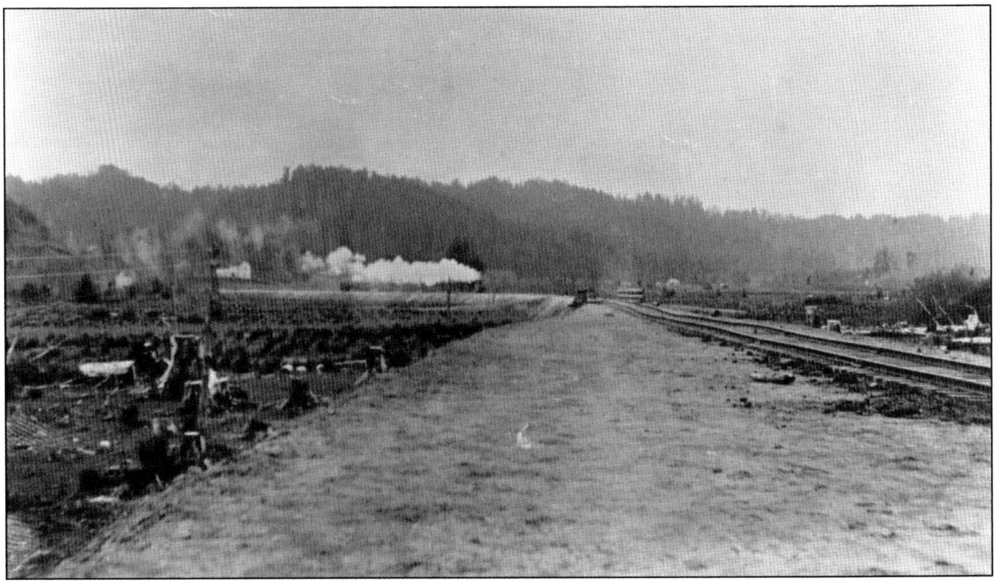

This is a 1916 photograph of the first train arriving in Reedsport. The Reed farm is on the far left, while the Decker Point Farm is on the far right. The first sawmill was constructed on this railroad right-of-way.

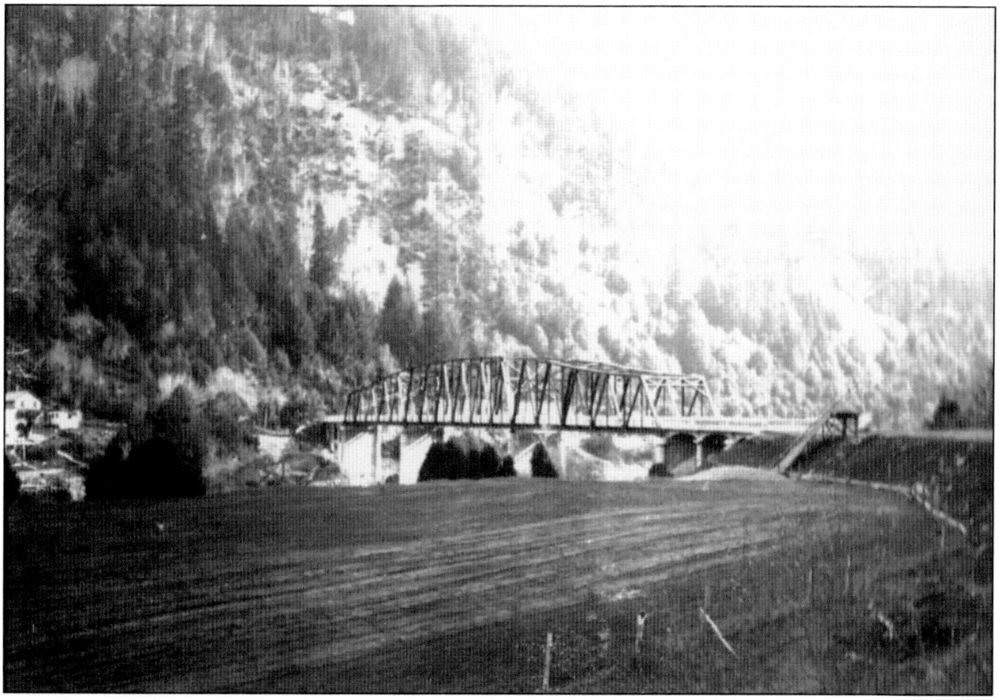

This is a 1928 photograph of the Scottsburg Bridge that spanned the Umpqua River. The bridge cost $150,000 to construct in the late 1920s but was almost lost in the 1964 flood when floodwaters almost rose above the level of the road. (Courtesy of Sunnie Heddon.)

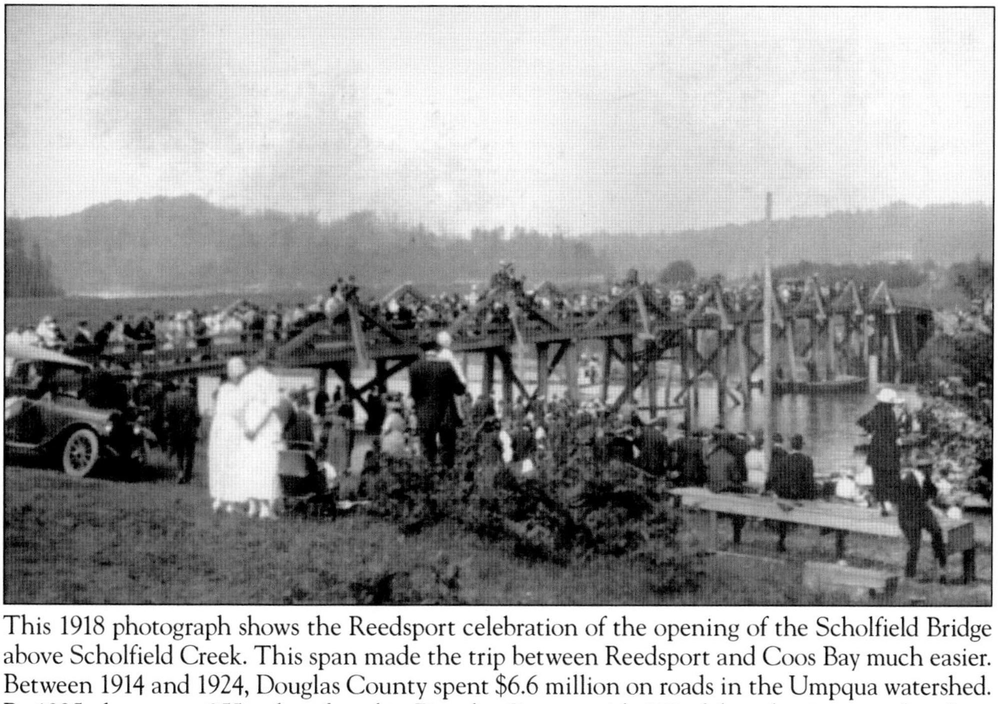

This 1918 photograph shows the Reedsport celebration of the opening of the Scholfield Bridge above Scholfield Creek. This span made the trip between Reedsport and Coos Bay much easier. Between 1914 and 1924, Douglas County spent $6.6 million on roads in the Umpqua watershed. By 1925, there were 955 miles of road in Douglas County with 602 of them having gravel surface. The current Scholfield Bridge opened in 1953.

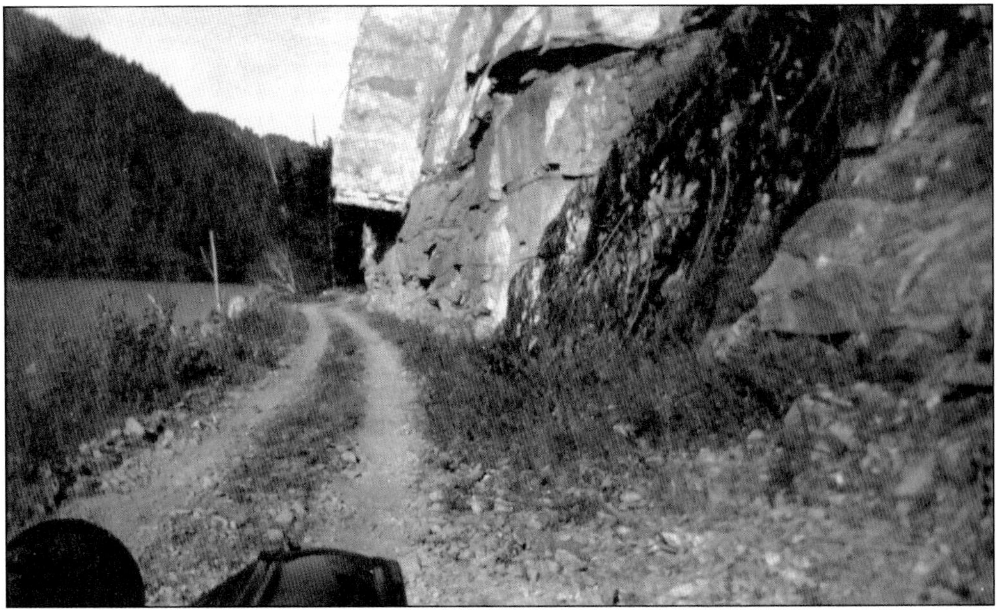

These c. 1929 photographs show Mill Creek on Highway 38 between Reedsport and Scottsburg. The photograph above shows the highway being completed before the covered bridge was constructed, while the photograph below shows the bridge completed. Highway 38 had recently been completed, giving Reedsport a road from the Willamette Valley to the coast, and providing another way to ship goods out of the area. Reedsport's gravel plant grew when it was being constructed, as all the gravel used on the road from here to Drain came from the Reedsport plant. An Umpqua ferry system had its slip just at the bottom of the picture of the uncompleted road. During World War II, there was a "coyote hole" filled with explosives on the other side of the bridge. If there was an invasion, the bridge was to be blown.

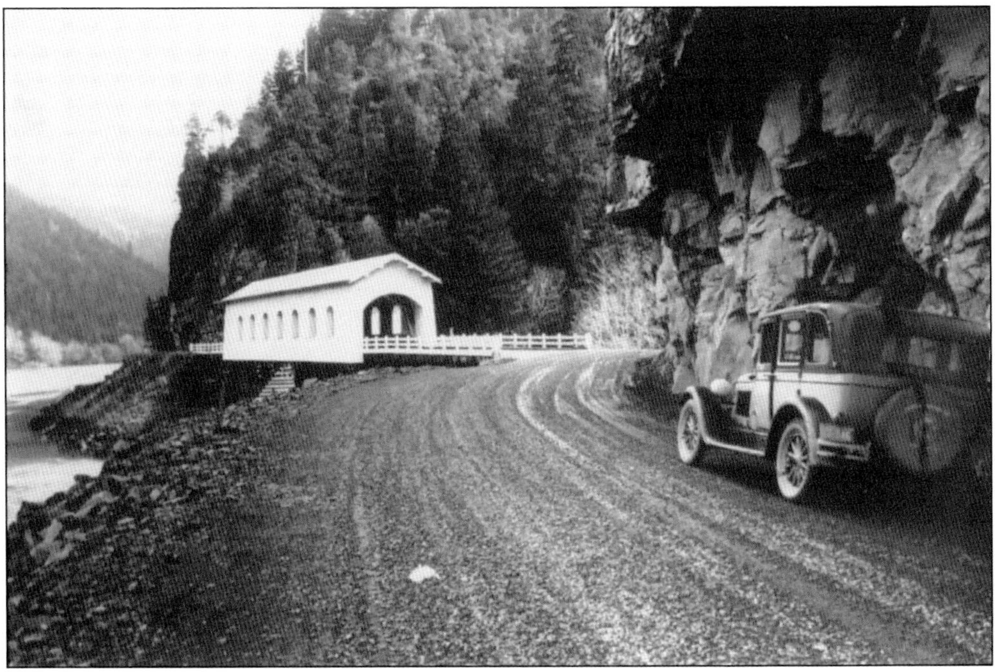

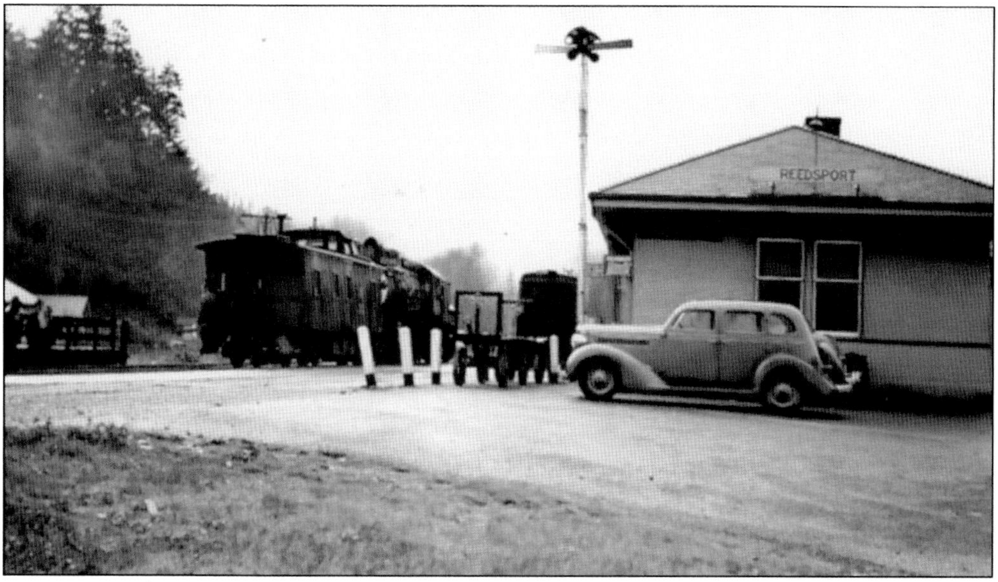

In 1916, Southern Pacific Railroad completed a line from the Willamette Valley to Coos Bay, going through Reedsport and bypassing Gardiner. This c. 1925 photograph shows the original train station, which was located on Winchester Avenue, near the railroad tracks that still exist. Over 500 men were employed in constructing the railroad through Reedsport.

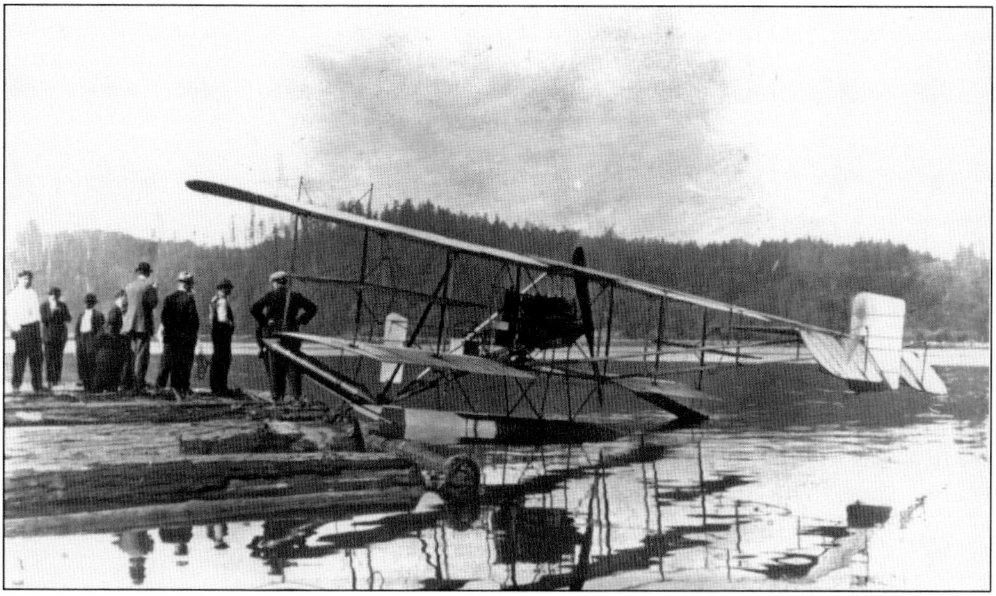

In 1913, Vern Gorst and Ed Steele flew a record-breaking airplane flight from Coos Bay, Oregon, to Toledo, Oregon, on the Oregon Coast. The plane made a stop in Gardiner on the way home to show the locals what the new transportation looked like. Vern Gorst's son would drive a Model T around their field at home so that his father would know where to land.

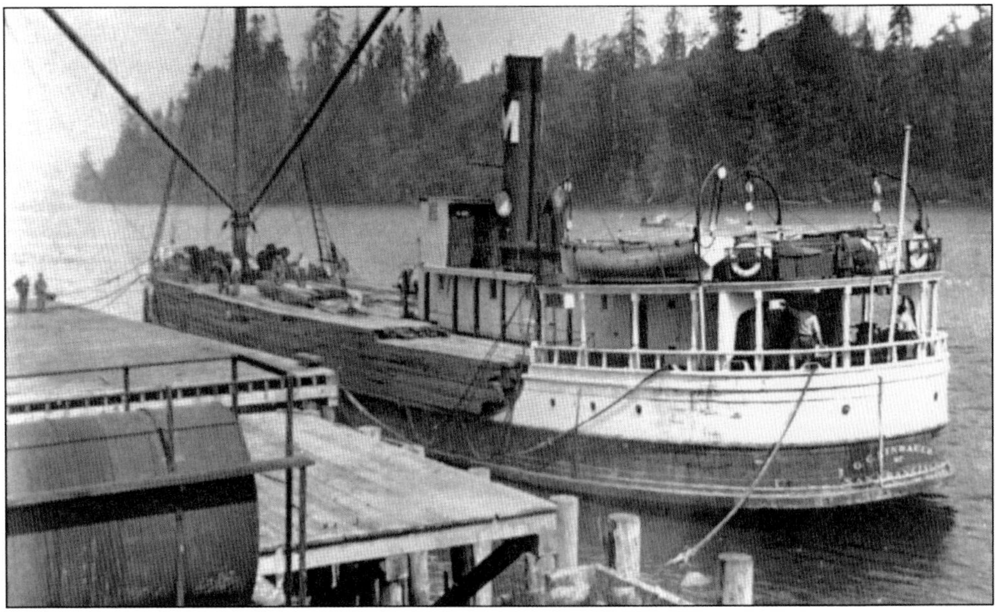

Reedsport has always transported cargo from its boardwalk. This is a c. 1930 photograph of the cargo ship O.G. *Sinbauer* out of San Francisco. It is moored to the boardwalk riverfront across from Bolon Island. It is loading a shipment of lumber that has been locally milled and is ready for export.

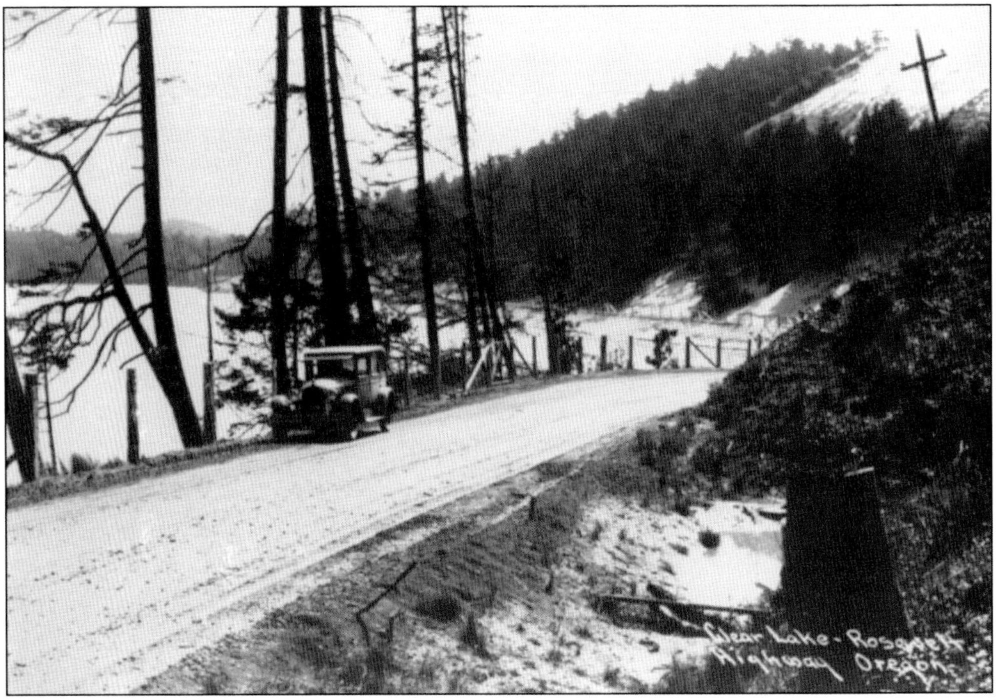

Part of the problem of constructing Roosevelt Highway, now Highway 101, around Clear Lake was how to prevent the sand dunes from spilling over on to the road. This image shows Highway 101 in the 1930s. Note how the dunes are encroaching on the pavement. The Civilian Conservation Corps spent many hours battling this issue during the completion of the highway.

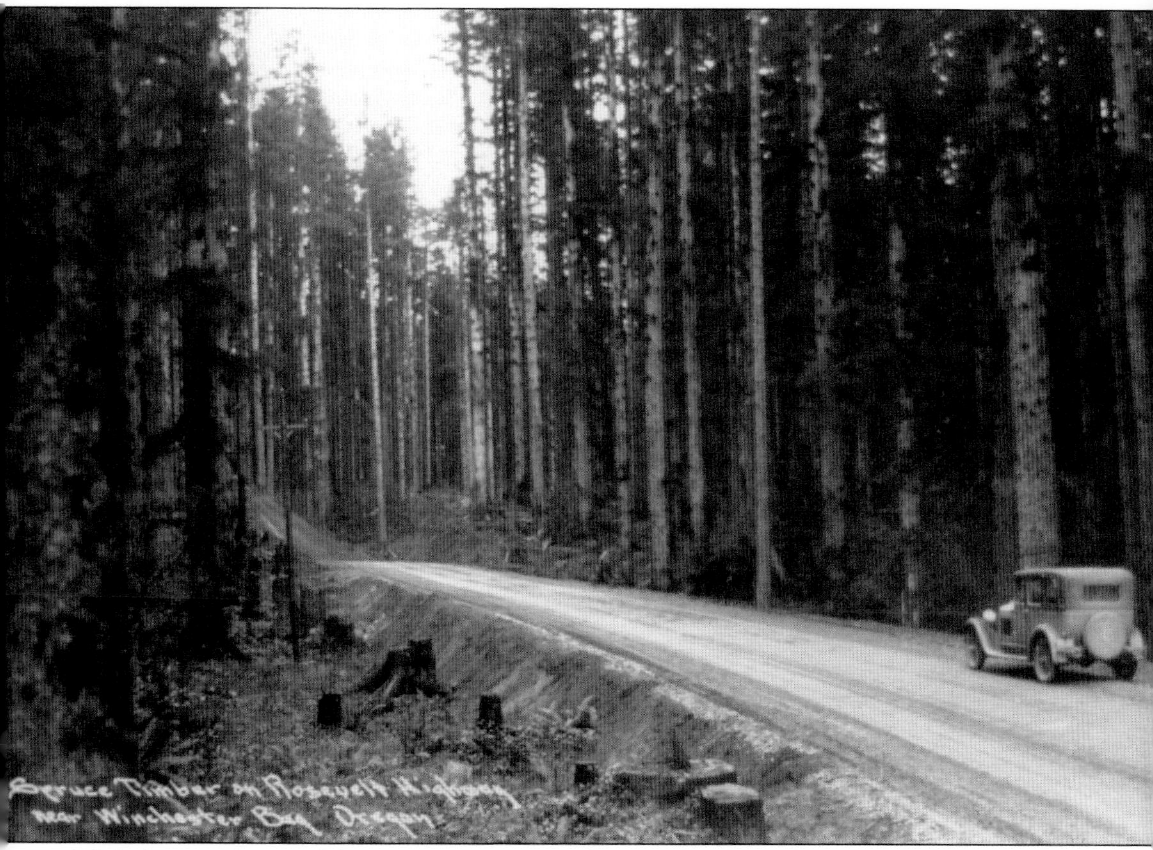

With the completion of the Umpqua River Conde McCullough Bridge in 1935, the Roosevelt Highway, later Highway 101, was completed with the bridges up and down the coast allowing an unbroken road to go from Astoria to Brookings. This is a c. 1932 photograph of the Roosevelt Highway near Winchester Bay.

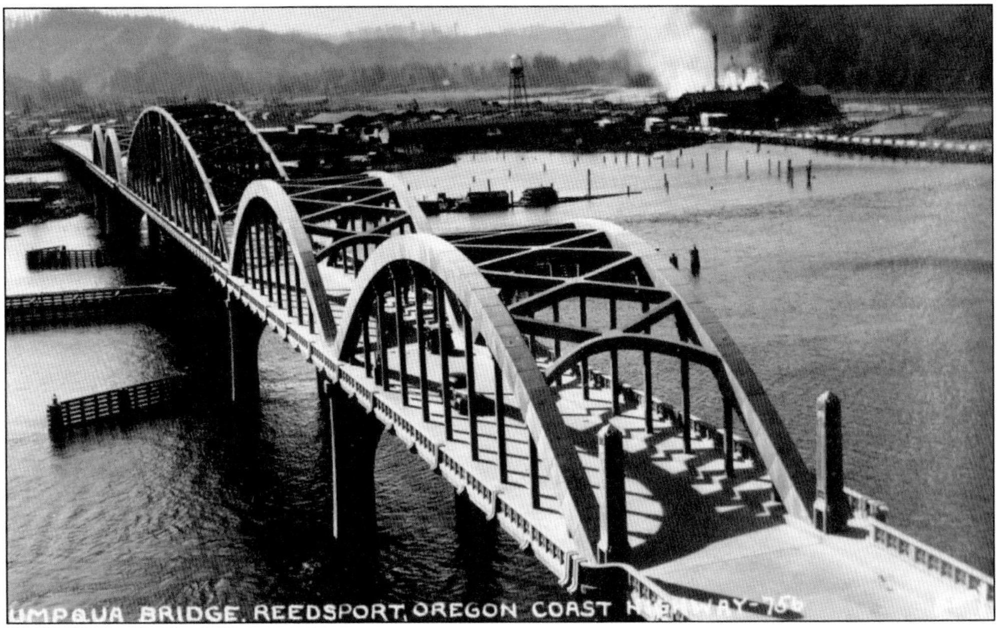

The Umpqua River Bridge was opened to traffic on July 2, 1936, and was one of five bridges on the Oregon Coast designed by Conde McCullough. All had soaring spires, gorgeous arches, long viaducts, wide roads, and wide sidewalks. These bridges insured the connection of the Roosevelt Highway on the Oregon Coast. The Umpqua Bridge had 430-foot swinging tress for a drawbridge to accommodate the wide, shallow navigation channel. It was 2,206 feet long and had a 27-foot wide roadway. The total cost of the Umpqua project was $549,818.81. The construction of the bridge employed an average of 125 men on 30-hour workweeks with an average payroll of $2,500 per week. President Roosevelt was rumored to be coming to commemorate the opening of the bridge, but was never able to make the trip. Consequently, the Umpqua River Bridge had never had a formal dedication until 2011 at its 75th birthday.

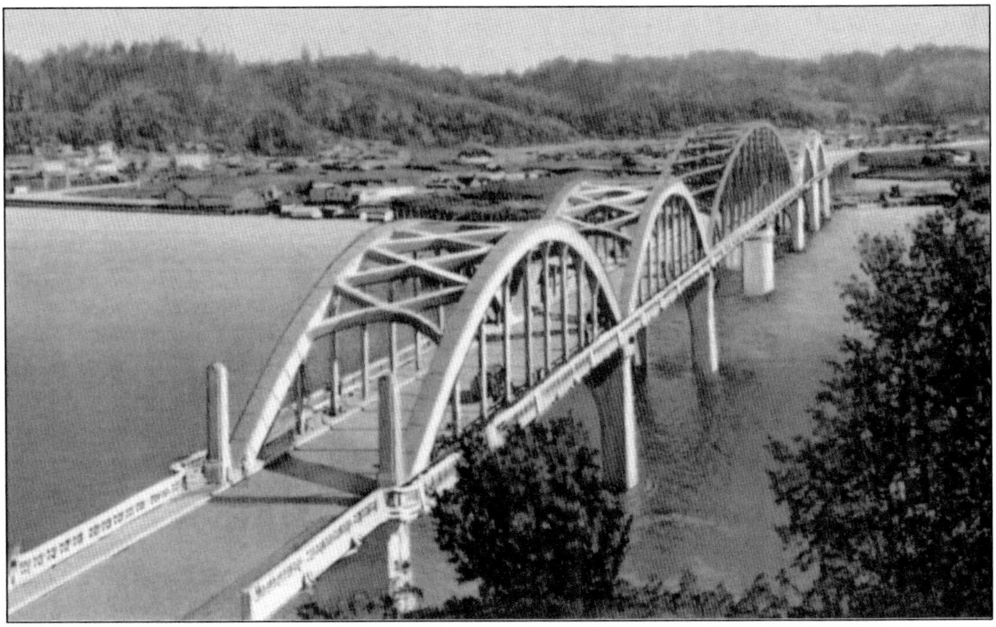

Eight

Disasters

The Oregon Coast has been shaped by one natural disaster after another. Earthquakes, floods, fire, and wind have all had a place in the formation of the Lower Umpqua River area. Through their oral history, local Native American tribes first recorded a massive tsunami in 1700 that decimated the northwest coast from California to Canada.

Floods, of course, have always been a part of the Umpqua River. The massive flood of 1861 washed away the town of Scottsburg, and was followed by a series of floods in later years that had a great impact on the Reedsport's growth and prosperity. Locals did not call the annual flows floods, but merely referred to them as high water. The flood of 1964 was so dramatic that there was between $4 million and $5 million damage, 500 citizens were temporarily homeless, 2 were arrested for looting, and there was one death. There was even the threat of typhus in the aftermath.

Snow and ice have also caused issues through the years. In 1928, the Smith River froze solid. Turkey farmers had to pull their products to town on sleds. Ice and driftwood added so much weight to the bridges that dynamite had to be used to save them. The snow of 1969 dumped three feet of snow on the town, resulting in the collapse of many roofs.

Wind and fire have also impacted the area. One of the first recorded major fires was in 1868, when a fire started in Greenacres, also known as Wells Creek, and burned on the north side of the Umpqua River to Mill Creek. It then jumped the river and burned to Coos Bay, incinerating 300,000 acres. In 1966, an employee of Umpqua Navigation, while hauling logs, started the Oxbow Burn. Eventually, 44,000 acres burned. In 1962, the Columbus Day storm, known as the "Big Blow," was a result of Typhoon Freda. It was the most powerful extratropical typhoon to hit the Pacific Northwest in the 20th century.

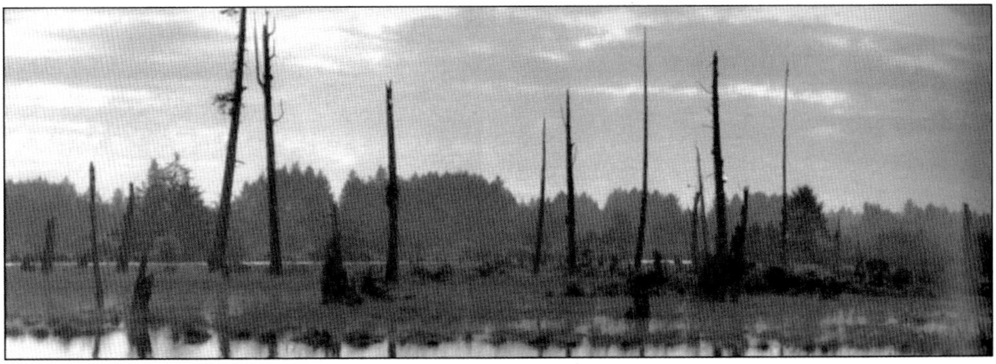

A massive tsunami struck the Central Oregon Coast at 9:00 p.m. on January 26, 1700. Since then, scientific research has discovered that it registered between 8.7 and 9.2 on the Richter scale, and might have been up to 30 feet tall and traveling at 200 miles per hour. It struck the coast all the way from northern California to Alaska, leaving devastation in its wake. Up and down the coast of Oregon and Washington, dead forests can be found around tidal marshes. Prof. Brian Atworth from the University of Washington has shown that tidal mud entombed leaves and stems in growth position before they had time to rot, proving the time line of this potent tsunami. It has also been established that such events occur roughly every 300 years.

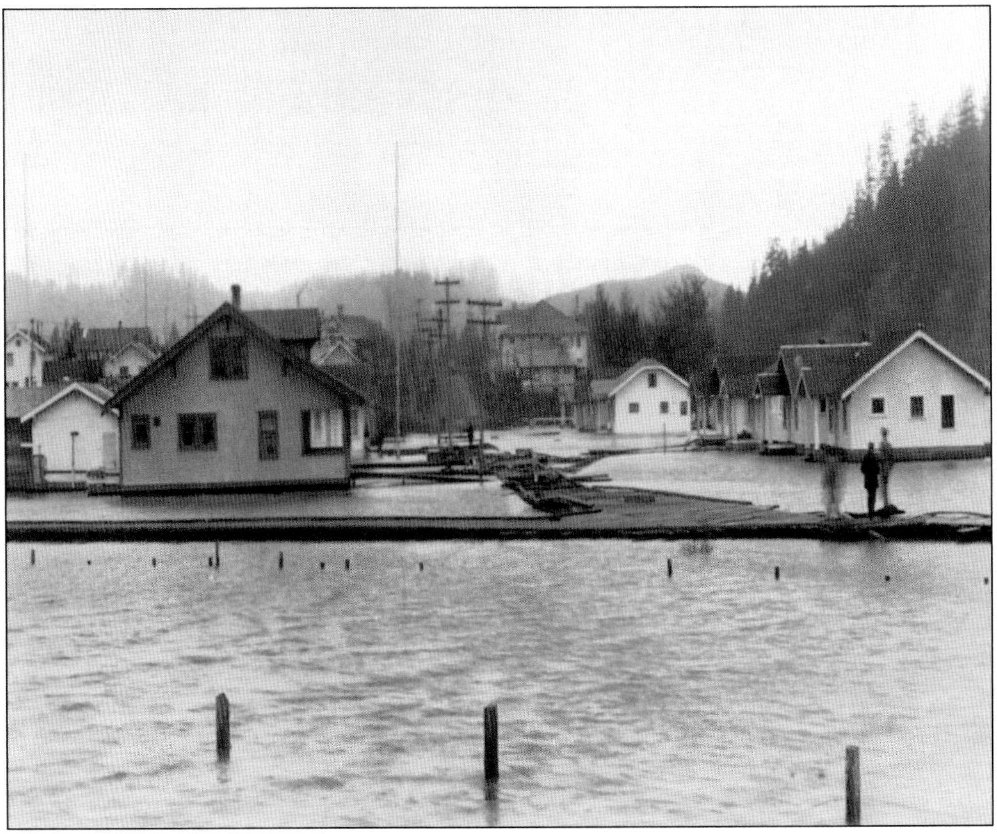

This is a photograph of the 1922 flood, where the water rose as high as the boardwalk. Tenth Street is under water in the foreground, with the Murphey home on the left. The second house from the right was the Edgar Stevens grocery, with the high school in the far background of this image. (Courtesy of Carole Plagmann.)

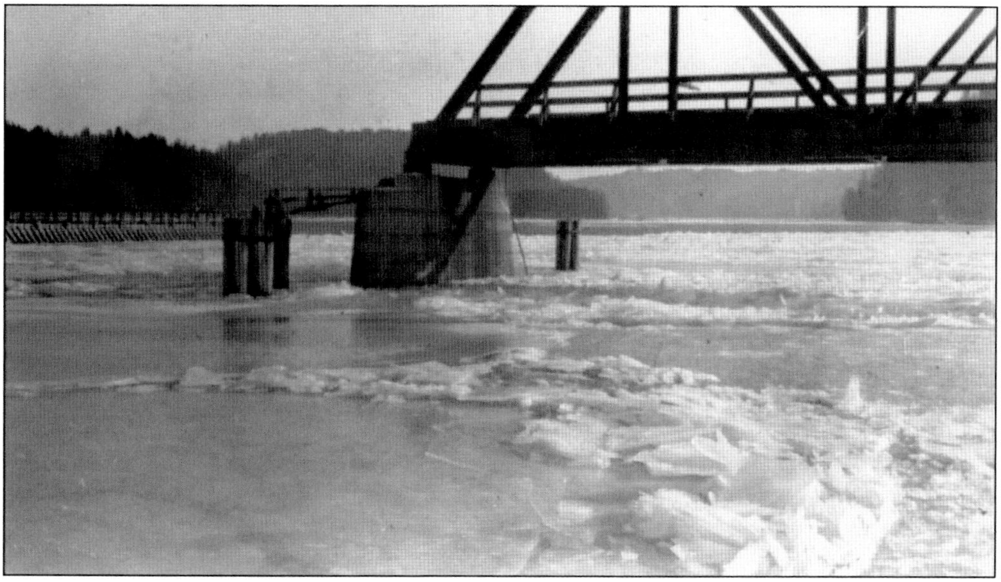

The year 1925 brought a series of storms, including a cold snap where ice floes piled up against the Railroad Bridge, threatening the bridge structure with its weight. Fortunately, the cold snap did not last long enough for the ice to do damage, and the threat of losing the bridge was forgotten. This 1925 photograph shows the ice floes and the snow that posed problems for this structure.

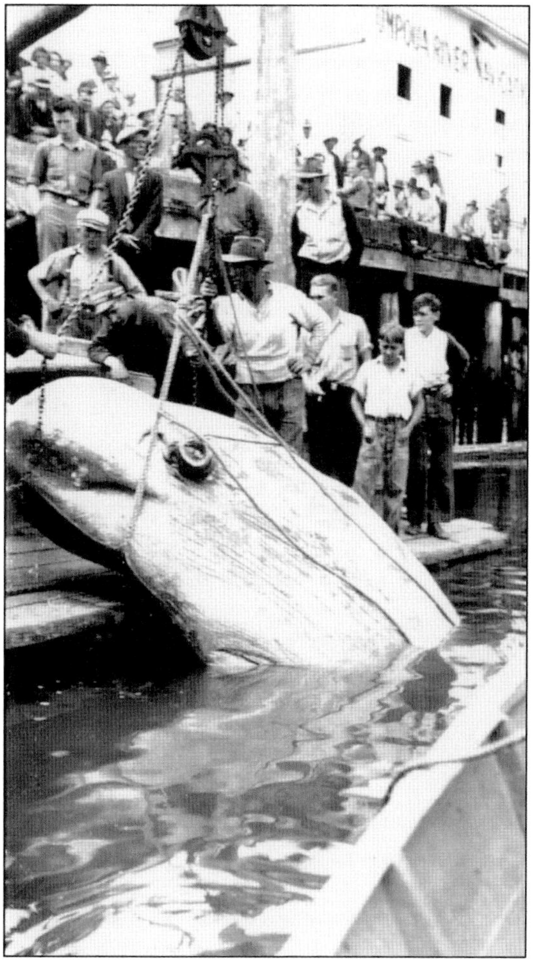

In the 1920s, another kind of disaster impacted Reedsport. A gray whale had come up the Umpqua River and died before it could return to the ocean. The whale carcass was in the river long enough to start to decompose before Reedsport residents, pictured here around 1925, could haul the carcass to the waterfront and lift it from the water near Umpqua River Navigation.

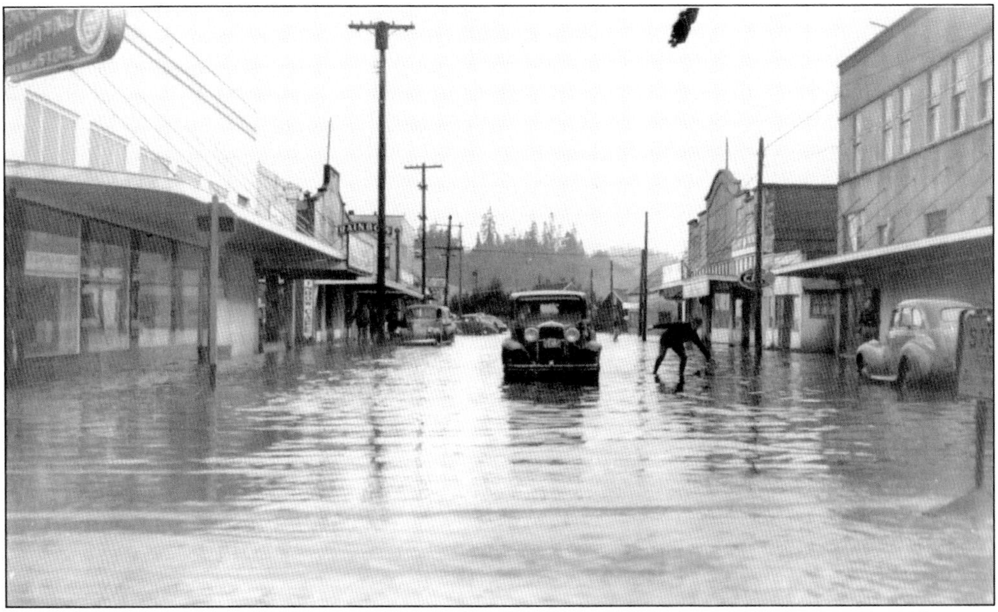

In 1927, Reedsport suffered one of its worst floods, damaging downtown businesses and homes. Before the floodwater receded, there was more than four feet of water in town. During the flood, Reed, who tried to monopolize the real estate market in town, was asked how real estate was selling. He answered, "By the gallon."

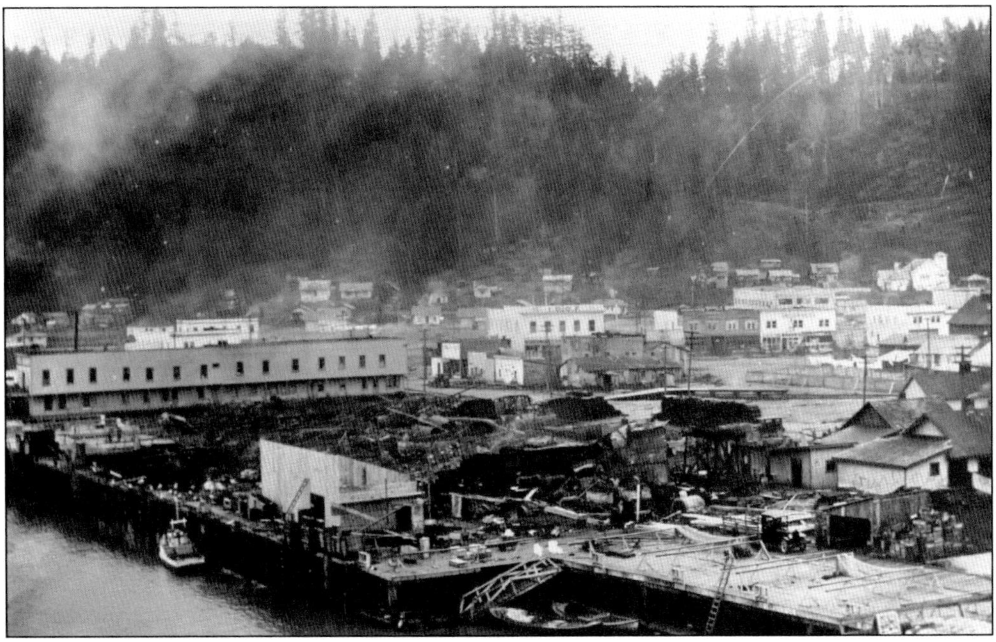

This 1926 photograph shows the aftermath of a waterfront fire that destroyed the Ed Franklin Store and the Chase Fish Cannery on the waterfront. This is the approximate location of today's Umpqua Discovery Center in Reedsport. Fires were a predictable problem with the number of wooden buildings and the amount of flammable material stored in them.

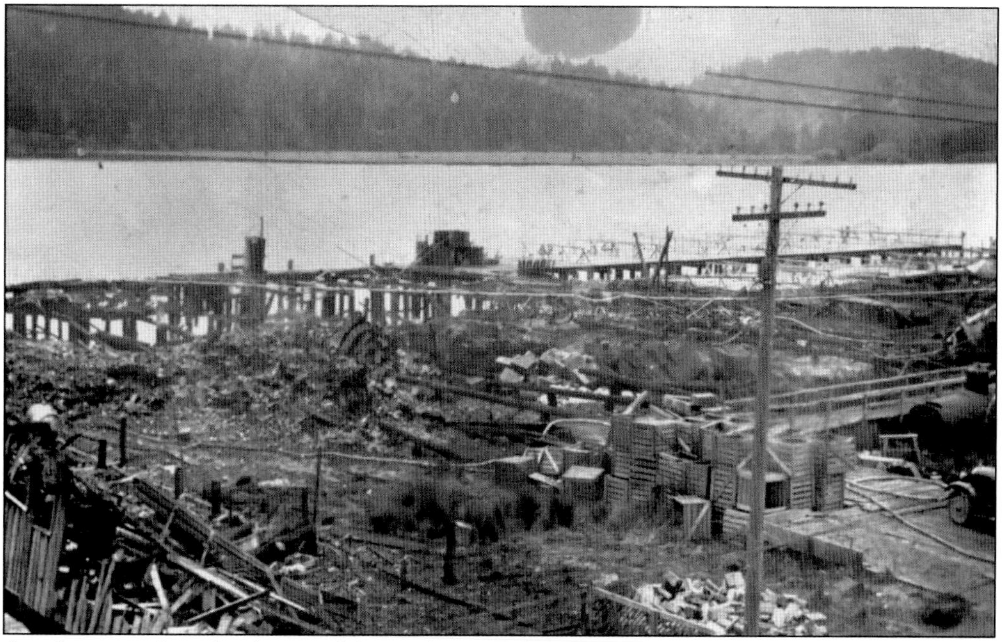

Another waterfront fire destroyed the Anderson Fish Packing Plant in 1926. This 1926 photograph shows the aftermath of the fire on the boardwalk. The skeleton of the waterfront boardwalk is visible in the middle of the image. Fish crates that were not destroyed by the blaze are at the bottom of the photograph to the right.

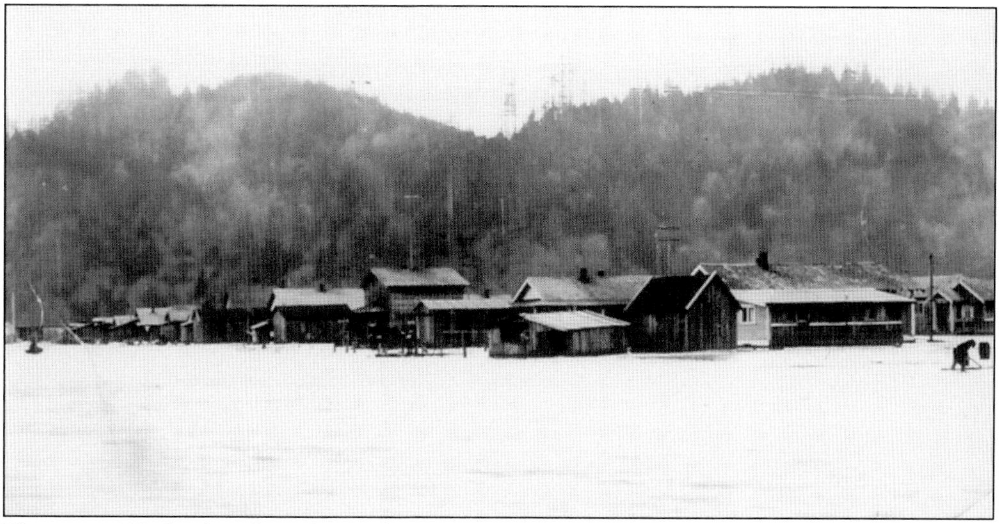

The year 1927 also found Reedsport shivering under the impact of snow and ice. The temperature dropped to seven degrees below zero for three days. It was so cold that the entire Smith River system froze over. Farmers up the Smith River walked on the river ice to get to town. Turkey farmers carried their birds on sleds down the river in order to get them to market. This photograph is of Reedsport housing near what is now Champion Park, looking west toward Scholfield Creek. The heavy rains prior to this caused logs and drift wood to pile up on the Railroad Bridge, adding weight to the structure and causing the potential for serious damage. Workers in town used dynamite to break up the driftwood and managed to save the bridge without doing any damage to the structure.

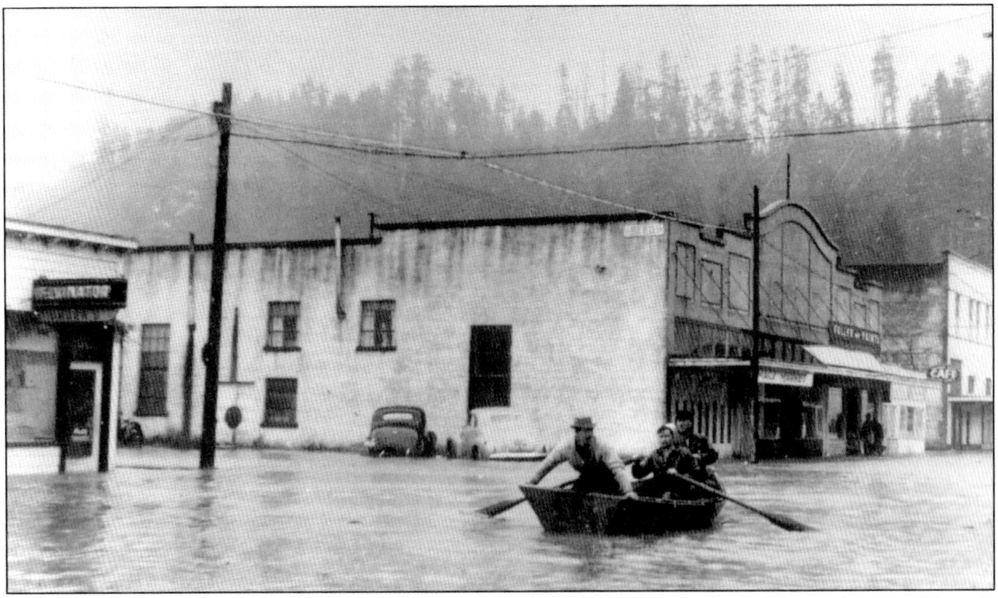

This is a photograph of the 1934 flood. The water was only one and a half feet deep on Fourth Street. During floods, rowboats were used for transportation. Al's Market, run by Frank Taylor, is on the corner behind the rowboat with the Thompson Café. The Square Deal is located to its right. The last building on the right is Burdick's Drugstore with Crestview Heights in the far distance.

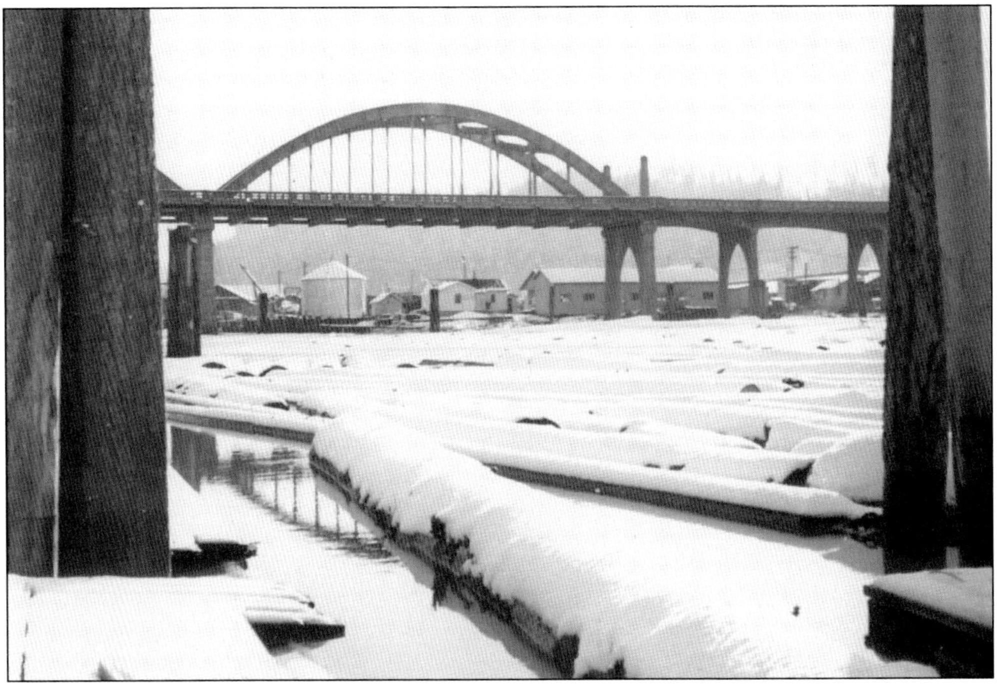

This is a 1949 photograph of the Umpqua Bridge from Hubbard's Mill. In January of that year, a cold snap brought ice and snow to the Reedsport Area. Up to a foot and a half of snow fell on the coast, coating the logs that were floating in the Hubbard Mill Pond at that time. (Courtesy of Nan Hansen.)

The Columbus Day Storm of 1962, otherwise known as the Big Blow, was a cyclone that ranked among the most intense to strike the Pacific Northwest since 1948. The peak winds were felt at Oregon's Cape Blanco, where wind gusts in excess of 145 miles per hour were measured. Some reports put the peak velocity at 179 miles per hour. The storm decimated much of the Hinsdale timber holdings. It was estimated that one in four trees in Reedsport and Gardiner blew down with power lines and telephone lines down throughout the area. Students were sent home at 2:00 p.m. before the winds struck at 2:45 p.m. Hundreds of trees blew down at Lake Marie and at the campground at Tahkenitch Lake.

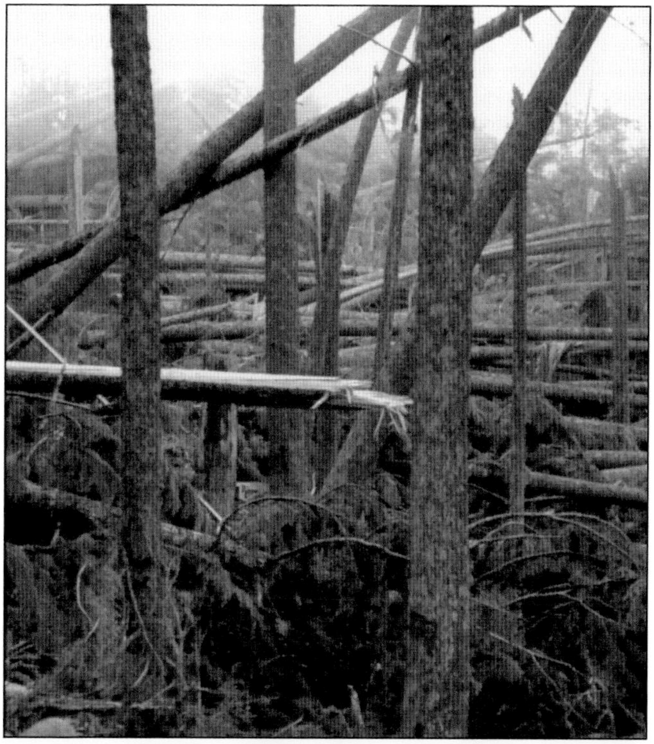

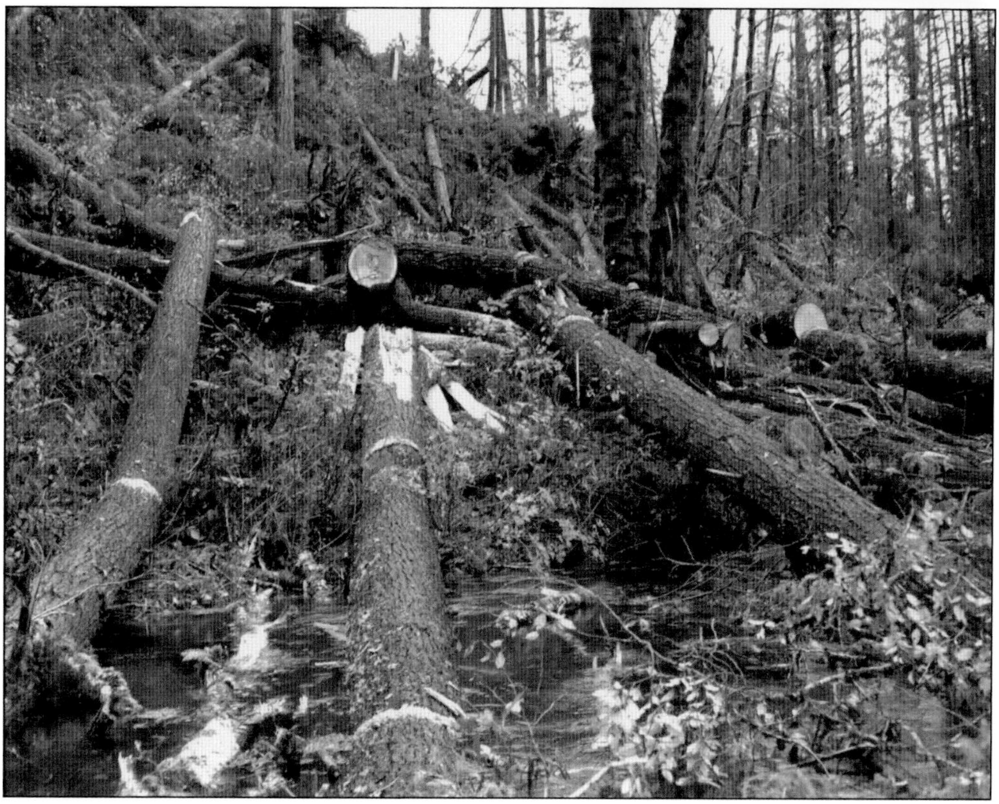

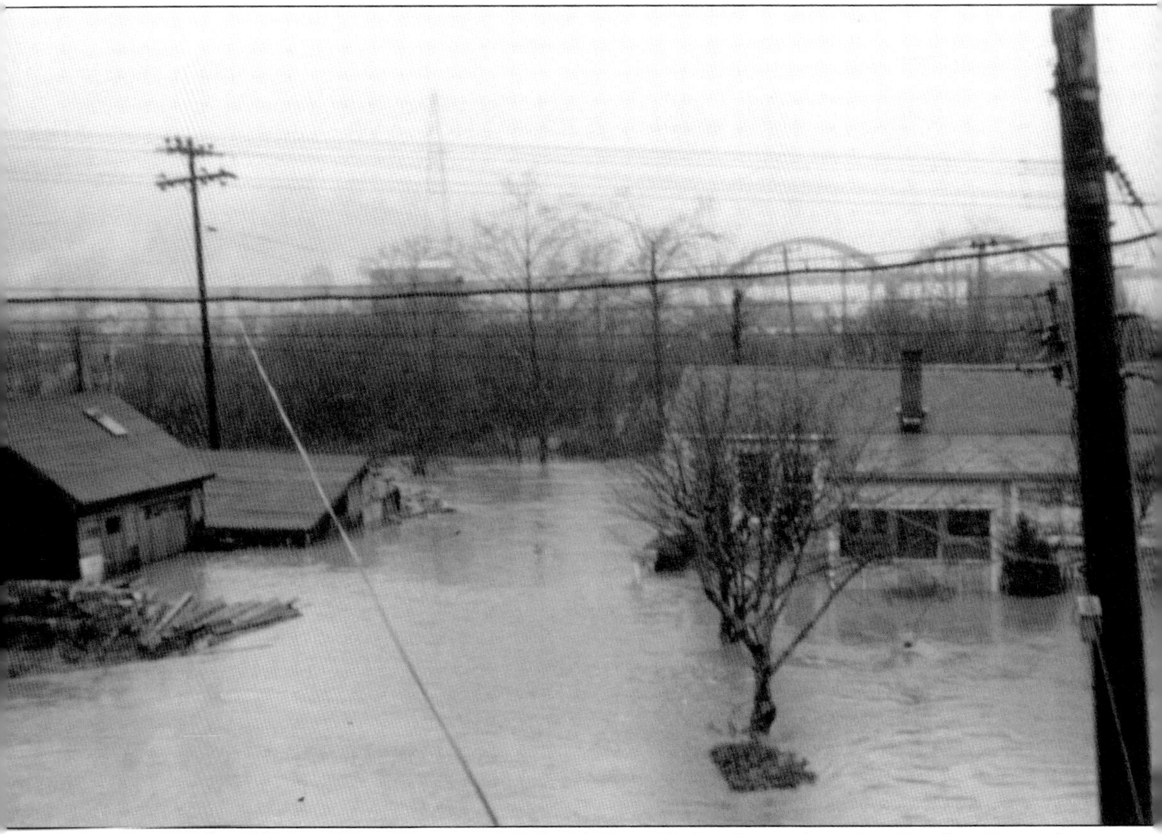

The 1964 flood hit Reedsport exceptionally hard. From Friday, December 18 to Sunday, December 27, 1964, Reedsport received as much rainfall as in one year. Mild temperatures melted the snow pack, and the wind and tides created a perfect opportunity for a massive flood. Water was eight feet deep in Reedsport. A total of 325 families and 50 businesses were affected. (Courtesy of Lewie Bachmeier.)

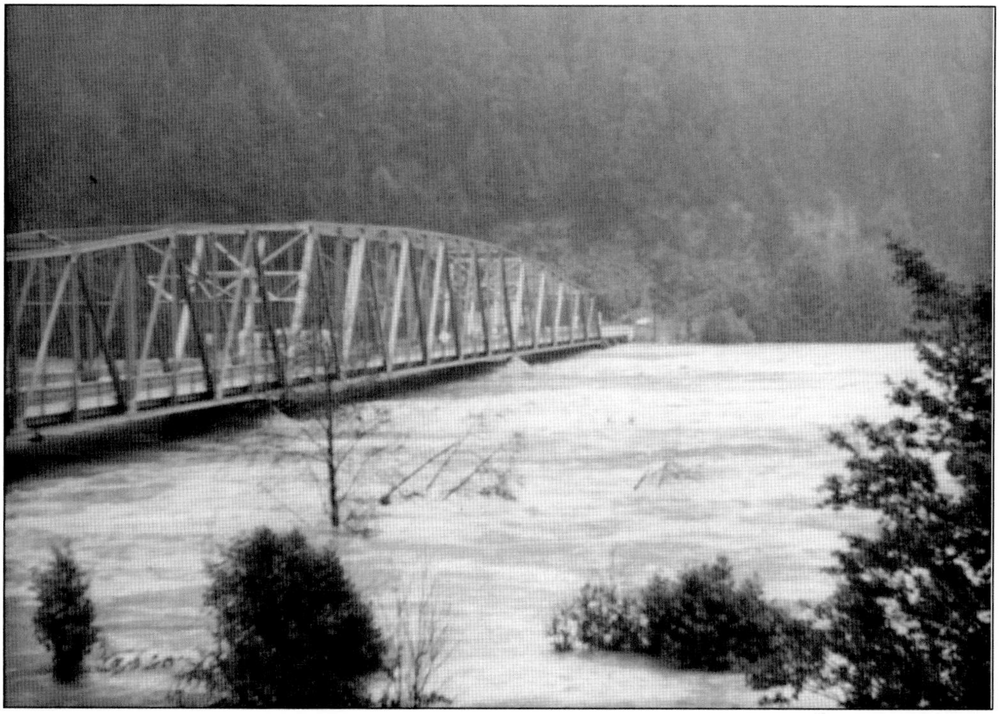

The Scottsburg Bridge is pictured during the 1964 flood. The water is almost to the highway, 45 feet above the normal river level. December rainfall was as high as a normal year. This was roughly equivalent to the flood of 1861, which washed away the town of Scottsburg and undermined the first Umpqua River Lighthouse.

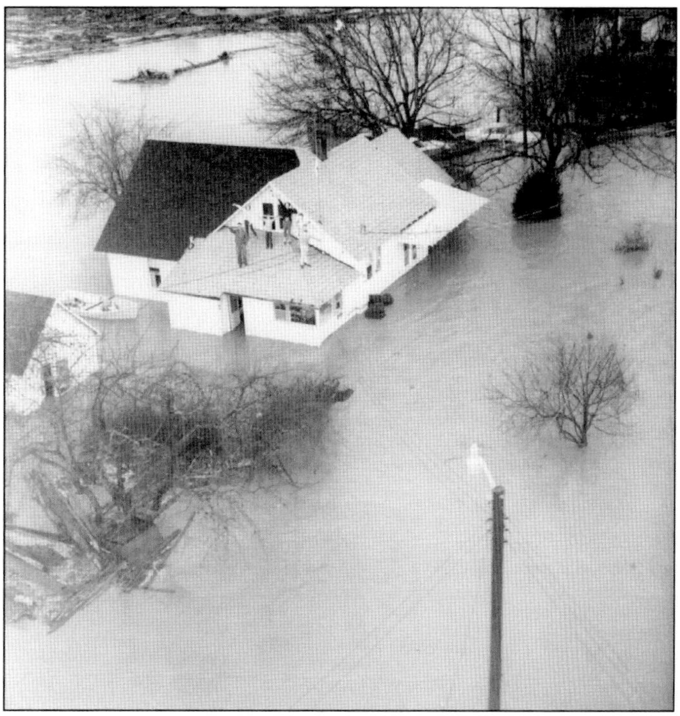

In 1996, another major flood hit the Reedsport area, causing mudslides and closed roads. The natural disaster was caused by warm and heavy "Pineapple Express" rains following major snowstorms in the Cascades. Under such a combination of conditions, the Pineapple Express rains create enormous snowmelt in just a few days, overloading Oregon rivers.

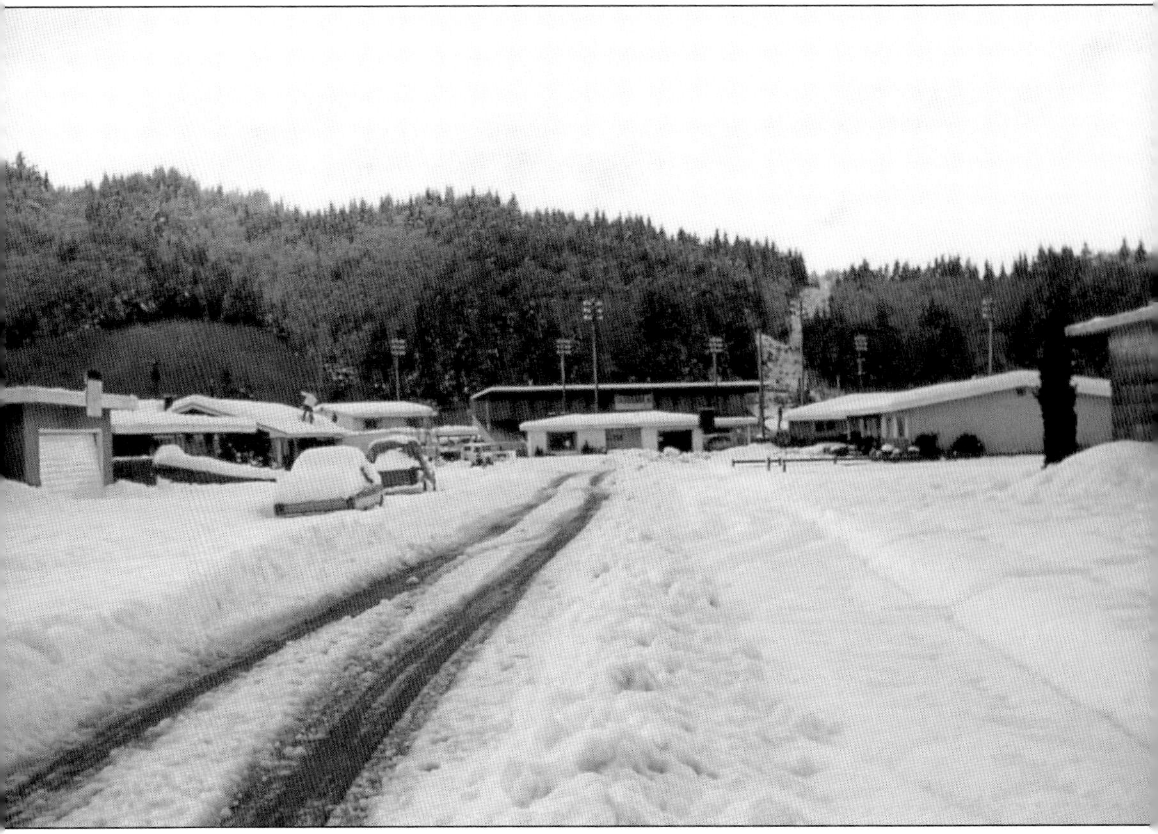

In January and February 1969, strong storms with snow, ice, wind, and sleet hit Oregon statewide. Roseburg received 43.7 inches of snow in an eight-day period. Reedsport received nearly three feet. This is a photograph of High Street, where, after school was over, students were hired to shovel snow off roofs so that they would not collapse. (Courtesy of Gerhardt Kaufmann.)

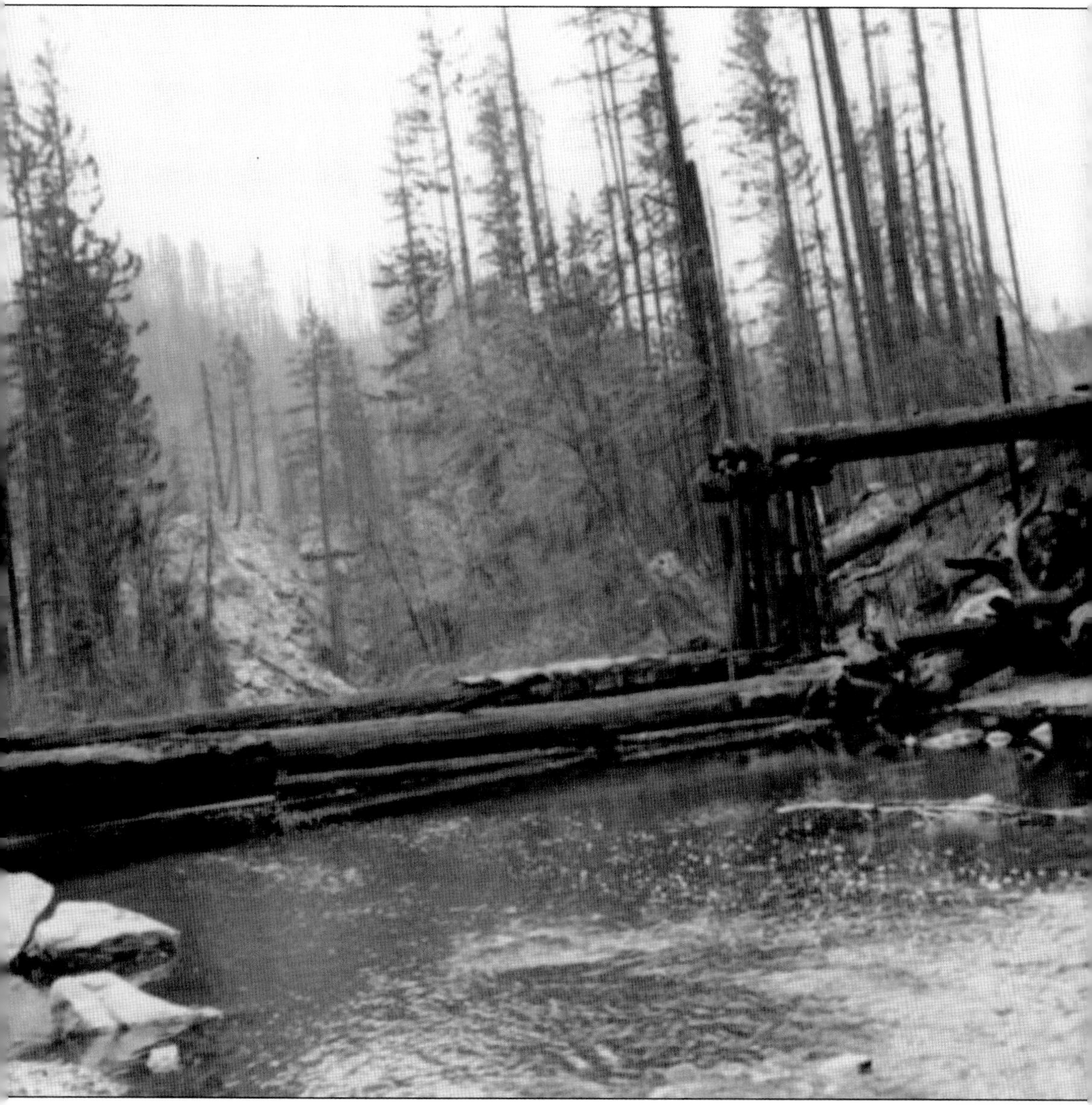

In August 1966, an employee of Umpqua Navigation started the Oxbow Burn when his equipment created some sparks and ignited the dry brush. Before the fire was extinguished, 42,274 acres of timber had burned. At its height, the fire was estimated to burn 2,000 acres an hour. A fire management team of 1,000 firefighters along with equipment was used to suppress the flames. Steep terrain and heavy smoke made the use of aircraft very dangerous. This photograph shows the damage at Club Creek, a tributary of the Smith River. At the time, it was considered the fifth-largest fire in Oregon since 1910. It was ultimately decided that Hinsdale had to pay for the cost of the firefighting. (Courtesy of the Oregon Department of Forestry.)